D0882634

Diploma Mills

Diploma Mills

How For-Profit Colleges Stiffed Students,
Taxpayers, and the American Dream

A. J. ANGULO

Johns Hopkins University Press

Baltimore

© 2016 Johns Hopkins University Press
All rights reserved. Published 2016
Printed in the United States of America on acid-free paper
9 8 7 6 5 4 3 2 1

Johns Hopkins University Press
2715 North Charles Street
Baltimore, Maryland 21218-4363
www.press.jhu.edu

Library of Congress Cataloging-in-Publication Data
Angulo, A. J.
   Diploma mills : how for-profit colleges stiffed students, taxpayers, and the
American dream / A.J. Angulo.
       pages cm
   Includes bibliographical references and index.
   ISBN 978-1-4214-2007-3 (hardcover : alk. paper)—ISBN 978-1-4214-2008-0
(electronic)—ISBN 1-4214-2007-4 (hardcover : alk. paper)—ISBN 1-4214-2008-2
(electronic) 1. For-profit universities and colleges—Corrupt practices.
2. For-profit universities and colleges—United States—Finance. 3. Student
loans—Corrupt practices—United States I. Title.
   LB2328.52.U6A64 2016
   378'.04—dc23   2015034017

A catalog record for this book is available from the British Library.

*Special discounts are available for bulk purchases of this book. For more information,
please contact Special Sales at 410-516-6936 or specialsales@press.jhu.edu.*

Johns Hopkins University Press uses environmentally friendly book materials,
including recycled text paper that is composed of at least 30 percent post-consumer
waste, whenever possible.

APR 2 9 2016

To my parents

CONTENTS

The sign read, "Closed Until Further Notice." That's what one hundred or so college students read as they arrived early one Monday morning at their institution during the fall term of 1978. But these weren't average college students and this wasn't an average college.[1]

Students of Lacaze-Gardner Business School in Washington, DC—nine hundred in all—came from the most disadvantaged areas across the city. Many struggled as single parents, living day to day on public assistance. Lacaze-Gardner, a for-profit college, offered them a way out of poverty by promising them careers in management, accounting, "key-punch" operations, and a variety of technical fields. What they knew about the school came from radio and television advertisements as well as "sales reps" who sold them the hope of a better future. What they didn't expect to read that morning was a sign telling them those hopes and promises had come to an end.[2]

Daniel Grossman, owner and operator of Lacaze-Gardner, had become the target of an FBI investigation in November 1978 for fraud and the misappropriation of $2 million in federal student aid he'd received the year before. He abruptly fired all twenty-one instructors over the weekend and closed the school's downtown office. This move dealt a major blow to students who had signed all the necessary documents and followed all the instructions the school had given them, including taking on debt that went far beyond their wildest expectations. "I was shocked," stated Candida Butler, a twenty-five-year-old student with two children, "when I went down to Lacaze for the first time and they told me the tuition was $2,900 [approximately $11,000 in current dollars] for nine months. But I decided to pay it because I needed some basic math and English courses. The school was close to where I work and the sales rep told me I could get a federal grant." She reported signing a sheaf of blank documents on her first day of school and discovered administrators had used them to fraudulently apply for federal student aid on her behalf. Her goal, like many of her peers, was to gain basic literacy skills to improve her life prospects. Lacking these basic skills, students relied on the school to handle the paperwork. What they soon learned was that Grossman and his staff had little intention of providing them with a high-quality education. As one former instructor and whistleblower described it, "All they wanted to do was get the kids in school. From then on they expected us to just perform a babysitting service." Lacaze-Gardner, now defunct and forgotten, left a lasting mark on the life prospects of its former students. It also reflected a much broader trend involving thousands of for-profit colleges and universities (FPCUs) that emerged over the next few decades. Industry insiders acknowledged that many of these FPCUs were engaged in predatory practices and poverty profiteering.[3]

Predatory lending practices have come under intense scrutiny in recent years due to the subprime mortgage crisis. Researchers, policymakers, and business leaders have all taken various positions on the matter—from identifying these practices as the cause of the global economic meltdown of 2008 to suggesting that poverty profiteering doesn't exist. Lately, the focus has shifted to an impending subprime student debt crisis. Pundits and the financial press predict the next major downturn in the economy could result from the $1.2 trillion student debt bubble looming large over the still-fragile global financial markets. Debt from FPCU students and graduates happens to make up a disproportionate amount of this bubble. While only 11 percent of the overall college-going population attend for-profits, they represent 44 percent of the student loan defaults. Policy analysts continue to argue over what this outsized portion of debt means. Some say it's a reflection of pressing economic needs among the student demographic served by for-profits. Others point to exorbitantly high tuition rates in the FPCU sector.[4]

What's often overlooked in these kinds of analyses is the long history of interplay between national policy and predatory behavior critical to understanding current debates over the for-profit industry. Those who write about FPCUs have tended to focus on present trends and patterns—the commercialization of traditional higher education, or the for-profit subsidiaries of nonprofit colleges and universities, or select case studies about faculty, governance, and curriculum at stand-alone for-profits. None have looked at the topic with the goal of producing a substantive history with an eye toward the long view that could help us put recent events within their broader context.[5]

Diploma Mills was written to address this need. It offers a sweeping exploration of the rise and dramatic expansion of FPCUs. It begins with the palpable tension between traditional colleges and their proprietary counterparts in early America and ends with US senator Tom Harkin's provocative hearings on Corinthian Colleges, the Apollo Group's University of Phoenix, and dozens of other for-profits in 2012. Between these bookends emerges a history of real-world struggles between elites and the impoverished, majorities and minorities, the powerful and the marginalized, the traditional and the upstart, the physical and the virtual. It's a history that intersects with some of America's most crucial conversations—social, cultural, political, legal, and economic—past and present. It's also a history littered with institutional competition, congressional investigations, government subsidization, and class litigation exposing the noble intentions as well as deceptive strategies that have long defined FPCUs. In the last quarter of the twentieth century, whistle-blower testimony captured by investigative reporting and congressional hearings reveal a history shot through with small-time criminals as well as large-scale, well-connected institutions guilty of industrial-sized fraud. This pattern continued during the first decade and a half of the twenty-first century—only bigger. For-profits expanded in size, scope, and enrollments with the help of Wall Street and federal student aid. FPCU campuses appeared along highways and in strip malls, while their ads and web portals popped up online, capturing hundreds of thousands of new applicants. Along with all of this growth came "creative" private student-lending schemes that became the subject of litigation at the state and federal level. Record-breaking lawsuits—in the multi-billion-dollar range—continue to wind their way through the courts, with the FPCU sector's predatory lending and deceptive practices as recurring themes.[6]

That's not to say all for-profits have engaged in questionable practices. Some have succeeded in meeting genuine postsecondary needs overlooked by other forms of higher education. But this book argues that FPCUs have had an unusually scandal-rich past. Key goals, motives, and incentives make for-profit institutions fundamentally different from traditional, nonprofit colleges and universities. Their institutional DNA has been cut from a different cloth and many remain unaware of how the variation has affected the higher education gene pool. *Diploma Mills* offers the first single-volume narrative history designed to provide a historical context for understanding why for-profits and their distinctiveness have mattered to students, taxpayers, lawmakers, and the financial aid industry.[7]

Without question, scandals make for great reading, and the following chapters contain plenty of them. But two more compelling reasons motivated this project from start to finish, reasons attuned to what most of us—whether we're part of the general public, investor class, policymaking set, or academic community—want to know about the origin and development of for-profit higher education.

The first has to do with wanting to get a handle on the basic contours of and potential lessons derived from FPCU history. Among the tribe of historians who call higher education their specialty, virtually all would admit they've ignored the for-profit industry, now a $35 billion Goliath, for far too long. The same can't be said about the origins of traditional colleges and universities. Scholars have spilled much ink over the last few decades in their quest to understand how one of the nation's greatest assets came into being, beginning with the founding of Harvard (1636), William and Mary

(1693), and Yale (1701). Classical undergraduate colleges of the early American and Revolutionary periods, as the story's commonly told, gave way to more forward-looking institutions like the Massachusetts Institute of Technology and graduate-focused universities like Johns Hopkins. Thanks to this line of research, we know much about the evolution of public and private higher education, especially when it comes to major milestones like the *Dartmouth College v. Woodward* ruling of 1819. Through *Dartmouth,* the US Supreme Court delivered a landmark decision in American contract law allowing private, nonprofit colleges to flourish. The modern university, in its public and private forms, emerged out of a confluence of traditional and innovative higher learning. The universities we recognize today began to take shape, in part, through federal legislation—such as the Morrill Acts of the nineteenth century—and, later, through Gilded Age philanthropy, the GI Bills of the forties and fifties, and the Higher Education Act of 1965.[8]

Historians have had good reason to take an interest in traditional US higher education. Colleges and universities of this nonprofit variety consistently dominate the top spots on international rankings. Faculty research productivity has tended to outstrip, by large margins in some cases, the work conducted comparatively around the world. This productivity has inspired investigations into improving instruction for undergraduate and graduate students as well as service to local, regional, national, and international communities. As such, the American system of higher education has attracted significant scholarly attention and nearly 1 million international students every year.[9]

But when it comes to for-profits, there's been a serious gap in our understanding about where these institutions came from and how they've developed over time. The void hasn't changed much, despite the work of economists, sociologists, and higher-education researchers on the topic over the last decade or so. What this means is that contemporary debates over FPCU regulation and legislation have occurred without a basic historical context. *Diploma Mills* highlights why this lack of context is a problem and how we might be able to get our national conversation about for-profits out of its present rut. It offers a guide to some of the most important accounts available about the turbulent rise of FPCUs in American history. It also provides a way to gauge lessons learned and relearned from past experiences with the industry.[10]

The second driving force behind this project has to do with the way FPCU history casts new light on American social, political, and economic life. Throughout the periods examined in this book, for-profits have drawn Americans into debates over cherished values and assumptions about education and the public good.

Some on the left of the political spectrum have seen for-profits as a form of access to higher education for severely disadvantaged poor and minority populations. They see these populations as falling through the cracks of the traditional, nonprofit system and as having turned to FPCUs for the job training necessary to break intractable cycles of poverty. They draw on New Deal and civil rights era political traditions to advocate for the sector as a remedy to past economic and social injustices. In this light, the single parent who's dependent on public subsidies can prepare for a better future by acquiring skills training from for-profits in order to enter the workforce. Aspiring chefs, nurses, or truck drivers can find programs tailored to meet their needs and help them along the path toward becoming contributing members of society. Advocates from the left have viewed FPCUs as part of the fabric of the welfare system and social safety net assisting those limited by life circumstances, location, and program options. For-profits, they argue, play a role as critical as that of Social Security and Medicare. From this perspective, FPCUs have identified an overlooked opportunity for serving the public good.

The Congressional Black Caucus typifies this position coming from the left. Its members have historically sided with for-profits, ostensibly because many of these institutions work with disadvantaged minority communities. They applaud FPCUs for offering training to those without the skills, background, or preparation often associated with success in other forms of higher education. This is no small matter. In poll after poll, Americans consider colleges the most important vehicles for fulfilling the American dream of upward social mobility and self-improvement. For these reasons, many on the left have identified for-profits as places to combat inequality, level the playing field, and give the marginalized a chance to participate in the American dream.[11]

Those on the right of the political spectrum have also cheered the rise and expansion of FPCUs, but for different reasons. Favoring privatization, they tend to see nonprofits as inadequate to the task of educating the public—whether poor, middle class, or wealthy. This position views public institutions as inefficient and ineffective when compared with competitive private enterprise. It's a perspective based on an American political tradition of free-market advocacy drawn from the writings of Adam Smith, Herbert Spencer, Alfred Marshall, Ludwig von Mises, Milton Friedman, and others. The dramatic growth of the for-profit industry beginning in the mid-1970s coincided with market-based reforms popularized by Margaret Thatcher and Ronald Reagan. Privatization was in; the public sector was out. And those on the right saw FPCUs as a way to expand the private sector in concert with their ideas about competition, free markets, and entrepreneurialism. These institutions formed part of a broader movement to incorporate greater choice across the board through voucher systems and charter schools as alternatives to public "monopolies," as they called them, in education. FPCUs offered a higher-education analog to their reform proposals at the elementary, middle, and secondary levels.[12]

For many on the right during the last quarter of the twentieth century, postsecondary education needed competition from for-profits to make them more limber and responsive to the needs of businesses and the marketplace. They valorized the work of "edupreneurs" who risked their capital in education markets. Privatization served as a countervailing force to ever-expanding public institutions they viewed as complacent, bloated, and of little contemporary relevance. In this vein, Friedman once called the state financing of colleges and universities the "great scandal of our times." He and his circle pronounced the end of the New Deal era and anticipated a brighter, market-based future through the expansion of institutions like FPCUs. Here, also, the idea of the American dream appears, but with a different meaning. Market-oriented advocates have embraced FPCUs as expressions of the country's founding principles based on certain inalienable rights—ones that, by extension, allow for the freedom to innovate, compete without excessive government intervention, and, if possible, make a profit.[13]

The question this book seeks to answer has to do with how well any of these views—left, right, and center—have fared when placed in a broad historical context. The answers offered in the following chapters are based on a wealth of newspaper accounts, archival documents, court papers, state and federal investigations, research reports, and other primary and secondary sources. Taken together, these sources show a formidable gap long in the making between the real and the ideal on the matter of for-profits, particularly when it comes to beliefs held most dear in American social, political, and economic life. This book argues that the rich historical record of concern and debate over what the profit motive means for post-secondary education points to one unmistakable conclusion: Too many students, taxpayers, and governments at all levels haven't come out ahead in their dealings with FPCUs. Rather, they've been "gypped" by "diploma mills," as a mid-twentieth-century University of Michigan dean once put it, and this book takes its title from such observations repeated throughout the nation's history. Their concerns, largely forgotten, dampened, or ignored over time, have been expressed in almost every conceivable form—from the literary to the legal—for hundreds of years.[14]

Diploma Mills is their story. It's organized around major milestones in the origin and development of this complex, wide-ranging, and multifaceted industry. The goal here is to take readers on a quick jaunt through time and across the country, with stops at key for-profit colleges and universities, visits with well-placed insiders and observers, and access to the court rooms, halls of Congress, and other settings where FPCUs have been hotly contested. It's a journey intended to provide readers with a critical understanding of how these institutions emerged from obscurity and have expanded to become a multi-billion-dollar industry. It's a history that begins with edupreneurs who worked the cobblestone streets of colonial American cities.

Diploma Mills

CHAPTER ONE

Commerce

They've gone by many different names—writing schools, merchant academies, commercial colleges, business schools, career centers, proprietary universities, technical institutes, and for-profits. This book calls them for-profit colleges and universities, or FPCUs. They're a form of higher education that has always appeared alongside traditional public and private nonprofit institutions. Sometimes for-profits have gathered on the margins or in the shadows of their nonprofit peers. At other times, they've taken a large share of center stage and the public's attention. Their numbers, in terms of institutions, enrollments, and profitability, have ebbed and flowed depending on the needs and contexts of the era. Throughout their long and storied past in America, whatever their name and whatever the period, one thing has remained constant: they were founded to make money.

During the colonial period, nine traditional colleges and universities received charters for granting degrees. About the same number emerged around the time of the American Revolution. The harsh conditions faced by the first few waves of colonists made founding a college an unlikely project, especially with its course of studies made up of mostly Latin and Greek. Survival, not Ovid and Cicero, was foremost on the minds of early settlers. Agricultural skills and local knowledge, the kind shared among native populations, would've come in handy for the many who lost their lives battling brutal New England winters or the miasmatic swamps of southern colonies. Despite these harsh realities, colonial colleges offered a classical curriculum filled with the words and worlds of ancient civilizations, leaving little or no room for practical knowledge.

In doing so, however, they addressed a different kind of practical need. They served as advertisements and symbols of progress that backwoods outposts used to coax potential newcomers who had good reason to question the viability of the colonial experiment. They worked as psychological salves for those who did make the trip across the Atlantic, replenished the human stock, and felt betrayed by false advertising. They maintained social order, produced homegrown leaders, and trained the clergy. In short, these institutions served many purposes—and, at times, blurred distinctions between private and public institutional forms—but none of them came into existence with the express purpose of making anyone a profit.[1]

Profit seekers found a different niche in colonial and revolutionary America. Master artisans with expertise, hard won or merely claimed, took on apprentices and taught individual students specific trades. Learners paid for the lessons through their labor. The apprenticeship, particularly the indentured kind, took the form of a contractual, proprietary relationship that established the obligations of each party. In one contract from 1676, a master agreed to "teach and instruct, or cause to be taught and instructed in the art and mystery as mason," a particular apprentice for twelve years and five months. The apprentice, in return, worked for the master during the same period. Other profit seekers devoted themselves solely to instruction and opened schools catering to groups of students and providing less formal, far shorter terms of instruction. In 1709, a proprietary school for adults in Boston claimed to teach a wide range of subjects. Advertisements mentioned everything from "Writing" and "Arithmetick" to "Surveying" and "Navigation" and even bit of "Astronomy." All this, they announced, could be had at a little shop near the "Mitre Tavern in Fish-street" at the Boston Wharf.[2]

Legal and medical education also took a largely proprietary, apprenticeship form during the colonial and revolutionary periods. With few regulations, if any, to dictate otherwise, the length, quality, and content of study for these professions varied greatly, depending on what the master knew. Variations in legal and medical training continued until the professionalization movements of the late nineteenth and early twentieth centuries. For most of American history, as a result, those with experience and an entrepreneurial spirit could take on apprentices or open an FPCU with the goal of training the next generation of attorneys and physicians without much in the way of external oversight. An entrepreneur named Tapping Reeve opened one such proprietary school in 1784 to provide legal education in Litchfield, Connecticut. He followed the same pattern as other lawyers in educating apprentices in his own office. But Reeve's popularity grew, and he moved his instructional practice to a separate location to handle increasing demand. The school's explicit purpose was to make the owner an income by charging students tuition for lectures and quizzes—all without awarding a single degree. When it closed in 1833, a decade during which states abolished the few formal requirements that existed for law apprenticeships, Litchfield Law School could boast having one of the largest and most successful for-profit programs in the country.[3]

Aspiring physicians followed the same career trajectory, although those with greater resources sometimes finished their training at European institutions. The University of Edinburgh was a particularly popular destination for the well heeled of this group. The more common practice, however, was for apprentices to begin around the age of sixteen and continue their training over a period of five to seven years. During this time, the youth would "read medicine" in the master's library, make observations on the doctor's rounds, and pay for these experiences by working for the physician as a servant, caretaker, and bill collector. Apprenticeships and proprietary schools forced the first medical colleges founded in revolutionary America, those affiliated with traditional institutions, to reduce their graduation requirements because states didn't require a degree to practice medicine. In this context, students had little incentive to pursue bachelor's or doctoral degrees of "physic." Degree-granting medical schools had few faculty, sometimes just one or two, and scarce resources, generally due to a lack of support from boards of trustees. In the end, these formal schools borrowed heavily from the apprenticeship system and continued to do so well into the nineteenth century.[4]

While a wide range of tutors and proprietary schools served the demand for professional education, the best-known FPCUs of the colonial and revolutionary eras were called "reading and writing" schools. These schools filled a significant gap for aspiring merchants looking to trade with Europe. Traders needed elaborate calligraphy skills with the quill pen to write successful letters to buyers and sellers across the Atlantic. That was their business face. Those wanting to be taken seriously learned penmanship skills in order to build trust with potential business and trading partners. Many turned to these reading and writing schools to prepare them for mercantile life since traditional colleges tended to hold practical studies at arm's length. Benjamin Franklin, among other revolutionaries, weighed in on the notable gap in American higher education and came out in favor of entrepreneurial institutions organized to meet the demand. He argued for formal courses of study "fitted for any business, calling, or profession" in his *Proposals for the Education of Youth of Pennsylvania* (1749). Franklin believed practical education was critical to the pursuit of happiness. His proposals led to the creation of the Philadelphia Academy and, later, the University of Pennsylvania, but in both cases traditionalists took over and steered the curriculum from the shoals of practical studies.[5]

As if responding to Franklin's original call, the number of institutions of public and private nonprofit higher education increased exponentially during the nineteenth century. Communities across the country used traditional and multipurpose colleges as a way to boost local economies. The institutions served as beacons of progress and civilization as settlers moved westward. Given the oversupply, rapid expansion, and quantity-over-quality mentality characteristic of the exponential growth, these colleges had mixed results. Many came and went before leaving much of a mark, but the college-founding mania kept driving the relentless upward tick. In 1790, there were 19 nonprofit colleges. That number grew to 50 in 1830, 250 in the 1850s, over 500 in the 1860s, and 811 in 1880.[6]

FPCUs followed suit. Nineteenth-century reading and writing schools transformed into "commercial colleges" and "business colleges" and appeared like mushrooms on the higher-education landscape. Trailblazers opened their doors in the 1830s and 1840s and kept a local flavor by taking on personal or area names followed, in almost every instance, by "Commercial College": Foster's (Boston, 1832), Bartlett's (Philadelphia, 1834), Sawyer's (Boston, 1838), Duff's (Pittsburg, 1839), Comer's (Boston, 1840), Jones's (St. Louis, 1840), Howard (Marion, Alabama, 1842), Crittenden's (Philadelphia, 1844), Schofield's (Providence, 1846), French's (Boston, 1848), Paine's (New York City, 1848), and Browne's (Brooklyn, 1849). Then came a surge of big-city and small-town commercial colleges in the next two decades. Some of note include Bell's (Chicago, 1850), Gregory's (Detroit, 1850), Bryant and Stratton's (Cleveland, 1853), Soule's (New Orleans, 1856), Oberlin (Oberlin, Ohio, 1858), Eastman's (Poughkeepsie, New York, 1859), National (Wheeling, West Virginia, 1860), Garden City (San Jose, California, 1862), Dirigo (Augusta, Maine, 1865), Leddin's (Memphis, 1865), Parish's (Peoria, Illinois, 1865), Janesville (Janesville, Wisconsin, 1866), Hurd's (Fayette, Iowa, 1867), Packard's (New York City, 1867), and Western (Topeka, 1867), among many others. Although the nature of the overall market—mostly small, tenuous, and tainted by fly-by-night operations—makes it difficult to read the data, the US Commissioner of Education placed the total number of FPCUs at 129 in 1878. Other estimates have ranged from several hundred to over 2,000, when including Canadian institutions, with a combined annual for-profit student population of approximately 240,000 by the last decade of the nineteenth century.[7]

With all of this growth, both traditional and for-profit institutions underwent a great deal of change. Cracks in the classical curriculum began to surface with reports published by Yale in the late 1820s. These reports defined the truly educated gentleman as one well versed in the classical languages, taught by way of recitation, and prepared with the mental discipline to pursue whatever studies or careers college graduates desired. The publications acknowledged the creeping expansion of the sciences into college catalogs and argued that the best course of action was to keep classical languages at the center of the curriculum.[8]

Despite Yale's significant influence on American higher education, traditional nonprofits continued to evolve and diversify. These classical institutions created separate schools of science in the 1840s to address demand for biology, chemistry, physics, and engineering, or, as more generally described at the time, natural history and natural philosophy. But pressure to change the core of American higher education intensified. Specialized scientific institutes, such as Rensselaer Polytechnic Institute and the Massachusetts Institute of Technology, kept the staunchest classicists awake at night wondering how far this push for practical studies would go. The passage of the Morrill Land Grant Acts of 1862 and 1890 gave the kind of answers hardened traditionalists had feared. Senator Justin Morrill's legislation provided federal funding based on the sale of western lands inhabited by Native Americans to create agricultural and mechanic institutions or to reform existing colleges for the purpose. As such, the classical college, based on the English model of undergraduate instruction, began to appear quaint, but backward-looking, especially after the founding of the German-styled, graduate-centered Johns Hopkins University in 1876. By the end of the nineteenth century, the contours defining the modern American university had become visible and distinct. The classical college had given way to a new form of higher education that fused traditional undergraduate studies with scientific, practical, and graduate education.[9]

Piecing together these elements became an ad hoc affair, but one element was notably missing from this fusion of nineteenth-century institutional forms: the for-profit model. FPCUs found their own way through this upheaval by largely focusing on aspiring business professionals. This was a demographic that even the most forward-looking of the nonprofits avoided for fear of soiling their reputations.[10]

Traditional nineteenth-century colleges avoided business studies, in part, because of long-held Western views about the separation of knowledge and money. The pursuit of knowledge has almost always represented a noble, pure, and, for centuries, literally monastic calling; the pursuit of money, by contrast, has conjured images of the craven and depraved. Scholars—those filling the ranks of most nineteenth-century colleges—who spent their lives reading, thinking, and writing about classical literature generally shared a dim view of the business world and the people who moved within it. Their skepticism had deeply entrenched roots. The Socrates they taught questioned the ethics, value, and wisdom of chasing after fame, power, and riches. These ancient dialogues, often ending with a red-faced aristocrat angered by some Socratic exchange, reminded readers of the corrupting influence of money generally. But nowhere was Socrates's message more pronounced than in the special antipathy he reserved for sophists who charged high fees for their lessons. He chided those who made fortunes from instruction, suggesting that financial incentives corrupted what they actually taught. Did sophists provide what students genuinely needed? Or did the act of making a profit corrupt the lessons themselves, driving sophists to teach what students wanted to hear in order to maintain satisfied clients? Socrates made his position clear, dismissing sophists as untrustworthy merchants of knowledge.[11]

Such positions critical of money's influence survived through the ages and made their way in one form or another into the traditional nineteenth-century college. The history of early Christianity they taught presented "money changers," particularly those near places of worship, in the least flattering light. If Dante's *Inferno* made an appearance in the undergraduate course of study, it would've been hard to miss the seventh ring of hell, reserved for violent, murderous sinners as well as usurious lenders who choked and gasped due to the weight of purses fastened around their necks. If they read Shakespeare's *Merchant of Venice*, Shylock—history's most famous financial villain made out of Elizabethan cloth but interwoven with ancient and medieval fabric—would've been there to reinforce the message. Moral philosophy and, later, political economy, sometimes taught by the college president, might discuss the birth of finance in Florence and the stock exchange in Amsterdam in the age after Shakespeare. But these developments did little to temper even the popular writings of Adam Smith that could be found in the nineteenth-century American college curriculum. Often cast as the original advocate of markets and the wealthy, Smith had great reservations about the moneyed class. He warned of "avarice" and "vain-glory" among businessmen who threatened the social order. To his mind, they should "always" be treated with great "suspicion" because they aim to "deceive and even to oppress the public" for the sake of profits aligned with their interests.[12]

For these reasons, nineteenth-century classicists had little in common with financiers and brokers, especially the Jay Goulds of the era and those who aspired to follow in their footsteps. Many loathed the idea of soiling traditional college campuses with for-profit schemes or commercial studies. As the *Scientific American* put it, the public viewed FPCUs with contempt for serving little purpose other than "lining the pockets of their proprietors."[13] From across the Atlantic, a report about commercial education in the United States by the British Parliament came to the same conclusion: "When it came to be generally believed that there was 'money in it,' there soon grew up an unprincipled exploitation of the field of business education, which has left a lasting stigma on the name 'business college,' and has done much to disgrace and discredit an honorable profession."[14]

Traditional colleges kept a safe distance from studies that would mark them as commercial or business oriented, although a slow, weak trickle of "separate" and "partial" commercial course offerings appeared at Notre Dame (1842), Hillsdale (1855), and Wake Forest (1869). Catholic colleges, in particular, were more amenable to this than others. It took pressure across nearly the span of the century to yield the first university-based school of business in America, and even then it appeared as a separate school affiliated with the University of Pennsylvania and funded through a special endowment established by industrialist Joseph Wharton.[15]

Another reason traditional colleges kept commerce out had to do with the questionable business practices of the largest for-profit commercial schools in the country. Henry Beadman Bryant and Henry Dwight Stratton started their first FPCU venture in Cleveland in the mid-1850s and soon after began expanding across the country. They set their sights first on Buffalo, Chicago, and Albany. By the end of the Civil War, they had a chain of over forty campuses.[16]

The problem with Bryant and Stratton's enterprise wasn't its sheer size, but rather how it became one of the largest chains in America. Their business strategy focused on opening colleges in cities where other for-profits had already made their start. Existing institutions signaled for them a demand and market for commercial studies. As they entered each new city, a familiar pattern began to emerge. "Proprietors of the other schools," according to one account, "were either required to sell out at a sacrifice or the attempt was made by competition to force them out of the field." Bryant and Stratton won few friends by acquiring local establishments and turning them into branches of the franchise. It also didn't help that the chain followed a policy of charging local operators 30 to 50 percent of their profits for the privilege of becoming part of the corporate family. During the Civil War, the company's franchise managers met in New York to stage a revolt against the chain's practices and heavy-handed contracts. It failed. Their protests fell on deaf ears and the initial insurrection was squashed. Even so, local operators followed with a protest letter blasting the unfair agreements that had "enriched its founders and conferred honor upon their names" at the expense of the "individual and collective efforts" of those handling the affairs at the local level. The agreements left them in "comparative obscurity and indigence." For these managers, Bryant and Stratton had created a for-profit business model that involved what we might now call hostile takeover practices. Dante, to many a scholar's mind, had reserved a special place for these kinds of businessmen.[17]

A third reason for the clear separation between nonprofits and for-profits had to do with the advertising campaigns of nineteenth-century FPCUs. For-profit business and commercial colleges earned a reputation for making inflated claims and offering a direct path to riches through short courses in penmanship, bookkeeping, banking, commercial law, telegraphy, and stenography. Coleman National Business College in Newark, New Jersey, claimed to be the "cheapest and best," with endorsements from "the most prominent business and professional men of the state and nation." Bryant and Stratton's Commercial College advertised special facilities "that cannot be surpassed by any institution of the kind in the United States" and that provided students "influence and advantages that cannot be obtained in any other way." Their courses offered a single "step" from the classroom to "positions of honor and responsibility" in established business firms.[18]

Many other nineteenth-century FPCUs offered students the moon, and Eastman Business College of Poughkeepsie, New York, was one of the most flagrant. Founder Harvey G. Eastman, cousin to George Eastman of Eastman-Kodak fame, regularly spent $1,500 to $3,000 for full-page newspaper advertisements. The cost of one Eastman advertisement exceeded the annual salary of Harvard's president during most of the 1850s and 1860s. This was at a time when book-keepers made six to eight dollars per week. These ads promised courses "to fill every demand of a business career . . . in the least time at the smallest expense." Not to be outdone, Bryant and Stratton made extravagant claims for those wanting to study at home. They claimed young men and women could "easily acquire a thorough and practical business education" through their program, endorsed by "thousands." Even for those engaged in home study, success was imminent. "Our students," stated Bryant and Stratton, "secure salaried situations." Job placement guarantees were common, although frowned upon by critics who charged that the guarantees were "not carried out in good faith." Students eager to begin this journey toward riches with a mere ten-cent introductory lesson likely failed to discern the subtleties of guarantees and inflated claims.[19]

Coleman, Eastman, Bryant, and Stratton started a trend that forced even tiny, remote nineteenth-century for-profit business colleges to make lavish claims. St. Paul Commercial College described itself as an "international" school offering "the sure road to success" (Figure 1.1). Graduates, they claimed, assumed "lucrative positions" upon graduating. What's more, although faculty at prominent classical colleges expressed grave insecurities at the time when com-

BUSINESS EDUCATION.

YOUNG MEN, PREPARE FOR BUSINESS—THE SURE ROAD TO SUCCESS.

The ST. PAUL COMMERCIAL COLLEGE is one of the
Institutions comprising THE

GREAT INTERNATIONAL CHAIN

OF

BUSINESS COLLEGES,

Embracing near fifty first-class Institutions in the U. States and Canadas.

A FULL SET OF TEXT BOOKS AND BLANKS, embracing every
needful variety of *Business Forms*, prepared expressly for this
chain of Colleges.

Most thorough, comprehensive, and practical course of instruction ever introduced, and many thousands of the graduates
of these Colleges, both male and female, are filling lucrative
and responsible stations of trust.

*Three Hundred Professors, Teachers, and Lecturers employed,
thus making it the greatest educational enterprise in the world.*

**The St. Paul Business College is the Oldest, the Largest, and
the Best in the State.**

PROF. W. A. FADDIS, an Educator of upwards of twenty-five years,
Resident Prin.

ALL THE DEPARTMENTS FAIRLY REPRESENTED.

Book Keeping, Commercial Arithmetic, Commercial Law,
Penmanship, Business Correspondence, Business Practice, Political Economy, Banking, Phonography, Orthography, Detecting
of Counterfeit Bankbills at sight, Card Writing, the Customs
of Trade, &c., thoroughly taught and illustrated.

Any Person Purchasing a Life Scholarship for the Commercial Course will
receive such instruction in the English branches as they desire, without extra
charge.

COLLEGE ROOMS OPEN DAY AND EVENING. Those unable to
attend during the day can receive a full course of instruction at
the Evening Sessions.

*The College Rooms are centrally located in the most pleasant part of the
City, and command charming views of the River and surrounding Bluffs.*

Life Scholarships issued in St. Paul, good throughout the Chain.

For Circulars, giving full particulars, Address—

W. A. FADDIS, or,
BRYANT & STRATTON BUSINESS COLL.,
ST. PAUL.

10

FIGURE 1.1. St. Paul Business School Advertisement. *Source:* J. W. McClung,
Minnesota as It Is in 1870 (St. Paul: McClung, 1870), 10.

paring themselves with their European counterparts, this Minnesota
for-profit described itself as "the greatest educational enterprise in
the world" without hesitation.[20]

While the marketing side of for-profits promoted myths to attract
students, commercial college faculty contradicted these claims as
soon as students arrived, although most likely after they paid their

tuition. The popular *Counting House Book-Keeping* (1864) text by Bryant and Stratton faculty warned students of the "extent of mental labor" expected of their students. "The great foe to true progress in all ages," they argued,

> has been mental slothfulness; and so prone are we all to this condition—so willing to let others do our thinking—that we are constantly in need of some impelling force which shall develop the dormant faculties, and enable us to realize the true idea of education. We have little faith in the "learning-made-easy" method of treating a science so eminently worthy of the best mental efforts, and requiring in its application such thorough comprehension as well as such nice distinctions.[21]

At bottom, such faculty knew students came with inflated expectations of success and delusions about the ease with which they could achieve that success. The first order of business, as reflected in the textbook's introductory comment, was to disabuse them of promises made by promotional literature luring students to their institutions in the first place.[22]

With commercial college faculty finding fault with the advertisements, it's not surprising that critical observers blasted FPCUs across the board during the mid-nineteenth century. "Nothing of greater use than the subjects included in the curriculum of the public schools," stated one critic in the pages of a popular magazine, "can be learned in the so-called business or commercial colleges, which, in so far as they undertake to teach the practical details of business life, are misleading, to say the least, in the opinion of all the merchants with whom we are acquainted." Others compared the business college to the "plumbing school" with disdain, while still others spoke of "sham degrees" given for professional studies and the "absurdity in going to a Commercial College to *complete* a business education." These institutions, as critic and author Alfred Holbrook put it, created a "false idea" about knowledge, human nature, and the proper course of practical study. They emphasized "cramming the memory with facts, definitions, rules, observations and remarks" or "preparing for business in working at arithmetic and penmanship." This, to the Holbrook's mind, was the "climax of absurdity."[23]

In addition to questioning the quality of commercial education, critics scoffed at what the era's institutions charged for their intellectual goods. Ohio's Orwell Normal Institute, a teacher training college, branched out into business education to provide an alternative to the overpriced courses on penmanship, mathematics, and other studies found at for-profits. "The Business Course," Orwell announced, "is calculated to furnish young persons who have not two or three hundred dollars to spend at a commercial college, with such training as when once engaged in business, speedily to comprehend its details." J. H. Goodwin, author of the best-selling *Improved Book-Keeping and Business Manual* (1882), also thought tuition rates at for-profits had far outstripped their worth. Having sold tens of thousands of copies of his manual over the course of fifteen editions, Goodwin leveraged his name recognition to speak out against overpriced and overrated commercial colleges. "The young man," he advised, "who spends from six to sixteen months and from sixty to six hundred dollars to learn book-keeping in a business college is—to put it mildly—throwing away both time and money."[24]

Others went a good bit further than Orwell and Goodwin in their criticism of mid-nineteenth-century commercial colleges. George E. Pond, who wrote for the magazine *Galaxy*, railed against the "sham degrees" these outfits conferred on their students: "To what a pass have degrees come in America! Colleges multiply like cockle over the land—or, rather, academies that take unto themselves the name of universities, and fling their diplomas broadcast. No writing-teacher dubs his school of penmanship with any less pretentious title than Commercial College or Calligraphic University." Frustrations with the proliferation of degrees, institutions, and courses of study—partial, full, classical, commercial, traditional, modern, collegiate, university, technical, technological, scientific, graduate, public, private nonprofit, and for-profit—had reached a tipping point for those who longed for the old-time college. The for-profit penmanship school was the last straw in a sequence of changes in American higher education across the century.[25]

Concern over the odd, uneasy place of for-profit institutions in American life reached beyond the desks of social critics and appeared in popular culture of the era as well. Robert Louis Stevenson, with coauthor Lloyd Osbourne, wrote *The Wrecker*, a late nineteenth-century comedy that pokes fun at the "absurdities" of a "sound commercial education." The "yarn" starts off with a young Loudon, the story's protagonist, leaving for a commercial college. He's being sent by his father, an unhappy businessman, who believes the college will forever alter his son's chances of success in the business world. From the boy's perspective, the father "no doubt considered he was putting me in a straight line for the Presidency and the New Jerusalem." Just before leaving him at the steps of the train cars, the father turned and said "Loudon . . . I am now giving you a chance that Julius Caesar could not have given to his son—a chance to see life as it is, before your own turn comes to start in earnest."[26]

For Stevenson and Osbourne, *The Wrecker* becomes a vehicle to present the nineteenth-century commercial college as an "absurd place of education." Loudon's courses included a smattering of bookkeeping and modern languages. But he and other students spent the vast majority of the day learning how to "gamble in produce and securities." The whole business was "cold-drawn gambling without color or disguise. . . . I thought I had never beheld a scene more disagreeable." Students received "college paper" that functioned like poker chips with which to practice speculating on exchanges. These chips, sold upon graduation, represented the student's success with market speculation. This is what they spent their days doing, inspiring for Loudon a comparison with Charles Dickens's *Oliver Twist*: "If there was ever a worse education, it must have been in that academy where Oliver met Charlie Bates."[27]

Even potential defenders knew something had to give if commercial colleges, with their courses of study typically ranging from six weeks to three months to three years in length, could rightly call themselves by the name "college." Henry Clews, a nineteenth-century financier and Wall Street fixture, questioned the value of for-profits for those looking to follow a similar career path. To this question, he brought a wealth of experience that included training clerks, organizing a "Committee of 70" influential citizens and investors, breaking up a major investment corruption ring led by William "Boss" Tweed, and serving as an economic adviser to President Ulysses S. Grant. His *Fifty Years in Wall Street* memoir recounted a lifetime of observations on the needs and shortcomings of America's business and investment firms. From his point of view, commercial colleges distracted aspiring young bankers and business owners from the qualities necessary for success. Early in the century, Clews recounted, "the parents of such a youth who were intent upon getting him a start in an office . . . were obliged in most instances to pay fifty dollars the first year for the privilege." Paid apprenticeships got many business leaders their start, he argued, and the public had misplaced its hopes in commercial colleges. What mattered most were the dispositions learned, not where they learned them. Too many wanted to get rich quickly "by some imaginary rapid-transit route." The young read about the Vanderbilts, Goulds, and Astors—as well as the advertisements of for-profits—and thought a short course in penmanship would get them there, but Clews believed they really needed "sufficient energy, fixity of purpose, patience, self-denial and self-control, frugality, and economy." It's not about genius or, worse still, becoming "an accomplished college professor," but rather cultivating "the habit of feeling at home wherever their lot is cast." If commercial colleges could achieve such a thing, they would've had Clews's endorsement. But he was skeptical the developments underway in both for-profit and nonprofit business studies would meet these needs.[28]

Of all the defenders of the era's commercial colleges, James Hodges stood among the most broad-minded and thoughtful. He, too, knew business needs from an insider's perspective and identified important shortcomings in the offerings of most commercial colleges. Unlike Clews, however, his point of view was driven less by Wall Street and more by Washington, DC.[29]

Hodges, a one-term (1885–1887) mayor of Baltimore and local business leader, came up through the ranks of commerce as an apprentice. Although he started a course of legal studies, he dropped out due to a death in his family. After an apprenticeship at a commercial house in Baltimore, Hodges started a successful import company, became a member of the city's Board of Trade, the president of the Mercantile Library Association, and a director of the National Union Bank. As mayor, he took a special interest in education—opening five schools, assisting with the passing of a school loan resolution, and appropriating funds for the construction of a high school for African Americans.[30]

When it came to commercial colleges, especially after his term in office, Hodges recommended these institutions not only as vehicles for individual prosperity, but also as a means to bring business leaders into the political process. He believed England owed its "wealth, power, dominion, and influence" to patient, deliberate commerce and held this up as a model to counter the "hot and eager haste" among American youth "rushing rashly" into the business world. Hodges argued that "business education for the commercial classes" was needed to "methodize" their minds for the "constantly-changing conditions of trade." Without commercial education, "many of them never rise to success as businessmen, or to places of high usefulness in commercial employment. Gross ignorance and inexperience are the primary-producing causes of many honest commercial embarrassments . . . and have caused many disastrous failures. And a faulty system of book-keeping has absolutely ruined and driven into bankruptcy many worthy merchants whose lack of commercial education rendered them incapable of detecting the villainy or ignorance of their clerks."[31] Commercial colleges, according to Hodges, offered no sure or "royal" road to success, but they certainly increased the chances and could prevent common, fateful errors in basic accounting.[32]

More importantly, Hodges saw in commercial colleges the possibility of producing graduates who could serve as viable contenders for political office, even without the prestige of a classical education. Commercial and financial legislation, he argued, required the guidance of those best informed about the consequences of such legislation. "Who are better qualified to do this," he asked, "than intelligent and experienced business men?" The classical college might expose future leaders to ancient languages, history, philosophy, and higher mathematics, but, in Hodge's experience, graduates of traditional institutions often appeared lost in a business firm. They turned to the "errand boy" for instruction on the rules of the trade and lamented the time "wasted at college" that could've been spent more productively preparing for a life in business. At the same time, Hodges proposed a remedy to a critical problem with nineteenth-century commercial colleges: their narrowness. The standard penmanship and bookkeeping instruction found at these institutions provided an "eminent service," he noted, but they didn't go far enough to prepare future leaders. In addition to the practical courses of study, Hodges also wanted to see students wrestle with "great questions involving the destinies of states and the welfare of nations, that once were decided on ecclesiastical or dynastic grounds, [and] are now decided on commercial." He longed for commercial interests to be represented in state and federal offices. "I cannot help thinking," he added, "that if we had a few less lawyers and a few more merchants in our State assemblies and in Congress, the country would be much the better for it." He wanted what the French had in the practical, business-oriented Ecole Spéciale de Commerce or what the German states had with the Commercial Academy of Vienna.[33]

Hodges's ideal commercial college curriculum included elocution, modern languages, political history, commercial law, and commercial geography. With that, in addition to practical knowledge of accounting, insurance, finance, and trade, the nation would see the rise of "not merely successful merchants, but intelligent citizens, public servants, and legislators." The business schools appearing in nonprofit colleges and universities in the final years of the century began to satisfy such needs. But for-profit commercial and business colleges had for decades attempted to fill the gap, however narrow in scope, for hundreds of thousands of students throughout the century. In 1895 alone, over 96,000 students enrolled in for-profit commercial schools. That same year, nonprofit colleges and universities reported a total enrollment of 97 students in business-related courses of study.[34]

The hundreds of thousands of students served by FPCUs throughout the nineteenth century took their training in countless directions. Some took a commercial course of study on the way toward a political career. George K. Anderson, president of the Exchange Bank of Titusville, Pennsylvania, got his start by attending Duff's Commercial College in Pittsburgh during the 1850s. He used his bookkeeping skills for Kirk and Rhodes, "well-known and prominent car builders of Rochester, Pennsylvania," and later for his own retail grocery business. But after these two ventures, he ran for office and became a senator in the state's legislature. William W. Lawson followed a similar path in the state of New York. After attending public schools in Buffalo and finishing a course of study at Bryant and Stratton's Commercial College, he worked for machinists, butchers, and ultimately a stock dealer that bought and sold cattle. He was elected to the state assembly in the 1870s for two terms and later served as sheriff of his county. Henry H. Koch did the same. He had a grammar school education, worked at a family sawmill for three years, and then studied at Bryant and Stratton's. This gave him skills to work as a bookkeeper and retail salesman for Buffalo's boot and shoe dealers. Koch opened his own retail store in the same industry that became a success in the area. After gaining commercial recognition, he entered political life as representative of the tenth ward in Common Council and later as sheriff of Erie County.[35]

Other nineteenth-century for-profit graduates served at various levels of government, journalism, or education. Thomas W. Davis, a graduate of Bartlett's Commercial College in Cincinnati, worked in the iron industry as a financial manager. After the Civil War, he took his bookkeeping skills with him to the office of Internal Revenue Collection for a district in Pennsylvania. Harrison G. Otis, a graduate of Granger's Commercial College in Columbus, Ohio, ran a newspaper and printing plant, moved to Washington, DC, managed the Government Printing Office, and later became the head official of the US Patent Office. Otis then returned to journalism as a part owner of the *Los Angeles Times* and as president and general manager of the Times-Mirror Company. James E. Scripps, a graduate of Bell's Commercial College in Detroit, became the owner and operator of the highly successful *Evening News* (later, the *Detroit News*). He turned his fortune into a philanthropic enterprise that funded projects in California, including Scripps Institute of Oceanography and Scripps College. J. G. Adams, a graduate of Iron City Commercial College in Pennsylvania, used his commercial training to help with the expense of completing a traditional course of study at Waynesburg College in 1870. A few years after graduating from Waynesburg, he became the superintendent of schools in Jasper County, Indiana. Harrison Soule, a graduate of Gregory's Commercial College in Detroit, worked as an accountant for the Michigan Central Railroad Company for several years. In the 1880s, he left the industry to serve as treasurer of the University of Michigan.[36]

A small number of the era's for-profit graduates made untold fortunes too, but, as economists often point out, it's never clear how much of an individual's success can be attributed to inherited traits, formal and informal training, and sheer chance. Before making their Gilded Age empires, Andrew Carnegie, John D. Rockefeller, Harvey Firestone, and Frederick A. Goodrich attended for-profit commercial and business colleges. In each case, the luck of being in the right place at the right time contributed in some measure to their success. Goodrich, for instance, started out at the Mound City (St. Louis) Commercial College and later finished a course of studies at the Northern Indiana Normal School in Valparaiso. He worked for Charles Himrod, an iron company in Chicago, as a bookkeeper and salesman. After being transferred to Detroit, the company's silent partner withdrew and Goodrich became owner, general manager, and treasurer of the company that took his name. In other cases, chance had just about everything to do with newfound success, eclipsing the influence of for-profit training. As one account of serendipity depicts, "Three brothers with educations obtained at Western Commercial College as their only capital, came to this [Alleghany River] oil region four years ago. Now they hardly know what they are worth." While the biggest names to come out of for-profits were extreme outliers, the idea of similarly striking it rich after a short course of studies motivated more than a few applicants.[37]

The reality, however, was that most of these nineteenth-century for-profit graduates neither failed nor amassed giant fortunes. As such, business colleges served a diverse body of students. Many used their bookkeeping skills to run local businesses. Some entered politics, government, journalism, and education. A select few became legends in the business world. They were all young, aspiring entrepreneurs at one time who thirsted for success and turned to the commercial college as a way to help slake their thirst.

Those who owned and operated the kind of commercial colleges these students attended, meanwhile, came from diverse backgrounds and followed equally diverse career trajectories. Some had little or no formal academic training. Bell's Commercial College was started by Digby Bell, who grew up in the Caribbean, apprenticed as a sailor at the age of twelve, and spent the first several years of his career at sea. He followed that period with a stint in agriculture near Detroit, buying and selling grain and feed. After "tiring of that drudgery," he decided to start a commercial college in 1850s Chicago. He moved to New York after a few years to work in a brokerage business. For Digby, the commercial college was one of a series of passing for-profit ventures.[38]

For others, like Ira Mayhew, the commercial college played a meaningful role within a broader, well-developed vision for nineteenth-century American education. Mayhew received an antebellum classical education from common schools and the Union Academy in Belleville, New York. He taught at the academy after graduation and, after several years of teaching, accepted a series of administrative appointments. Some of these included serving as principal of Adam's Seminary, principal of Wesleyan Seminary, president of Albion Seminary and College, superintendent of Jefferson County Schools in New York, and state superintendent of public instruction in Michigan. He received an honorary degree from Middlebury College, in part, for such publications as *Means and Ends of Universal Education* (1860) and a practical work on bookkeeping that went through sixty editions over ten years. Mayhew founded Albion Commercial College in 1860 as part of a lifelong career in education. After a fire destroyed his school, he moved the operation to Detroit, renamed it Mayhew's Business College, and later sold it to Spencerian Business College. It later turned into Goldsmith Business University, Detroit Business University, and ultimately Detroit Business Institute.[39]

For-profit college leaders of the nineteenth century, at least those like Mayhew who spent more than a passing moment in the field of education, understood that their institutions intersected with some of the greatest challenges and concerns of American society. They knew that their colleges were caught in the crossfire over debates about professionalization, regionalism, feminism, and industrialization.

Professionalization was serious business in the nineteenth century. Scientists, physicians, and teachers wanted it, as did lawyers, engineers, business leaders, and academics in every discipline. At the start of the century, however, virtually none of them had it. The drive for professionalization began as a vague desire to separate the quacks and charlatans from the experts and authorities. The difficulty came in deciding where to draw the line. Those who accepted apprenticeships in preparation for their trade and career did so without assurances about consistency or formal requirements in terms of what an apprenticeship should entail. Professionalization pushed various fields to define and standardize training, specialization, codes of conduct, governing bodies, societies, organizations, and publication outlets. The most prominent professional associations came into existence for this purpose, including the Association of American Geologists (1840), which became the American Association of Geologists and Naturalists (1842) and later the American Association for the Advancement of Science (1848). The American Medical Association (1847) appeared around the same time. So did the National Education Association (1857), American Social Science Association (1865), American Bar Association (1878), and the American Society of Mechanical Engineers (1880).[40]

The professionalization of business came later than the rest, and this delay affected the development of commercial colleges. Professional societies, conferences, journals, and academic courses for those in business came in the early twentieth century. Some of the most important organizations for accountants as well as those in finance, management, production, and marketing didn't appear until the mid-twentieth century. Without an organizing body, little consensus developed around requirements for the preparation and training of aspiring business professionals. Leaders in the world of commerce brought the same laissez-faire attitude they had toward the marketplace to their own professional development.[41]

This lag in nineteenth-century business professionalization cut both ways for proprietary commercial colleges. On the one hand, it allowed them the freedom to experiment. There were no expectations, at least none that were standardized and policed by professional societies, as to what a business education entailed. While many offered similar courses in penmanship and bookkeeping, the length of programs could vary wildly and the content of these courses could take on different forms. Institutions offering six-week courses could claim to provide the same programming as those offering three-year courses without professional repercussions, sanctions, or loss of recognition. On the other hand, the lag in professionalization kept these colleges in the shadows—barely acknowledged by their nonprofit, traditional counterparts or, worse, dismissed as disreputable profit-making machines. Those pressing for standards in the nineteenth-century for-profit industry expressed great frustration with the state affairs. As trade magazine *Manufacturer and Builder* described it in the 1870s, there were obvious problems with "business preparation for young men in this eminently practical age. It is especially the absurd notion that scholarship is valuable alone to the professions, and that a few years of mechanical work in memorizing facts and formulas, are all that is needed for success in business, especially commercial affairs."[42] Such periodicals lamented that "in many instances studies are selected at random" and that, as a result, "proper classification becomes an impossibility." The aspiring bookkeeper, banker, or broker had little to go on in terms of distinguishing good from bad programs.[43]

Ira Mayhew, of Albion Commercial College and later Mayhew's Business College, understood the push for professionalization and its potential impact as well as anyone. To his mind, "Young men expecting to become lawyers or physicians, hence appropriately attend the Law School or the Medical College, in order to receive that necessary preliminary training without which they cannot reasonably hope to attain success." "So persons," he continued, "intending to become book-keepers, or to engage in merchandise, or in any of the numerous commercial pursuits of the country, should attend a well regulated Commercial College, and for a like reason." At the same time, Mayhew had an unclear admissions policy that would have worked against professionalization or standardization across institutions. To attend his college, he wanted students to arrive with a "common English education." If lacking this, students would still "do well" with a basic, "preliminary education." If lacking this, some "arithmetic" and "reading and writing" were the only "essential" requirements. It might be inferred from the catalog that, if students paid the $100 tuition for the fourteen-week course, even these requirements could be waived.[44]

During the 1850s, professionalization took a backseat to regionalism and nationalism as for-profits got swept up in the storm brewing between North and South. In the decade before the Civil War, a form of southern nationalism emerged and shaped discussions about the best forms of instruction for southern students. With Harriet Beecher Stowe's *Uncle Tom's Cabin* (1852), the Kansas-Nebraska

Act of 1854, the *Dred Scott v. Sandford* (1857) decision, and John Brown's raid (1859) as a backdrop, some turned their attention to what commercial colleges could do for the South.[45]

When Soule's Commercial College opened in New Orleans at the height of these regional tensions in 1856, the local community enlisted the institution to do much more than prepare bookkeepers. They also asked it to play a critical role in domestic and international affairs. "At this moment," read one editorial, "when the South is struggling to preserve her social and political station, there is no agency which will do more in so short a time as to improve her commercial intercourse with other countries. . . . For this, the college of Col[onel] Soule is admirably adapted." Advocates of the southern cause wanted the institution to train youth in the region in modern languages and skill sets necessary to expand their trade, largely cotton, with buyers abroad. This would reduce dependency on northern markets and increase commercial and financial autonomy. What southerners also believed commercial colleges like Soule's could do was help cultivate allies through foreign trading partners should a civil war erupt. The for-profit, as such, fell into the broader social, political, and economic feud that ultimately engulfed the nation in civil war.[46]

Before the war, although more successfully after it, women fought for a place in traditional American higher education. For-profit operators, understanding this need and seeing a market, catered to the women's needs long before classical colleges opened their institutions to full coeducation.[47]

The trend in nineteenth-century traditional colleges was to either prohibit women from admission or offer a separate school or separate session for them to attend. The resistance to coeducation had much to do with tradition (e.g., religion), social norms (e.g., separate spheres), and even science (e.g., public health). Arguments formed around these and other values to close off much of traditional higher education to women, despite the existence of long-standing female seminaries of higher learning that offered women rigorous liberal arts education. Scientific studies, in an age increasingly deferential to scientists, gave a progressive twist to the traditionalist point of view. Edward Clarke, Harvard professor of medicine, for instance, claimed to have evidence of the poor health conditions of women who attempted a classical course of college studies. In *Sex in Education* (1873), Clarke theorized that classical studies were harmful to female reproductive organs. American women had to make a choice: either Homer or healthy children.[48]

Commercial colleges, all the while, had more freedom to experiment with coeducation. Since mid-nineteenth-century women represented an increasing share of the urban workforce, filling industrial, medical, and educational roles, training for them in these areas served a direct purpose. For this reason, coeducation posed less of a problem and controversy in for-profit settings. Those that did admit women, in some cases, also gave them a tuition reduction. In the 1860s, the "ladies" of Michigan's Albion Commercial College could enroll at "reduced rates, and enjoy the benefit of the full course of instruction." Although Albion had a "Ladies' Department," women shared the same facilities and lectures "as do gentlemen, and enjoy in common with them all the privileges of the Lecture Room and Library of the Institution. Becoming accomplished Book-keepers, the quiet duties of the Counting-room are befittingly open to them." During the same period, Boston-based Comer's College, unlike Albion, described exactly how much of an incentive they gave female students. Comer's offered women "a discount of twenty per cent from the terms for gentlemen" and claimed "the course of instruction is precisely the same." Women could also apply on equal terms for twelve scholarships the college offered students needing assistance.[49]

Some commercial colleges run by women in the mid-nineteenth century kept the public informed about gender, business, and the role of for-profits in women's prospects for employment. McIntyre and Kidder's in Boston, led by Sarah McIntyre, had a decade of experience in preparing ladies for bookkeeping and sales when they described their institute to a women's magazine. "It was at first," they acknowledged, "difficult for ladies to obtain such situations; but as those who did succeed gave entire satisfaction, others were induced to give them a trial; and now they are very generally employed in our retail stores, at prices varying from four to eight dollars per week, and a few at a still higher salary."[50] The conditions, they stated, were "not so unhealthy as needlework," although the typical bookkeeper worked ten hours per day. What's more, McIntyre and Kidder told their students to expect less pay than their male counterparts, even though female workers tended to be "superior to men in faithfulness in the performance of duties." The owner of a Brooklyn commercial college stated as much when he said that women "are not so well paid as male book-keepers. Much depends on the kind of friends a lady has to secure her a place." With low pay expectations, preferential treatment and reduced tuition rates made enrolling more appealing to women.[51]

Low wages paid to both male and female workers of the mid- to late nineteenth century created widespread labor-management disputes that, like professionalization, regionalism, and feminism, raised new questions about the role of for-profits colleges. The rapid industrialization of factory production, railway and steam transportation, telegraph communications, oil refining, and steel manufacturing generated tensions between owners and workers that resulted in violent conflicts. Textile weavers, shipbuilders, shoemakers, coal miners, cigar rollers, railway operators, machine assemblers, field hands, and dockworkers organized strikes across the New England landscape throughout the nineteenth century. From the mill strikes in Lynn, Massachusetts, in the 1830s to the ironworker strike in Homestead, Pennsylvania, in the 1890s, Americans lost lives and property over disputes about proper compensation and working conditions.[52]

Advocates of commercial colleges saw a role for these institutions in the nineteenth-century struggle between labor and capital. In "Some Experiments in Co-operation" (1876), Charles Barnard, contributor to the popular magazine *Scribner's,* argued that for-profits could help ease tensions between the classes: if companies provided commercial courses to laborers, their employees would have greater sympathy with owners. "Give the working man a business education," he explained, "and he learns to see and understand the laws that govern the movement of wages and interest." Although Barnard suggested that companies should give "the laborer a share in the guidance and profits of the work," business leaders of the era tended to dismiss profit sharing as a fanciful experiment. These leaders associated profit sharing with the kind of experiments tried by Robert Owens and other utopianists, despite share plans enacted by Procter and Gamble and N. O. Nelson Manufacturing Company. More important for Barnard was the expectation that for-profits would train workers how to appreciate "the causes that bring about a reduction of wages." Through a commercial education, workers learn "patience and wisdom," or, more bluntly, docility: "He comes to see the folly of a strike, and finds out for himself the plain and simple path every industry must follow, if it is to declare good dividends." Commercial and business colleges, as Barnard understood them, could dissolve the conflicts that existed between laborers and capitalists by turning laborers into capitalists or, at least, by training them to think from the capitalist's perspective.[53]

Nineteenth-century commercial colleges ultimately succeeded in securing a foothold in American higher education. They were successful despite the disdain from traditional institutions, the self-inflicted wounds caused by misleading advertising, the dispositions of students who wanted easy paths to riches, the unfavorable reviews by social and literary critics as well as FPCU advocates, and the diverse career aspirations and trajectories of those who attended and operated these institutions. Commercial colleges, of course, represented only one of many kinds of practical schools, proprietary or otherwise, in operation in the nineteenth century. Others included lyceums (e.g., Gardiner, 1822), mechanic institutes (e.g., the Franklin Institute, 1824), institutions for the disabled (e.g., National Deaf-Mute College, 1864), distance education programs (e.g., Correspondence University of Ithaca, 1883), and barbershop training academies (e.g., A. B. Moeler of Chicago, 1893)—all of which beg for further attention and exploration. But the commercial college branched off from the rest, creating a niche characterized by the absence of philanthropic or public support. This niche, with its fiercely independent approach to the way it targeted and catered to aspiring businessmen and women, established by far the dominant formal for-profit model of the century.[54]

In the end, these commercial and business colleges did more than simply find a place in the established order. They created new possibilities and responses to some of the most provocative concerns of nineteenth-century America, including professionalization, regionalism, feminism, and industrialization. Along the way, they taught hundreds of thousands of students about penmanship, bookkeeping, and commercial law and practices. They struggled to define the nature of business professionalism and were swept up in the era's disputes between North and South, men and women, owner and worker. The nineteenth-century commercial college, in short, reflected the multidimensional character of American society, especially when it came to the challenges and concerns faced by for-profits as they entered the twentieth century.

CHAPTER TWO

Competition

Despite a remarkable period of growth and expansion throughout the nineteenth century, FPCUs faced serious, industry-busting threats at the start of the twentieth century. Threats from all directions suggested the for-profit's era might have come to an end. A tidal wave of professionalization efforts in law, business, and medical education as well as expanding trade and technical education at nonprofit secondary and postsecondary institutions began to sink FPCUs as it swept across the country. Operators of proprietary institutions witnessed the rise and dominance of graduate schools approved by professional organizations at a time when the fate of institutions increasingly rested on such approval. Professional societies and organizations began wielding the power to name institutional winners and losers, a power not lost on the for-profit sector. FPCU owners also feared a significant drop in enrollments as a new breed of two-year colleges and public high schools flush with state and federal funds for practical, career-oriented studies attracted large numbers of students and supporters. The secure niche FPCUs enjoyed in the past—the one overlooked by traditional institutions—no longer looked so secure as competition from all sides increased. But, then again, few elements of American life appeared stable during the Progressive Era.[1]

For-profits entered the twentieth century with the same unsettling concerns facing most Americans, concerns having to do with rapid increases in urbanization, industrialization, and modernization. Vast new fortunes displaced old ones as cheap, immigrant labor expanded the workforce and ran factories that used increasingly complex technologies. Titans of industry ushered in an era of immense change generating uncertainty about the future. Was the country headed into a utopia of production of goods desired by the masses? Or was it creating a dystopia of factory wage slaves who lived in squalor and were oppressed by their corporate masters? The nation craved progress, but notions of progress in social, political, and economic terms multiplied, complicating the nature and character of the "progressive" age. In the end, *reform* was the watchword of the era and it evoked images of humanitarian concern for the disadvantaged and disenfranchised as much as economic efficiency for the most well off.[2]

For profit-driven colleges and universities, all of this Progressive Era change and reform looked ominous. Out of this tumult, three competition-related threats, in particular, rocked the FPCU world: early twentieth-century profession building in law, medicine, and business; institutional diversification and specialization; and government involvement in education. These changes brought about the greatest flux for proprietary postsecondary institutions. They exposed the for-profit's vulnerabilities, shined light on FPCU practices, and reminded the public of important distinctions between for-profits and nonprofits that had characterized the two since their inception in early America.

The earliest example of the professionalization clampdown on twentieth-century FPCUs began with the founding of the Association of American Law Schools (AALS) in 1900. This organization immediately picked up where the bar left off, spelling trouble for proprietary legal education not accustomed to serious oversight and scrutiny. Late in the nineteenth century, only one-fifth of all attorneys admitted to the bar each year had attended law school. The American Bar Association (ABA) at the time took a stab at requiring a standardized course of study for aspiring lawyers, but the attempt failed miserably. Disagreements within the bar made it impossible for professionalization advocates to produce a firm resolution on admissions, instructional methods, and graduation requirements. In this fog of disagreement, however, ABA members came together on one important point.[3] They categorically rejected for-profit legal instruction and passed a formal resolution on the matter, making their rejection an official position of the ABA: "Further, we believe that law schools should not be operated as commercial enterprises, and that the compensation of any officer or member of its teaching staff should not depend on the number of students or on the fees received."[4]

Despite this flat rejection of FPCUs from the late nineteenth-century legal community, the bar's internal conflicts weakened the organization's ability to control legal education. Competing cultures of practice emerged as a result, leaving an opening for proprietary institutions. On the one hand, defenders of the apprenticeship model preferred practical instruction within the context of the "ideal" law office. These defenders of the status quo wanted faculty with practical experience. On the other hand, the emerging modern American university began to embrace its affiliated, but once-marginalized, law schools and other professional programs. The process of integrating law schools into the academic community brought about new cultural values based on the German scientific (*Wissenschaft*) ideal. The Germanic model paved the way for the rise of university-based career law professors who used case-based methods and the law library as their laboratory to teach reasoning and theory. Increasingly, university-based programs, with their theoretical emphasis, began to replace proprietary schools focused on day-to-day law office needs in the service of advocacy and justice.[5]

From the outset, the AALS recognized these competing law school cultures and sided with the nonprofits. Critics of the for-profit approach wanted the AALS to expose the chaotic, unsystematic nature of the law office approach to training lawyers. The scope and sequence of the curriculum, they argued, depended too heavily on the cases the master's office received. The apprentice had no assurance of a broad, complete, or sequential training in law. Since most law offices specialized in such areas as tax, real estate, or patent law, the apprentice could expect to learn a specialty but not necessarily much else. The drift toward "formalism," as some historians have described it, meant increasing pressure from law schools and the ABA to standardize requirements for admission to the bar.[6]

The AALS advocated formalizing legal instruction while FPCUs fought to preserve the apprenticeship system. The dustup between these two interest groups, however, was woefully lopsided, although it didn't start out that way. For most of the last half of the nineteenth century, traditional law schools occupied a minor place in the legal community and had virtually no role in ensuring professional competencies or entry into practice. Bar associations—as well as personal relationships formed between aspiring lawyers and the established judicial circuit—served as the primary gatekeepers. The dramatic change disrupting all of this came in the form of an overwhelming demand for legal training at the turn of the twentieth century. Demand far exceeded the supply of law offices willing and able to absorb students. As a result, the number of university-based law schools grew from 1,200 students in twenty-one schools in 1870 to 4,500 students in sixty-one schools in 1890. Between 1890 and 1910, these nonprofits doubled in number (Figure 2.1). Overcrowding of offices and traditional schools, along with the rise of prominent law firms focused on corporate clients rather than personal relationships with bar members, produced Progressive Era calls for change and reform.[7]

From 1900 onward, the AALS gained confidence in its quest to unseat for-profit apprenticeships. The organization drew increasing strength from both the demands for reform and the swelling enrollments at university-based law schools. AALS supporters also received a boost from state lawmakers who began passing laws (or, in many cases, reinstituting laws from the antebellum period) requiring at least an apprenticeship for entry into the profession. State officials, over time, used these laws to make nonprofits the preferred alternative to the old system. The AALS gained further momentum from Alfred Z. Reed's investigative report, *Present-Day Law Schools*. This study was sponsored by the Carnegie Foundation, a philanthropic organization founded by Andrew Carnegie for "the advancement of teaching." The report added fuel to the reformist's fire by expos-

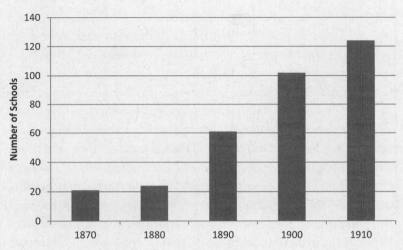

FIGURE 2.1. University-Based Law Schools, 1870–1910. *Sources:* Robert Bocking Stevens, *Law School: Legal Education in America from the 1850s to the 1980s* (Chapel Hill: University of North Carolina Press, 1983), 76; William Johnson, *Schooled Lawyers: A Study in the Clash of Professional Cultures* (New York: New York University Press, 1978), 133; *Handbook of the Association of American Law Schools and Proceedings of the Seventeenth Annual Meeting Held at Chicago, IL, December 30–31, 1919* (Washington, DC: Association of American Law Schools, 1919), 41.

ing great unevenness in legal instruction across the country. Some proprietary schools, Reed stated, "profited" by doing "little more than to provide the training needed to pass superficial bar examinations. . . . No authority made their relative merits clear." The report highlighted distinctions between kinds of institutions, grouping them into categories that ranked proprietary schools as "low entrance" or "short-course" schools and nonprofit programs as "high entrance full-time schools." At first, the AALS's efforts and the Carnegie report made little difference. Enrollment increases in AALS member (25 percent) versus nonmember institutions (100 percent) during the period from 1901 to 1917 suggested that FPCUs had dodged the first major professionalization bullet of the century.[8]

For-profit legal education continued to survive into the 1920s and 1930s, but so too did the demands for reform during these decades. As late as 1927, for instance, no state required attendance at a law school to practice law. Instead, regulations called for an apprenticeship or some evidence of training, whether formal, informal, proprietary, or nonprofit. Up to that point, those who had received some instruction and could pass the bar exam earned the right to practice law. During the following decade, a few states, like West Virginia, Colorado, Kentucky, and Wyoming, began enforcing a minimum numbers of years of legal training to enter the profession. Even these states, though, couldn't agree on one, two, or three years as a minimum requirement. Discrepancies among state requirements eventually brought the ABA and AALS together to create professional standards. The associations started publishing lists of approved institutions, attracting the attention of state legislators wanting to burnish their Progressive Era reformist credibility. During this period, only one-third of law schools in operation received ABA-AALS approval. As a result, enrollments at unapproved institutions dropped precipitously, by approximately 10,000 students, between 1928 and 1935.[9]

The fatal blow for unapproved, unaccredited for-profits in legal education, however, came from soldiers returning from World War II. These veterans received federal funding to attend postsecondary institutions of their choice. The vast majority of those who chose to enroll in law schools went to ABA-AALS approved institutions. Tens of thousands followed this path, including veterans and traditional students, in the forties and fifties. By then, only an estimated 14 percent of the law school student population attended unapproved schools. Federal support allowed aspiring lawyers to choose higher quality, nonprofits over marginal, unapproved, unaccredited, and proprietary programs by a landslide. With students voting with their feet, the era of the for-profit law school as the profession's dominant institution came to an end.[10]

Like proprietary law schools and apprenticeships, for-profit business colleges benefited greatly from the period before the early twentieth-century professionalization movements. These for-profits offered courses in accounting, finance, marketing, management, and other areas without oversight from professional associations. They also benefited from the lack of interest in commercial studies shown by those in traditional higher education. The FPCUs filled a niche with their penmanship, bookkeeping, and commercial law classes. As long as traditional colleges and universities ignored these areas, for-profits could count on a steady stream of new applicants. All of these advantages began to evaporate at the turn of the century as the modern university took shape and as business leaders jumped on the professionalization bandwagon.[11]

Operators of early twentieth-century commercial and business colleges likely saw the writing on the wall. After the Wharton School at the University of Pennsylvania came programs at the University of Chicago and the University of California in 1899. Over the next decade, New York University, Dartmouth, and Harvard all added undergraduate or graduate programs in business. Around the same time, the American Association of Public Accountants appeared. Their *Journal of Accountancy* became a monthly in 1905. The American Association of University Instructors in Accounting (1915) later gave rise to the American Accounting Association (1917). Their journal, *The Accounting Review*, became a staple in the profession in 1926. The Association of National Advertisers was founded in 1910 and the American Marketing Association (and their *Journal of Marketing*) in 1937. The professionalization of management occurred under the auspices of engineering associations and organizations until it broke off to form a separate Administrative Management Association (1919) and the American Management Association (1925).[12]

Steeper competition from nonprofits and increasingly sophisticated scholarly outlets for business studies meant an almost certain end to early twentieth-century for-profits in business education, especially those following old school models and principles. The tremendous leap in the number of nonprofit business programs and enrollments mirrored an interest in advanced, specialized, and academic training in the field (Figure 2.2). The old for-profit institutions, with

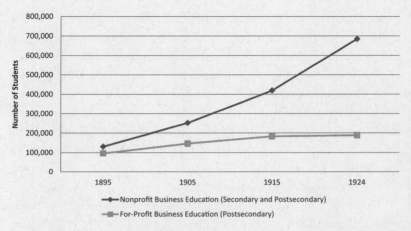

FIGURE 2.2. Business Program Enrollments, 1895–1924. *Source:* Rakesh Khurana, *From Higher Aims to Hired Hands: The Social Transformation of American Business Schools and the Unfulfilled Promise of Management as a Profession* (Princeton, NJ: Princeton University Press, 2007), 89.

their generalist courses of study, felt pressure to adapt, reinvent themselves, or perish.[13]

The same threats descending on proprietary legal and business education also fell on for-profit medical schools. Of the three—legal, business, and medicine—the American medical community underwent the most sudden and impressive professional upheaval during the opening decades of the twentieth century, leaving medical FPCUs in critical condition. Professionalization advocates in medicine cast for-profits in a particularly unfavorable light, putting both disreputable and disadvantaged schools out of business.

Big changes began in 1910, when Abraham Flexner's report for the Carnegie Foundation sent shockwaves throughout the entire medical community. The report, *Medical Education in the United States and Canada,* acknowledged the significant role past proprietary institutions and apprenticeships had played in training physicians. Even the few medical schools affiliated with traditional colleges, in most cases, operated as commercial enterprises without salary support from college treasuries. They were self-sustaining, running predominantly on student tuition and fees. Proprietary schools, especially those focused on producing high returns, generated pressure on all institutions to compete with one another for students. Competition of this sort created a downward spiral in requirements for admission and graduation. During the mid-nineteenth century, the University of Pennsylvania tried to lengthen its medical program from four to six months, acting on recommendations from the fledgling American Medical Association (AMA). Enrollments dropped like a rock. Students flocked to area proprietary programs offering shorter courses of study for the same degree. Penn faculty responded by completely cutting the undergraduate degree and reducing requirements for their doctoral degree to below what they used to expect for the bachelor's program. FPCUs taught traditional institutions that medical schools with the shortest programs attracted the largest number of students.[14]

Flexner also acknowledged the proliferation of medical institutions of all types during the decade before the twentieth century, noting that the total number, including ones founded purely as proprietary institutions, increased from 116 to 151 during the period. From his perspective, this growth had exacerbated the problem of wildly uneven programs of study. Many weaker institutions relied on tuition and fees and used strategies from a previous age to survive: reduce standards for admission and lower requirements for graduation. By the opening of the twentieth century, the downward trend in quality and standards created by competition clashed with Progressive Era professionalization movements. With a team of assistants, Flexner conducted a sweeping study of medical programs across the country. By the time they undertook the survey, many states had already instituted specific minimum education requirements for those applying to take state licensure exams. Requirements included graduation from a medical school that had upgraded from the common four-month curriculum to the newer three- and four-year programs. Some states required the new programs to offer clinical and laboratory experiences. In the last two decades of the nineteenth century, schools with multiyear courses of study increased from 27 percent to 96 percent. For Flexner, the challenge was in distinguishing between what schools advertised and what they actually offered. He approached his survey by building on the AMA's 1903 Committee on Education (later, the Council on Medical Education) report based on site visits, which found many medical colleges to be "absolutely worthless." Flexner started his own series of site visits in Baltimore by observing the teaching practices and facilities at Johns Hopkins University, considered one of the foremost medical schools of the era. With these observations in mind, he took his team to inspect the 155 medical schools across the country.[15]

Of all the institutional types he studied, Flexner found the greatest amount of fraud and misleading practices at for-profits. Based on the nationwide tour of campuses, Flexner concluded that it was virtually impossible for competent, well-staffed, and well-equipped proprietary medical schools to exist. In other words, for-profits had to go. They no longer served a useful purpose in an age of rapidly expanding scientific and medical knowledge demanding resources beyond those available to FPCUs. To his mind, institutions solely dependent on tuition and fees couldn't afford to maintain medical standards. Flexner's report documented how proprietary institutions violated their own admissions standards to fill empty seats, failed to invest in modern laboratory equipment necessary for basic medical training, and relied heavily on local physicians as part-time faculty rather than promoting long-term career professors who had vested interests in the success of the institution. The profit motive, in short, conflicted with the professionalization needs of the medical profession.[16]

Some of the proprietary medical institutions hardest hit by Flexner's *Medical Education* report were those serving marginalized communities. Many for-profits catering to aspiring black physicians, for instance, didn't last long after the publication began to make its rounds. The report generated bad publicity for institutions already experiencing financial strain. The ones in the worst shape were distinct from missionary-based, religiously affiliated programs established after the Civil War designed to train a corps of African American doctors to serve the southern states and elsewhere. For-profits, by contrast, had no formal ties to church or philanthropic groups and their sole purpose was to generate tuition-based profit from poor, marginalized African Americans. Flexner discovered a group of black, for-profit institutions—including Louisville National Medical College, Hannibal Medical College of Memphis, Chatta-nooga National Medical College, and others in Tennessee and Maryland—that failed to make the grade in terms of student suc-cess on state exams and quality of facilities. Flexner studied these institutions carefully and found false advertising, fabricated faculty credentials, and a failure to follow their own admissions and gradu-ation requirements. His report called these for-profits "ineffectual" and "in no position to make any contribution of value," accusing them of the kind of business practices later observers would call poverty profiteering.[17]

For those opposed to FPCUs, Flexner's *Medical Education* pro-vided all the ammunition necessary to do away with proprietary medical schools for good. It confirmed suspicions of fraudulent behavior traced back to the previous century. According to C. C. Fite, a late nineteenth-century secretary of the Medical Society of the State of Tennessee, his state's lack of FPCU oversight had attracted an unscrupulous, even criminal, element to the operation and man-agement of proprietary medical schools: "We have no laws bearing upon the practice of medicine. . . . Confidence men and all that ilk ply their 'trade' with no restriction whatever. A farmer boy too lazy to plow reads an old work on [medical] practice, or 'Every Man his own Doctor,' invests $6 in drugs and is a physician."[18] Flexner's site visits had turned up precisely such beliefs at FPCUs. He reported on for-profits that had operators without medical degrees, facilities without buildings as advertised, and graduates without reasonable chances of passing state board exams.[19]

Flexner wasn't alone in making the connection between suspi-cions of FPCU fraud and actual practices on the ground in early twentieth-century medical training. Arthur Dean Bevan, chair of the

Council on Medical Education, had conducted his own site visits. He tracked examination scores from medical schools across the country and drafted (but didn't circulate to the public) reports targeting specific institutions with the aim of helping them raise standards. Based on these visits, Bevan concluded that the great problem in the profession had to do with "medical schools conducted solely for profit." These were, as he put it, nothing more than "a menace" to the profession. Under his leadership, the Council on Medical Education pushed to have all for-profit medical schools excluded from recognition and recommended having them eliminated altogether.[20]

The work and commentary of Flexner, Fite, Bevan, and many others put medical FPCUs on the defensive. State agencies mobilized in response to calls for reform, and few proprietary schools of medicine survived the Progressive Era challenge, especially as students questioned the wisdom of enrolling in institutions receiving negative reports from independent reviewers. Within a decade of Flexner's Medical Education, almost half of all medical schools had closed, with the total number of institutions dropping from 155 to 85. By the early 1940s, the number had fallen to 77. The ones that survived were almost all nonprofit institutions affiliated with established colleges and universities or patterned after them.[21]

While professionalization brought an end to many FPCUs, those that remained faced an equally troubling threat from Progressive Era trends having to do with institutional specialization. Higher-education reformers at the start of the twentieth century produced ambitious and enthusiastic plans for reforming, altering, and creating new institutional structures within American postsecondary education, some of which came to fruition. Out of this rush of experimentation came the two-year college.[22]

William Rainey Harper, president of the University of Chicago, spearheaded a two-year college movement in the last few years of the nineteenth century that carved out a space for them within the existing school, college, and university system. This new institu-

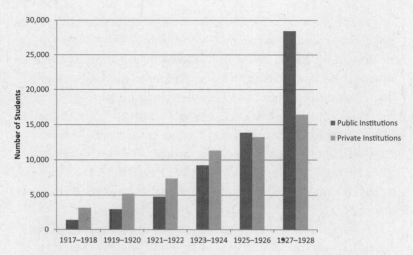

FIGURE 2.3. Junior College Enrollments, 1917–1928. *Source:* Steven G. Brint and Jerome Karabel, *The Diverted Dream: Community Colleges and the Promise of Educational Opportunity in America, 1900–1985* (New York: Oxford University Press, 1989), 26.

tional breed was Harper's response to two demands. The first came from university faculty wanting advanced training and specialization to occur earlier in the undergraduate course of study. The second emerged from pressures created by real and perceived inadequacies of entering college freshmen. Harper turned to the two-year ideal as a way to address both issues and established the first junior college at the University of Chicago in 1896. The idea spread slowly at first, with the founding of Joliet Junior College and two others by the end of the first decade of the twentieth century. But by 1919, the total number had jumped to fifty-two (Figure 2.3).[23]

Joliet set a precedent for granting higher-education access to those without the resources or background necessary for entry into traditional four-year institutions. Two-year institutions initially provided transferable, liberal arts education for students continuing on to a four-year program. The dominant motive for advancing the junior college movement, according to George Zook in 1922, then chief of the higher education division at the US Bureau of Education and later lead editor of *Higher Education for American Democracy,* "appears to me to be economy in education." The two-year college reforms, as he saw it, could bring about a "reduction in the total number of years devoted to elementary and secondary education," which would be "a great boon to professional students." As such, the junior college represented an accelerated pathway for those seeking to enter professional studies. But leading proponents of these colleges didn't only have transferable courses of study in mind. The Lewis Institute (Chicago) and the Bradley Polytechnic Institute (Peoria, Illinois) offered two-year vocational and technical education as well.[24]

Harper and other two-year-college advocates began taking up ground familiar to FPCU operators. Both groups catered to the same student demographic—those who left secondary school and wanted a postsecondary education but were uncertain about completing a four-year undergraduate course of study. For-profits now had to compete with these new publicly supported and financed two-year institutions.[25] The American Association of Junior Colleges (AAJC) in 1922 made this competition official when it defined the colleges they represented as offering "two years of instruction of strictly collegiate grade. This curriculum may include those courses usually offered in the first two years of the four-year colleges; in which case these courses must be identical, in scope and thoroughness, with corresponding courses of the standard four-year college. The junior college may, and is likely to, develop a different type of curriculum suited to the larger and ever-changing civic, social, religious, and vocational needs of the entire community."[26] The shift in terminology from *junior* to *community* college occurred in the mid-1930s, emphasizing the second half of the AAJC's definition. By the forties, the scope of offerings expected from the community college was, as one report described it, "limited only by the vision, the energy, and the ingenuity of the college staff and by the size of their budget." With such a wide-ranging imperative, for-profits recognized that their days without such competition were numbered. But which FPCU offerings, programs, and institutions would disappear and how quickly remained unclear. The Great Depression and the economic challenges of the period prompted two-year institutions to diversify their offerings to include job-training programs. Community colleges were asked to serve on the front lines in the national fight against poverty and unemployment through vocational education. Institutional diversification continued after World War II as a result of the Truman Commission of 1948, and proposals for the expansion of nonprofit, publicly supported community colleges followed.[27]

While FPCUs competed directly with community colleges for students, new vocational and industrial secondary programs of the early twentieth century threatened to take an even larger share of potential for-profit enrollments. Practical secondary education, as noted in a 1906 Massachusetts report, raised "the most important question which faces the educational world today." What should be done, they asked, about children between the ages of fourteen and sixteen who left school and lacked skills necessary for entering an increasingly complicated and technical workplace? Vocational and industrial high school education offered one answer, but it also posed a series of additional questions about which kind of practical studies should be offered, to whom, in what fashion, and to what end. None of these issues had easy answers. Many of them had to do with expanding immigrant populations and increasingly specialized industrial needs. Some argued for requiring vocational high school studies; others wanted to create electives available to those who showed an interest in applied programs. Philosopher John Dewey gave a push to both positions when he urged diversification along vocational lines, although he advocated a view shot through with a contentious view of human nature and experience. He did so when suggesting that "in the great majority of human beings the distinctively intellectual interest is not dominant. They have the so-called practical impulse and disposition." With all this momentum, fueled by Progressive Era angst over urbanization, immigration, industrialization, and modernization, high schools expanded their technical and vocational offerings.[28]

FPCUs had largely been protected from this threat from below because, as late as the last decade of the nineteenth century, the traditional, college preparatory curriculum had continued to dominate secondary education. Members of the National Education Association (NEA) followed and, at times, generated heated debates over competing visions of high schools and their role in society. A segment of the NEA wanted to break with the college preparatory model and diversify the course of study to meet the needs of the more than 90 percent of high school graduates who didn't attend college. This group advocated a more practical, vocational, and technical education that had much in common, at least in terms of curricula, with the interests of FPCUs and proprietary apprenticeship programs. Another segment wanted to stay the course and maintain a strict focus on college preparation. To respond to these competing ideals, the NEA commissioned what came to be known as the Committee of Ten, led by Harvard's president Charles W. Eliot. The report they produced, in effect, maintained a prominent place for classical education while opening the door to modern languages, a broader range of social, scientific, and historical studies, and new purposes for the high school in Progressive Era America.[29]

By the end of the first decade of the twentieth century, Eliot had reversed himself on the issue. After having witnessed dramatic changes in the nation's industrial development, the idea of teaching ancient languages to students facing huge leaps in technological and scientific advancement simply no longer seemed tenable. He became sympathetic to the work of the National Society for the Promotion of Industrial Education (NSPIE), founded in 1906 with a wide swath of the public's support, from Wall Street to Main Street. Two years after the society's founding, Eliot made a formal address to the NSPIE. The talk focused on the need for practical, trade, and vocational schools for those children, fourteen years old and younger, "who are unfortunately obliged to leave the regular public school system." His response to the dropout problem, and the industrial needs of the Progressive Era, was to continue to specialize and diversify program offerings for students who had no plans to attend a four-year liberal arts college. What's more, he enlisted elementary school teachers to begin tracking students at an early age. Eliot wanted these teachers to "sort out the pupils and sort them out by their evident or probable destinies." With the college preparatory curriculum no longer foremost on the mind of Harvard's influential president, proponents of vocational education saw a bright future.[30]

This shift in secondary education programs meant much more competition for FPCUs. The greatest cause for concern along these lines came from federal appropriations to support new high school initiatives. Between 1917 and 1946, five key acts of Congress provided over $150 million to the industrial and vocational education movement. This funding threatened the very existence of FPCUs in this sector (Figure 2.4). If students received adequate training from tuition-free high school vocational programs, backed by federal subsidies, what need would they have for proprietary colleges and apprenticeships that offered similar training?[31]

The Smith-Hughes Act of 1917 was the first of five appropriations to inspire secondary education reform efforts that directly competed with for-profit career programs across the country. The act came out of a congressional commission charged with exploring ways to provide national aid to vocational education. Throughout the process, the commission, and the legislation that ultimately came from it, triggered sectional tensions in the halls of Congress. While deciding on which kinds of training to fund and how to distribute the funding, congressional leaders staked out positions representing the industrial North and the agrarian South. Those from southern states managed to take the lead in brokering vocational education legislation. In this case, Senator Hoke Smith and Representative Dudley Hughes, both from the state of Georgia, kept an eye on benefiting agricultural as well as social and political interests in their region, such as providing it with funds to support a segregated system of education. Given the congressional seniority system and the relative power of Smith and Hughes, agrarian interests won out. They succeeded in pressing a states' rights argument, especially

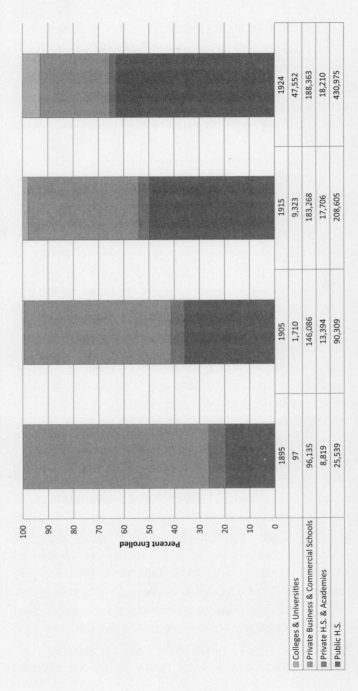

FIGURE 2.4. Secondary and Postsecondary Enrollments in Business Courses, 1895–1924. *Source:* Rakesh Khurana, *From Higher Aims to Hired Hands: The Social Transformation of American Business Schools and the Unfulfilled Promise of Management as a Profession* (Princeton, NJ: Princeton University Press, 2007), 89.

	1895	1905	1915	1924
Colleges & Universities	97	1,710	9,323	47,552
Private Business & Commercial Schools	96,135	146,086	183,268	188,363
Private H.S. & Academies	8,819	13,394	17,706	18,210
Public H.S.	25,539	90,309	208,605	430,975

on increasing state-level management of funds and reducing over-sight authority given to a proposed Federal Board of Vocational Education.[32]

When Smith-Hughes became law in 1917, the act established an ominous precedent for proprietary institutions. It created a multi-million-dollar channel of federal funding to public institutions serving a student demographic previously targeted by FPCUs. For a decade, Smith-Hughes turned on the vocational education funding tap. Half of the funding went to agriculture, 40 percent to trades and industry, and the remainder to home economics programs. The George-Reed Act of 1929 followed a similar path, but it split the entire appropriation equally between agriculture and home economics; in George-Reed, trade and technical training didn't receive provisioning. The George-Ellsey Act of 1934 dispersed funds in thirds: 33 percent for agriculture, 33 percent for trades and industry, and 33 percent for home economics. This distribution was repeated in the George-Deen Act of 1937 and modified slightly in the George-Barden Act of 1946. Collectively, these five pieces of legislation dispersed over $150 million to public high schools across the nation, creating a vocational education juggernaut poised to sink the FPCU.[33]

Even with the massive infusion of federal funding to competing programs—and the competitive challenges created by professional-ization and the two-year-college movement—FPCUs faced their greatest pressures from within. The threat had to do with the way proprietary institutions handled competition among themselves during the opening decades of the twentieth century. Investigations into questionable, unethical, and even illegal behavior among for-profits produced a surge of bad publicity, casting a pall over an al-ready beleaguered industry. The best-known internecine scandals came from proprietary business schools in major cities, but the problems they raised illustrated broader concerns the public had about profit motives in education. Reports about the industry found more than a few bad apples in major urban areas. They uncovered evidence suggesting that the profit motive itself conflicted with the very ideal of ethical practices in recruiting, retaining, and preparing students for the world of work, service, or further study. The scandals and controversies studied in these reports echoed the practices of earlier for-profit operators who advertised great success through easy course work.[34]

Among the most comprehensive and far-reaching early twentieth-century studies of trade and commercial FPCUs was one conducted by the City Club of Chicago. This nonprofit organization—founded in 1903 and born out of the Progressive Era desire to tackle social, political, and economic corruption—started looking into problems characteristic of for-profits in 1909. A special committee on vocational education gathered data over the next few years from nine states and over twenty major cities, including Chicago, Boston, New York, St. Louis, Philadelphia, Indianapolis, and Milwaukee. Philosopher George Herbert Mead, a leading pragmatist and founder of social psychology, served as chair of the investigation throughout and assisted the committee in completing its *Report on Vocational Training in Chicago and in Other Cities,* published in 1912. From the outset, the report identified "evidence" of the "unsatisfactory commercial training given in our private commercial colleges" and the "vast sums" students paid in tuition. Based on the data received, Mead and his colleagues concluded that FPCUs suffered from intractable problems rooted in the conflict between education and the profit motive. Institutions relying on student fees and tuition to survive typically showed greater concern for new applicants than for current students. With an estimated 25 to 35 percent of "gross receipts" paid out to solicitors, for-profits devoted a significant portion of their budget to competition-related expenses. FPCUs were, as the report put it, "under the necessity of keeping their attendance, to pay dividends on their capital, and therefore conduct a vigorous campaign of solicitation which extends even to the pupils in grammar schools." For this reason, the report turned to one of the for-profit's most notorious problems: solicitation.[35]

According to the 1912 City Club report, solicitation had to do with recruiting students for proprietary institutions. It was something unique to the for-profit industry, since no similar practice had emerged from public or private nonprofit postsecondary programs. The report blasted solicitors for their unscrupulous behavior:

> Most of the solicitors for these schools are working on a commission basis and tend, therefore, to be more interested in securing students than they are in telling the truth . . . in the amount of business they secure than in the maturity or fitness of the pupils they solicit. In very many cases the pupils, even from the fifth grade and up, are induced to leave the public schools for the purpose of taking a course in some business college.[36]

The committee described solicitation as a "serious evil in the community," given the way proprietary institutions used the practice to prey on the young. It lured children out of public schools, half of whom, at least in Chicago, never completed the eighth grade. It made promises to them about employment expectations that the for-profits couldn't possibly keep. And, in the end, solicitation resulted in "wasted years" and wasted money for children who statistically ended up in low-wage, unskilled jobs. The entire practice was based on "misrepresentation" benefiting proprietary institutions at the expense of the young and unwitting. To the City Club committee, for-profits had become "a source of positive injury to the children." The report found that FPCUs in Chicago alone enrolled an estimated 19,000 students who spent almost $1.5 million per year in for-profit tuition. The city, meanwhile, spent $1.1 million for the entire public high school budget, which served 17,781 students. These figures and other data collected by the report's authors indicated that students left public schools because of a lack of interest in their offerings, rather than a financial need, only to end up in an inadequate, "unsatisfactory" for-profit educational system.[37]

The City Club blamed competition for the problem of solicitation. Their investigation documented the way teachers and students in public schools felt about this "widespread" competitive pressure. According to interviews, teachers objected to the aggressive practice of extracting lists of public schools students, "one can not say how," in order to target children and their parents. The solicitors "canvass these families thoroughly and repeatedly," describing high school as a "loss of time" and the for-profit college as a "short cut to wage-earning." The "persuasion" of the solicitor, as one teacher described it, has managed to capture "my best pupils." Through the "indefatigable" work of these sales representatives, students also felt the heat generated by this competitive pressure. Of 862 students surveyed between 1909 and 1911 in ten high schools about why more students didn't continue on to high school, 565 put "the work of the business college agents" at the top of their list. "Perhaps parents wouldn't be so much against high school," stated one student, "if it were not for the agents that come around and persuade many parents to let their children go to business college." Another student reported having had "about ten agents who came to my house last summer" on ten separate occasions, many of whom called the student's plan to attend high school "foolish."[38] Then there were students who recognized the difference between public and proprietary institutions on this mark: "There is no one going from house to house telling of things they have in high school, and people don't bother to find out. I have had this same [solicitation] experience, only that my father, being a well-educated man and holding a good position, knew different, and I was compelled to go to high school."[39] When asked about the high school dropout problem, students gave similar answers. Out of nearly 500 student responses to this issue, 341 blamed for-profit "advertisements" and the "work of the solicitors" *within* the public high school. As one student put it, these sales representatives take the "easily persuaded" students and, according to another, "the more unlettered class of people." A dividing line had appeared between students with educated families who knew to question the claims of for-profits and those with families who knew no better.[40]

Operators of proprietary institutions interviewed for the City Club report had equally harsh words for solicitation and blamed competition for forcing FPCUs to cut costs and focus on raising revenues. The cost cutting resulted in "employing teachers who lack training" and "soliciting children," without regard for the quality of instruction or the likelihood of student success. "I will welcome the day," said one for-profit owner, "when every young man and woman who needs and wants commercial training can get it without having to pay the fee charged by special schools."[41] Other owners, who didn't go so far as to wish the end of the for-profit sector, acknowledged that profit motives had distorted the values, mission, and priorities of trade and vocational education. "Many of the proprietors," explained an operator, "care more for the dollars received as tuition than the kind of training they are giving; because of solicitation, we are getting our pupils too young and immature; the high cost of solicitation renders it impossible to provide high-class instructors."[42] For these operators, solicitation was a symptom of a much more important problem that could be traced back to the pursuit of profits and the way it conflicted with educational goals. The quest for increased revenues, as they saw it, affected everything for-profits did. It determined how they went about the business of recruiting students, setting the length of the curriculum, paying teacher salaries, and funding solicitation campaigns.[43]

The City Club concluded their report with the view that competition for student dollars had produced unacceptably low quality FPCUs in the early twentieth century. Of the institutions surveyed across nine states, "only a few of them are really efficient, and in every case the course is too short."[44] "The whole attempt," they continued,

is to drive the students through in as short a time as possible,
this being, of course, an attractive feature in the case of the
student who must be a wage-earner immediately after he
graduates; from his point of view the sooner he graduates
the better. The business colleges will take students ordinarily
without regard to age, though several maintain they take none
under fifteen years. They pay little attention to previous training
and do not take into account the natural adaptability or ability
on the part of the student, i.e., no attempt is made to inquire

whether the prospective student is fitted to become a business man either in a directive or directed position. All is grist that comes to the business college mill.[45]

City Club proposed a solution to all of the problems stemming from FPCUs and the profit motive in education: expand nonprofit trade, career, vocational, technical, and commercial studies at the secondary level. "This need," they insisted, "could be better met by public schools." Their report recommended publicly funded, tuition-free secondary programs backed by local and state support as the only reasonable alternative. The public sector, they argued, had efficiency advantages in not having to pay for solicitation expenses; had financial support to offer longer, more comprehensive, well-staffed programs requested by business leaders; and had the added benefit, as a public institution, of being able to integrate studies beneficial for "active life" as a citizen over and above that of a future employee.[46]

When the Chicago report came out in 1912, few could have appreciated it as much as New York's Bertha Stevens. As one of the era's leading experts in commercial studies for boys and girls, Stevens would've instantly agreed with the City Club's rejection of for-profits and praised its public rather than market-based solutions. She had long tracked the unemployment rates of for-profit college graduates and identified a large segment of these institutions as a fraud perpetrated on young, desperate, and unsuspecting students. The "honest school," she charged, "cannot guarantee positions," as many institutions had.[47]

For her own study, *Private Commercial Schools: Manhattan and the Bronx* (1918), Stevens interviewed 1,952 children and twenty principals in twenty-nine public schools within twenty-four districts. To this, she added an examination of the solicitation work of sixty-three for-profit commercial schools and at least twenty-two fly-by-night operations in the area that had opened and closed without much time for investigation. In addition, she gathered information on 1,682 students who had attended FPCUs since 1913. Based on this evidence, Stevens viewed revenue-focused competition as a "serious" problem responsible for forcing standards downward, reducing teaching quality, shortening courses, and advertising to students too young or unable to benefit from postsecondary instruction.[48] "The effect of competition," she noted, "is, too often, to concentrate all the energy and ingenuity upon methods of outwitting a rival, instead of using this energy and ingenuity in building up a better school and thus winning fairly by offering to students a better thing for their money. . . . The hottest rivalry is to be found in the relations of the private schools with each other."[49] Her investigation revealed evidence—documented, published, advertised, and experienced by students and their families—about the way rivals fought "with all disregard of truth and fairness." The "misdoings" of these institutions appeared frequently in documents gathered and testimony "enthusiastically" provided by interviewees.[50]

The unscrupulous, competition-born behavior of FPCUs Stevens exposed had much to do with fraudulent activity directed at students and other for-profits. Proprietary college students, for instance, received unmarked mailings from rival institutions. These mailings falsely warned them not to attend the school in which they were enrolled due an infectious disease outbreak at the students' institution. The noticed would be "signed" by the manager of the stricken school. Others, particularly female students, were victims of deliberately "unscrupulous" behavior by fly-by-night for-profits requiring payment in advance of instruction. In one of many cases, a group of one hundred or so women and girls "were cheated out of months of schooling and a good deal of money" when an operator collected advance tuition from students the day before the institution closed. Students interviewed in such cases called the proprietor a "crook" who had profited from their hopes of removing themselves from poverty.[51]

Stevens interviewed for-profit owners as well, but, to her mind, their replies were underwhelming. They asserted their right to exist because of historical precedent and their role as "discoverers and pioneers" in areas of education overlooked by traditional colleges and universities. They aspired to fill a niche by providing short, practical courses that could be completed in the kind of time frame (e.g., four to six months) suitable for those looking to transition quickly into the workforce. And they argued that they offered an educational alternative to those not suited for or not successful in the public school system. "Public school does right in keeping to ideals in education," one proprietor told Stevens, but "the private [for-profit] school must exist for the minority who cannot follow the ideal." From comments like these, Stevens picked up on a theme of fear. These owners and managers of FPCUs, at bottom, worried that a public system of vocational education might put for-profits out of business. The arguments advanced by FPCUs attempted to "justify an object which had in reality no aim beyond that of an opportunist's business enterprise."[52]

As with the City Club study, Stevens reserved her sharpest words for when she described the problems with solicitation. She found that "solicitors" in New York "work on a commission and have no other connection with the school which employs them. They can make verbal contracts which the school later may not uphold. Arguments used most effectively by agents are the shortness of the course, the futility of high school education or training, the undesirability of factory work, and the guarantee of a position."[53] On average, children reported receiving five to nine personal visits from FPCU agents. Solicitors gathered names and addresses by paying children in grammar schools to collect this information from their peers. These agents promised anywhere from two cents per name to eight dollars per page. While some received payment, children also reported never receiving a cent. In addition to hiring children to traffic in personal information, for-profits sponsored fake contests and awards to extract personal information from grammar school students and their parents.[54]

Both the City Club and the Stevens reports revealed competitive pressures and rivalries among for-profits that had a corrosive effect on education from the elementary to the collegiate level. It shifted priorities from instruction to recruitment, misdirected the energy of proprietors, consumed budgets toward unproductive ends, displaced quality instruction, and mislead students or, worse, left them with empty purses and empty promises. The recommendations coming from both reports focused on replacing for-profits with a more efficient, publicly funded version of vocational education at the high school level. As the City Club described it, students left school less because they needed to support their families and more because they disliked the strictly academic curriculum. By expanding their vocational curriculum, public schools could retain students with practical interests, providing them with a tuition-free program of study while also continuing to prepare them for "active life" as future citizens of a democratic society. Stevens came to the same conclusion about needing to build a public alternative to prevent the profit motive from eroding educational quality and opportunity. "Private commercial schools as a group," she noted, "are receiving too many and the public schools too few of the city's younger candidates for commercial instruction." In the process, FPCUs admitted children "too young and too unprepared" to benefit from their instruction, provided a curriculum "too short to be thorough," lacked basic English instruction desperately desired by business leaders, and paid "lower grade" teachers a pittance. A public alternative would give parents a far more objective measure of whether their children could benefit from vocational instruction. Such schools, not dependent on direct payment of tuition and fees, could give a "clear-cut, frankly explained refusal" to admit a boy or girl that would "deter many parents from investing money in private instruction."[55]

The calls to action from these two reports focused primarily on creating a public alternative to the for-profit model. That was the ideal solution they offered based on extensive research at the local, regional, and national levels. But they also pushed for interim solutions, asking states to take immediate action in regulating proprietary institutions already in existence. The misleading advertising and solicitation on behalf of FPCUs "could be eliminated if, by legislative provision, private schools were compelled to file at the State Department of Education samples of all advertising material, and the State Department were given power to censor it." Laws could also make it "illegal for schools to use published lists of names in endorsement of their work, unless definite addresses are appended and the date of attendance at the school is indicated." City Club members called on boards of education to clean up the pollution created by for-profits in much the same way inspections by "the City Board of Health" controlled sanitation in the cities. Stevens came to a similar conclusion when she urged states to regulate for-profits the way they regulated medical education, "issuing of State license" for those wanting to open a proprietary educational institution. The license would require standardized courses of study, standards for admissions, recruitment, and graduation, and the revocation of licenses for noncompliance.[56]

Reformers of the first few decades of the twentieth century, at bottom, wanted the state to intervene on the matter of FPCUs. They objected to the hands-off, laissez-faire handling of the for-profit sector's extreme business practices, which had begun to borrow from the most volatile and competition-driven parts of the economy. This was no small objection, given what a British observer once described as a "perfect orgy of speculation" on Wall Street during the Roaring Twenties. The Great Depression following the market crash of 1929 taught the markets a lesson about the absence of regulation and brought about increased government intervention in American economic life. But it took a war of global proportions to mobilize lawmakers on behalf of those most concerned about the financial, academic, and societal impact of for-profit colleges and universities at the local level.[57]

CHAPTER THREE

Control

FOR-PROFITS WERE THE LAST THING on the minds of most
Americans just before and during World War II. Attention had
turned to the nation's attempts to stay out of the Pacific and European conflicts. But then came Pearl Harbor and, the following day,
Roosevelt's "Day of Infamy" speech. The problems with for-profit
colleges and universities—the bad publicity from questionable,
unethical, and illegal practices; the targeting of grade-school children; the misleading advertisements; the defrauding of students;
and the many other scandals and controversies identified by citizen
groups—receded into the background. More important were the
men and women who left home to serve the country, especially the
1 million casualties of war and the more than 300,000 soldiers who
never returned. The $298 billion war mobilization effort, calculated
at $4 trillion in current dollars, came with strict controls that con-
sumed the public's attention, too. Government agencies regulated
crop prices for farmers, halted the production of hundreds of non-
essential products, and established rationing quotas for canned goods,
meat, coffee, tires, gasoline, shoes, and even toilet paper.[1]

Yet war mobilization and control over the economy had as much
to do with goods as it did with services like education and training.
Government intervention in this area was nothing new after the
popular Depression Era programs that had served over 5 million
unemployed American workers. The Work Projects Administration
(WPA), the Civilian Conservation Corps (CCC), and the National
Youth Administration (NYA) had already established a precedent for
federal funding of public and for-profit education during the thir-
ties. The National Educational Association applauded the public

support, but expressed concern over those institutions "run for profit. . . . They have no place in our system of education." Through the Federal Emergency Relief Act of 1933, nevertheless, states received $500 million to support a wide range of institutional types through "Emergency Education" and "College Student Aid" programs. All three agencies directed their resources to defense needs after the US entry into World War II. With 9 million workers still unemployed from the Great Depression, the WPA, CCC, and NYA funded the retraining of men and women to work with rivets, lathes, drill presses, machine tools, and milling machines for defense industries. Between 1940 and 1945, these agencies stimulated the creation of and enrollment in 13.5 million "Vocational Training for War Production Workers" courses. These studies prepared people for work in automotive, aviation, electrical, foundry, machine, radio, sheet metal, shipbuilding, welding, food processing, engineering, and science industries.[2]

By far the most important World War II–era intervention in American higher education generally, and FPCUs in particular, was the GI Bill of 1944. Also known as the Servicemen's Readjustment Act, it affected college and university expansion as well as regulatory control over postsecondary institutions.[3]

With almost 16 million veterans returning from war and entering the workforce, the GI Bill provided a way to ease their transition back to civilian life. The federal government subsidized home mortgages, provided veterans a monthly stipend for up to a year, and covered full tuition as well as living expenses for education and training. Over 2 million veterans went to college and another 5.5 million enrolled in job-skills programs through the GI Bill. Total enrollments doubled on campuses across the country. Veterans in the immediate postwar era accounted for as much as 49 percent of the overall US higher-education student body. To absorb the influx of funds and adult students, most institutions expanded their facilities, adopted a more corporate and less personal approach to administration, and revised their codes of conduct and parietals to accommodate adult and married students. In the process, veterans who went to college on the GI Bill paved the way toward democratizing higher education in America. Completion rates tripled what colleges had known in the prewar era, and these successes shattered perceptions about the intellectual capacities of veterans and the mystique of collegiate studies.[4]

While existing colleges and universities designed new dormitories, classroom spaces, and campus rules as a result of the GI Bill, FPCUs underwent a different but equally dramatic change. During the five-year period immediately after the signing of the Servicemen's Readjustment Act of 1944, for-profits experienced a 300 percent increase in terms of numbers of institutions across the country. The number of newly registered FPCUs—those created in the five-year period between passage of the GI Bill and October 1949—had reached 5,623. For many lawmakers, this startling development in American higher education raised serious suspicions and questions. They wondered about the sudden increase in the number of FPCUs organized to prepare individuals for war work between 1941 and 1945, as well as the dramatic rise in for-profits specifically catering to veterans. Who was running these new for-profits? Where did they come from and what background did they have? Did they have the best intentions for veterans? Could these new FPCUs be trusted with taxpayer-supported GI Bill monies?[5]

The wave of GI Bill–inspired FPCUs produced new dilemmas, first for state-level lawmakers of the 1940s and, later, for congressional leaders of the 1950s. States had primary responsibility for regulating, monitoring, and controlling for-profits since the GI Bill expressly prohibited federal agencies from exercising a supervisory role over educational institutions. This feature left accreditation and approval processes up to each state and, as a result, great differences began to emerge around the handling of these institutions. What they all shared in common, however, was the need to address increasing and widespread reports of FPCU fraud, abuse, and fly-by-night operations. Public outcry over these problems came with demands for legislative action. In response, states like Illinois, Maryland,

Michigan, New Jersey, New York, Oregon, and Pennsylvania passed new FPCU laws or amended old ones by 1947.[6]

Illinois commissioned one of the most extensive investigations of the late forties as lawmakers there prepared to revise statutes governing and regulating FPCUs. State representative Elroy C. Sandquist spearheaded the effort for the Illinois Legislative Council and learned that citizen groups in the state had long demanded stricter control of "private trade schools." For years, the Chicago Association of Commerce and Industry had decried the lack of "comprehensive and effective legislation in Illinois" and urged that "action should be undertaken in this direction."[7] According to investigations conducted by the Chicago Association's Committee on Education, "Numbers of the proprietary schools in various fields are substandard in many respects, and . . . their students are being victimized. This is due to poor instruction, inadequate facilities, misrepresentation of the benefits to be obtained, questionable contracts and exorbitant fees. A number of individual cases of unethical practices and inadequate services have come to the attention of the members of the committee."[8] What this citizen group wanted was legislation that would provide "adequate controls for proprietary schools" to discourage the founding of "improper organizations of this kind." According to the committee, the absence of these controls had turned Chicago into a "center of activity of many of the worst types of proprietary institutions which advertise on a national scale."[9]

Sandquist didn't see the problem in Illinois as a lack of *any* FPCU regulation. His report noted the existence of the Illinois Act of 1927, designed specifically to control correspondence, manual, and mechanic schools. The problem, rather, was in how ineffectual the decades-old law had become in light of FPCUs created after the GI Bill. State law lacked clarity on what counted as a proprietary school and what penalties the state could levy on for-profits guilty of defrauding students, taxpayers, and the government. Unlike statutes in Massachusetts, Michigan, Minnesota, New York, and North Dakota, the Illinois law also lacked control over FPCU sales and advertising. It failed to do what Minnesota, North Dakota, and Oregon already had underway—the licensing of sales agents (also described as solicitors) of for-profits. These states required each solicitor to post a $1,000 bond to head off the known problem of false promises and unscrupulous selling of for-profit education. In the case of Oregon, FPCU agents had to demonstrate "good moral character," evidence of "good reputation for honesty, truthfulness, and fair-dealing," and a record clear of felony and misdemeanor convictions having to do with "moral turpitude." The Illinois Act of 1927, meanwhile, had none of these provisions. Despite an amendment passed by the Illinois legislature in the early forties about student tuition recovery from dubious for-profits, the act had remained untouched since becoming law.[10]

Sandquist and colleagues in the Illinois state legislature felt pressure from their constituents to rein in for-profits. They knew applications for state approval from newly formed FPCUs during the mid-forties had created a blizzard of paperwork, a new set of regulatory challenges, and a firestorm of student complaints making statutes on the books appear weak and archaic. What they needed was a guide for planning their next legislative move. Sandquist answered this need with a report on how several other states had handled FPCU problems.[11]

Sandquist reached out to officials in Maryland, Massachusetts, New Jersey, New York, North Dakota, and Oregon for guidance. His correspondence revealed a similar thread of concern over FPCU practices across all states. Merle S. Bateman, director of certification, accreditation, and publications at Maryland's Department of Education, described the context in which his state had passed for-profit regulations in 1945 and again in 1947. It was largely in response to neighboring state activity to control the institutions. "The standards in New York, New Jersey, and Pennsylvania," stated Bateman, "were being tightened and it was feared that some of the less reputable schools would leave these states and try to operate in Maryland." Raymond A. Fitzgerald, deputy commissioner of education in Massachusetts, offered a familiar rationale for 1945 FPCU legislation pending in that state. "The intent of the law," wrote Fitzgerald, "is to protect the student against abuses connected with any phase of school operation." Massachusetts, no newcomer when it came to for-profits, had already passed a law earlier in the decade to deal with "several flagrant examples of such abuses." But Fitzgerald and others campaigned for additional measures to handle increasing complaints about predatory institutions.[12]

New Jersey's John A. McCarthy, assistant commissioner of education, complained of the "many malpractices on the part of private trade schools" throughout the forties. "This Department," he continued, "has had an opportunity of controlling the situations which were not favorable to the taxpayer of the State and one accomplishment was the preparation of a contract agreement under which there would be a specified registration fee and secondly a specified amount for tuition costs with a specified procedure for reimbursement for uncompleted portions of the training program." New York passed FPCU laws in 1947 to handle such claims. As E. G. Simmons, supervisor of private trade schools in the New York Education Department, explained it, the law corrected for "laxness in administrative procedures, questionable practices in the collection of tuition and low standards of instruction."[13]

North Dakota's A. F. Arnason, commissioner of the state boards of higher education and vocational education, encouraged Illinois in its efforts to rein in for-profits. Arnason recalled that, as early as 1942,

> we became somewhat concerned over the fact that fly-by-night private trade schools were making their appearances in neighboring states under the guise of providing training for war industries. Many of the operations were of the shoestring variety and we felt that North Dakota young men should be protected in case that operators of this type attempted to establish themselves in North Dakota. Unquestionably the Law served a good purpose in our State, as no one attempted to invade our State with the type of operation against which we were attempting to guard ourselves.[14]

The language used in North Dakota appeared again in correspondence with officials from Oregon. Rex Putnam, Oregon's superintendent of public instruction, said their FPCU law as amended in 1945 aimed at stopping the "'fly-by-night' operators." He followed by describing the law as "effective except in dealing with out-of-state correspondence schools which the attorney general has ruled are not subject to the act since such schools are in interstate commerce."[15]

For all states attempting to sort out problem for-profits within their borders, the issue of interstate commerce loomed large. Regulating companies across state lines was beyond their purview and required attention at the federal level. What these officials hoped for was an advocate on the floor of Congress. And in the early 1950s, they found one in a representative from Texas known as "Tiger Teague."[16]

While states conducted FPCU investigations and passed regulations, Texas representative Olin Earl Teague followed the problematic rise of FPCUs and knew the federal government needed to get involved, establish basic controls, and provide regulatory oversight. Teague was hardly the first at the national level to notice GI Bill abuses occurring at the state level. Congress had already amended the bill in 1946 to address select cases of "on-the-job" training fraud, misappropriation of funds, and unevenness in instructional quality. Congress had also passed amendments in 1949 to prevent veterans from using GI Bill aid for "avocational or recreational" programs of study. Both of these amendments highlighted problems with the bill as originally drafted and with the way unscrupulous operators took advantage of the lack of oversight. Both amendments, however, danced around the central problem with for-profits: rampant institutionalized fraud.[17]

It wasn't until early 1950 that Congress began to deal head-on with concerns over for-profits. Teague, at this point a forty-year-old representative with less than a handful of years in office, carefully tracked how two more senior officials handled the issue of FPCUs. The first, Senator Elbert D. Thomas, chaired the Committee on Labor

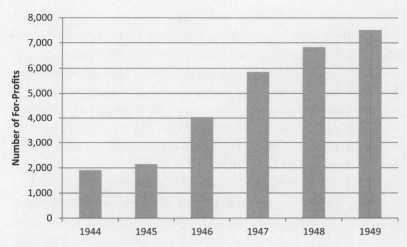

FIGURE 3.1. Total Number of For-Profits, 1944–1949. *Source:* For-profits on VA approval lists itemized in House Select Committee to Investigate Educational, Training, and Loan Guaranty Programs under GI Bill, US House Report No. 1375 (Washington, DC: GPO, 1952), 29.

and Public Welfare. The second, Carl R. Gray Jr., served as chief administrator of Veterans' Affairs (VA). Thomas, by then closing out a nearly three-decade career in the Senate, had requested from Gray a report on education and training under the Servicemen's Readjustment Act. What Thomas wanted to know was how bad the problem was with GI Bill fraud and corruption in general. Gray replied to the request in January 1950 by delivering a scathing report focused heavily on for-profits and their troubling rate of expansion (Figure 3.1).[18]

Gray's two-hundred-page VA report of 1950 dropped like a bombshell, and Teague couldn't have missed the rumble and roar it created. It started with a discussion of the origin and evolution of the GI Bill. They followed this with statistics about those who benefited from assistance for education and training, the kinds of programs and courses taken, the means of approving training institutions, and the "business relationships" the bill created between the

VA and educational institutions. The numbers demonstrated without equivocation that FPCUs had abused the system and the trust placed in them by veterans, taxpayers, and governments at all levels. The two figures, nine maps, four tables, and sixteen documents included in the appendix all suggested for-profits had to go. If they were not cut altogether, the next best option on the table was to enact strict regulations.[19]

The 1950 VA report included a wealth of data and case studies that would later inspire others, like Teague, to continue exposing fraud perpetrated by FPCUs. The VA acknowledged the existence of over 5,600 for-profits established after the GI Bill's passage as the source of "most of the problems encountered by the Veterans' Administration." The institutions had gained a reputation for charging wildly excessive fees for education of "questionable character." Given their high tuition rates, Gray predicted that the "great majority" of these institutions would pass out of existence as soon as GI Bill funds ran dry. For-profits, he concluded, preyed on veterans in order to extract a "quick and large return on invested capital" without much provided in return to veterans.[20]

Of all the allegations of fraud received by the VA and discussed in Gray's report, 78 percent had to do with for-profits. The reports led to the closure of 299 institutions, and the VA deemed another 399 unacceptable. Many other potentially fraudulent institutions, however, escaped undetected due to limited resources for investigations and site visits. Out of approximately 3,000 FPCUs surveyed, 40 percent had increased tuition rates by an average of 25 percent between 1944 and 1946. "Many of the institutions established subsequent to the act," Gray noted, "were using initial tuition rates which were well in excess of the rates claimed by older institutions offering similar instruction." As soon as the VA began requesting cost information from FPCUs in 1947, the for-profits revolted. They believed the VA had no authority "in any manner" to regulate the training of veterans. Despite the backlash—including three lawsuits filed by FPCUs to prevent disclosure of information, student protests organized or required by for-profits, and a series of congressional hearings—the VA won approval to move forward with the data-gathering effort. No less than 68 percent of a sampling of 2,265 for-profits immediately "reduced their rates" to "fair and reasonable charges" after the VA began requiring disclosure. The VA also recovered $5.5 million in "cash surplus accumulated in excess of the actual cost of instruction" as a result of increased transparency. Officials learned that, in some cases, for-profit operators had tried to hide schemes yielding a "951 percent" return on investment off of GI Bill funding.[21]

The for-profit fraud unearthed by Gray and studied carefully by Teague's circle went beyond grossly inflated tuition. Investigations revealed widespread inflated supply costs; the pocketing of income produced by student labor in practice workshops; instructional salary payments to corporate owners; duplicated administrative salaries for executives; the hiring of commission-based field agents who used "pernicious," high-pressure sales tactics; and unjustifiably long courses of studies to retain students through extended programs. "There is no doubt," Gray lamented, "that veterans' education has been an extremely lucrative and profitable enterprise for certain types of business men . . . [in] education and training of veterans for which honest value is not being received." Among the most egregious for-profit conspiracies to defraud the GI Bill program was the supply chain scheme. In this scheme, for-profit operators created dummy corporations. The operators then worked with wholesale tool and supply companies to have wholesalers provision the dummy corporation with discounted products. FPCU operators would turn around and "sell" supplies from the dummy corporation to the for-profit and, in the process, pocket an almost 100 percent markup in costs. In one case, the wholesale to retail price of a product purchased by a for-profit soared from $12,085 to $22,086 without the product ever changing hands. To call attention to the problems outlined in the VA report, Gray included brief, paragraph-long descriptions of 228 "typical examples" of FPCU fraud and thirty-eight reproductions of "misleading advertisements" found in periodicals across the country.[22]

The VA report created a stir in Congress and heightened Teague's interest in the topic, especially as reverberations hit the White House. President Harry Truman read Gray's study and, most likely, slammed a fist on the Oval Office desk at the for-profit fraud schemes that "blemished" the spirit of the GI Bill. Truman called out "certain kinds of trade and vocational training" with their "less than acceptable quality" for failing to "contribute materially" to the needs of veterans. Too many of these former servicemen, decried Truman, "have not received instruction which meets reasonable standards." The president wanted further investigation into the matter and commissioned a joint investigation between the VA and the US Bureau of Budget. In large measure, the joint report published in February 1950 condensed and summarized Gray's VA report findings.[23]

Senator Thomas, who'd originally requested the VA report, left office within a year of its publication and, shortly thereafter, so did Gray. While neither departure stemmed from the FPCU investigation, they left a vacuum of leadership Tiger Teague moved in to fill.

Inspired by the work of these and other senior officials, Teague cosponsored a GI Bill amendment in July 1950 designed to address the "typical" FPCU. The amendment had four elements. First, it required for-profits to have a one-year track record of independent sustainability before receiving any GI Bill funding. By requiring the waiting period, the amendment forced FPCUs to demonstrate their viability in the regular marketplace before receiving public subsidies. Second, for-profits now had to pass a more stringent test for approval if the number of non–GI Bill supported students at their institutions fell below twenty-five individuals or one-fourth of the total student population. The intent, as with the first element, was to establish whether the FPCUs could stand on their own without GI Bill support. Third, the amendment disallowed for-profits from creating new courses designed to prepare students for work in oversaturated fields or for which existing facilities and institutions already adequately served demand. By limiting the range of FPCU offerings, the amendment addressed competition in crowded fields and duplicated efforts across institutions. And the fourth element had to do with stricter student attendance requirements. Minimum standards forced FPCUs to keep track of the number of student contact hours for reporting and funding allocation purposes.[24]

The amendment passed and became Public Law 81-610, but it still fell short of what Teague believed the nation needed in order to deal with nationwide for-profit fraud. His continued interest in this area netted him one of his first leadership positions in the House of Representatives in late 1950: chair of the House Select Committee to Investigate Educational and Training Programs under the GI Bill.[25]

Under Teague's direction, the committee conducted a three-month study of the GI Bill. It focused on the "increasing number of complaints from various sources" about "widespread abuses" in educational programming. Committee members directed attention to both sides of the programmatic equation: the administration of the program from Washington and the fly-by-night operations across the country. Their investigation revealed "errors," "extravagances," "corruption," "larceny," and "administrative inefficiencies." The committee also focused on problems receiving significant "publicity," stemming in part from Gray's VA report and causing "widespread belief" in the public and Congress about where "the most flagrant abuses have taken place." The 228 "typical examples" identified by Gray in his 1950 study offered a starting point for the committee's three-month study.[26]

The Teague committee report of 1951 that emerged from the investigation first lashed out at the VA. It took the agency to task for not consulting with a single official in the US Office of Education on how best to administer the GI Bill's multi-billion-dollar education program. Teague criticized the VA for failing to "utilize the facilities or experiences of that agency" and failing to secure officials with the experience and background necessary to organize the education and training programs. Teague and the rest of the committee were stunned to learn that the VA's chief of the training facilities division, the person responsible for "inspecting and approving schools and training facilities for disabled veterans," had little more than a high school diploma, a one-year course in shorthand and typing, and no education-related work experience. What's more, they found others, like the former contract chief of the Education and Training Section, with equally lackluster profiles. With all the available talent in allied agencies, their résumés failed to impress. Teague's greatest concern with inadequate VA staffing had to do with failures in the efficient and expert administration of "sound educational policies."[27] Without experienced staff, the committee noted,

> the field of education and training for the veterans was thrown wide open for any individual who could establish the semblance of a school. . . . Existing regulations did not question the background or qualifications of any individual opening a school, and many of the new schools formed after the program was initiated were owned or headed by individuals not concerned with the question of whether or not the veteran was to ulti- mately receive training which would tend to make him employ- able upon graduation, but only as to how much money could be made.[28]

On this count, the committee referred to evidence presented in Gray's 1950 report, especially evidence of unjustifiably extended courses of study. It showed "many" new vocational and trade schools offering two-year programs for what established, better known, and more respected institutions gave to students over the course of a year. The obvious attempt by for-profits to "prolong tuition pay- ments" and studies, the committee determined, had little or no edu- cational merit for the veteran.[29]

The committee also blasted VA officials for bribery and irregular practices. Some had accepted direct payments or gifts, such as a "1946 Buick sedan," from school operators. Other VA officials se- cured thousands of dollars in undocumented or poorly documented loans from educational institutions or owned interests in the pro- prietary schools over which they had a supervisory role. All of this indicated a form of regulatory capture, and Teague wanted to shine light on these instances of corruption.[30]

But the for-profit supply chain fraud, according to Teague's 1951 report, was what dominated public and congressional interest. The dummy corporation scheme, the report stated, "is today considered one of the more controversial phases of the veteran educational program." The GI Bill had provided over $400 million in federal funds for supplies since the mid-forties, and the committee wanted to discern the difference between customary charges and wildly excessive fees (e.g., those yielding 951 percent returns). Through three days of hearings, they discovered that, "with few exceptions," every school in certain areas—like those training students how to make and repair watches, clocks, and other timepieces—had "conspired with" such companies as Chicago's C&E Marshall to defraud the government through a supply scheme. Rankled by the discovery, Teague committee members referred for-profit fraud cases to the US attorney general for possible "criminal prosecution" and other legal action by the US Justice Department.[31]

Along with investigating fraud, Teague had the committee prepare a sweeping evaluation of the for-profit sector from multiple perspectives. They consulted with "old-established trade and vocational schools" to determine a baseline for customary supplies charges in place before the GI Bill. They also requested information from state-level agencies on their procedures for approving new educational institutions. The committee reached out to the National Association of State Approving Agencies to collect data from their nationwide study of attitudes and perceptions of "on-the-job" training for veterans. Other institutions and individuals the committee surveyed included major veteran organizations, individual trainees, large corporations and companies, a select group of "representative colleges and universities," staff at VA field offices, and such educational associations as "the American Council on Education, Association of Land-Grant Colleges and Universities, and the American Vocational Association." Those surveyed were asked to describe abuses observed and offer recommendations on how handle them in the future.[32]

Looking forward, Teague saw the GI Bill's possible extension to Korean War veterans as the next opportunity to clean up problem areas with for-profits. "The committee," the report noted, "is of the unanimous opinion that further study and evaluation . . . is of necessity before any such extension is granted." Teague got his chance to keep at GI Bill problems through two more investigations: one as member of the Committee on Veterans' Affairs (1951) and another as chair, once again, of the House Select Committee (1952).[33]

As a member of the Committee on Veterans' Affairs, Teague requested William L. Ellis, the General Accounting Office's (GAO) chief of investigations, to conduct an audit of all educational operations related to the GI Bill. Ellis responded in July 1951 with, by far, the most detailed and extensive analysis to date. It gave Teague and other observers what they had long been waiting for. The Ellis Report of 1951 built on the work of earlier studies—the 1950 VA study and the 1951 Teague investigation and evaluation—to assess with painstaking precision the extent of FPCU fraud in the GI Bill system.[34]

Ellis's examination of for-profits began with an indictment of their overall efficacy. His numbers showed what many had suspected: privately operated, for-profit trade and vocational schools had a dismal record of success. According to the GAO's estimates, completion rates for veterans at these institutions stood at a mere 20 percent. Put another way, for-profits on average failed 80 percent of returning soldiers. These same schools, moreover, marked up tuition rates well beyond "customary" practice. For-profit operators frequently and unjustifiably set tuition at "the maximum allowed under the law," "entirely unrelated to their costs" and "far in excess of what the average citizen would be able to pay." Despite the high failure rates and excessive charges, FPCUs managed to stay open by way of "extensive advertising and promotional campaigns" designed to attract veterans who qualified for GI Bill support.[35]

Ellis's report then turned to all of the known forms and categories of FPCU fraud committed through the GI Bill. Fraudulent activity in this scheme fell under two general headings: frauds committed in relation to program costs and those committed through supply costs. For the first category, Ellis described the grossly inaccurate information FPCUs sent to the VA about tuition rates, student enrollments, and over thirty points of interests. "Cost figures submitted by [proprietary] schools," he explained, were

misrepresented or overstated; information withheld with respect to anticipated material increase in enrollment which would have caused a reduction in the rate; listing as expenses during base period items that would have been amortized over the period of school operations; use of incorrect enrollment figures in computing costs; failure of schools to maintain adequate records from which cost data could be verified; profits realized in excess of amounts authorized by VA regulations; tuition based on estimated, not actual costs; payment at rates in excess of those provided by contracts; tuition billed for periods prior to enrollment and subsequent to discontinuance; charges for periods when no instruction was given; tuition paid in excess of statutory limitation; tuition paid for unapproved courses; charges made for tuition rates in excess of those charged nonveterans; and duplicate payments.[36]

Ellis's report went on to highlight the second category of fraud and its twenty standard abuses related to supplies requisitioning found throughout the for-profit sector. These practices included the following:

Supplies not furnished as specified by contracts; veterans required to sign blank receipts for books and supplies, some of which were never furnished; no records available to substantiate payments made for books and supplies furnished veterans and billed to the Government; prices charged VA in excess of actual costs of books and supplies; payments made for books furnished in excess of course requirements; duplicate payments; payments made for books and supplies furnished veterans but not required for nonveterans pursuing the same courses; and no evidence available to support claims that books and supplies were actually furnished veterans as billed.[37]

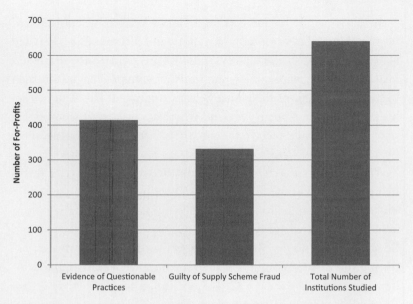

FIGURE 3.2. 1951 Study of 641 For-Profits. *Source:* General Accounting Office, *Report of Survey—Veterans' Education and Training Program* (Washington, DC: GPO, 1951), 10–12.

For both program and supply costs, Ellis detailed how and why these cases of FPCU fraud posed a "widespread" problem, rather than simply reflecting the work of a few bad actors. While gathering data for the report, for example, Ellis conducted his own study of 641 for-profit institutions. Of these FPCUs, 65 percent showed evidence of questionable practices (Figure 3.2). Of these, 80 percent were guilty of one or more of over thirty known program cost abuses. Thirty-one percent of the questionable for-profits, meanwhile, had committed one or more of the twenty known supply scheme frauds. As a result of his own limited sample, Ellis uncovered $7.5 million (approximately $65 million in current dollars) in fraudulent GI Bill charges and quickly recovered $1.4 million of these expenditures. By the time of the report's publication, the VA and GAO had launched active investigations into the remainder of unrecovered and questionable FPCU charges.[38]

By early 1952, Teague had read Gray's VA report, coordinated his own House Select Committee report, and digested Ellis's detailed GAO report. With the surveys, studies, investigations, inquiries, hearings, audits, maps, tables, and statistics in mind, Teague returned to his role as chair of the House Select Committee. This time, he set his sights on the Korean War and whether soldiers returning from that conflict should receive the same readjustment benefits received by veterans of WWII.[39]

The outcome was the Teague committee report of 1952, a document emphasizing the long-standing trouble created by the "rapid uncontrolled expansion" of for-profit colleges and universities. Teague opened with a warning to Congress: "A new act should be written extending educational benefits to veterans who served during the Korean conflict." Given the now well-known and publicized problems with the GI Bill, he called for "an entirely new act, rather than amendment to existing law." The committee's recommendations for the new act included, among other things, limiting courses to those offered "by public schools and colleges." If veterans couldn't access a public option, the new act could allow consideration of some FPCUs. But it's clear the committee had strong reservations against this. "Many" of these "proprietary profit schools," Teague concluded, offered training "of doubtful quality." Armed with extensive data to support their recommendations, the report didn't mince words: "Exploitation by private schools has been widespread." For-profits had a disproportionate tendency to falsify cost data, attendance and enrollment records, and charges for supplies, books, and tools. What's more, Teague's committee mentioned the "unethical" influence for-profits had achieved over VA officials. Through irregular practices such as gifts, loans, and ownership stake in for-profits given to officials charged with supervising FPCU practices, operators had engaged in bald attempts at regulatory capture. Based on investigations into GI Bill exploitation and abuse, Teague noted, "this class of schools" showed a demonstrable and "widespread" tendency toward "criminal practices." He cited roughly fifty FPCU-related criminal convictions—coupled with ninety pending criminal cases, a multi-million-dollar recovery of overcharges from "this class of schools," and the "many new cases" developing—as good reasons to warn against approving any for-profit college or university for GI Bill funding.[40]

To help fill out the picture of for-profit abuses occurring across the country, the 1952 Teague committee conducted hearings and field investigations—almost all of which had to do with FPCU fraud—in or related to cases in Illinois (Chicago), Kentucky, Pennsylvania (Philadelphia), Tennessee (Memphis, Nashville, and Murfreesboro), and Texas (Dallas, Waco, Houston, and San Antonio). It also requested reports and investigative support from dozens of institutions and thousands of individuals. Respondents included the GAO, the VA, the Federal Bureau of Investigation, the Justice Department, the American Legion, the Veterans of Foreign Wars, the Disabled American Veterans, and the American Veterans of World War II. To this, they added responses received from thousands of students, faculty, and administrators at nonprofit and proprietary programs.[41]

Based on all of this evidence, the 1952 Teague committee reaffirmed four key conclusions. First, they heard repeatedly that the "vast majority" of FPCU operators had "no previous experience" in education and training. The GI Bill had brought about an "influx" of a large number of non-educators into the sector who privileged making money—particularly from federal funds—over providing veterans with a high-quality education. Second, they revisited case studies highlighting the typical excessive cost claims characteristic of for-profits. Case studies included detailed descriptions of specific trade and vocational programs in electricity and refrigeration, tailoring, woodworking, dry cleaning, aviation, auto mechanics, radio and television broadcasting, dance, art, theater, meat cutting, upholstering, photography, watchmaking, business, and secretarial studies. Teague committee members held up these cases as representative of widespread "abuses and illegal practices on the part of the privately owned trade schools."[42]

The committee's third conclusion had to do with the now well-known use of dummy corporations by for-profits engaged in supply chain fraud. The descriptions—corroborating ones discussed in earlier reports—followed intricate webs of interlocking business, personal, and familial relationships. They also reported on the criminal indictments and investigations underway. And fourth, the Teague committee heard from students and employees themselves who testified about schemes to "falsify the attendance records" of "a considerable number of students." Many of these students had been recruited not through traditional admissions channels, but as a result of aggressive advertising campaigns conducted by for-profits. "This situation occurred most often and most blatantly," the committee stated, "in the case of profit trade schools which had been organized specifically to cater to veterans after the inception of the Servicemen's Readjustment Act." Examples included schools from different parts of the country. A small midwestern tailoring for-profit took out large newspaper advertisements promising a free suit for veterans and material for hundreds of dollars' worth of clothing fitted to the student's specifications. A southern automotive mechanics school offered all interested "GIs" free tools and free car repairs. An eastern trade school made similar promises in their promotional materials. This one promised an "opportunity of a lifetime" announced over a background image of more than fifty tools. These kinds of competitive pressures among "less scrupulous schools," the committee regretted, had created incentives that distorted the purpose of education and training for readjusting veterans. Extreme and aggressive advertising tactics by for-profits, they noted, threatened to turn the GI Bill into a massive get-rich-quick scheme for FPCU operators. From the committee's perspective, for-profits had eroded the undergirding ideal of the bill's original purpose: to create opportunities for veterans to break cycles of poverty and unemployment through concerted study and career preparation.[43]

Virtually none of the concerns raised by the Teague report of 1952 about FPCUs appeared in the committee's review of nonprofit colleges and universities. In the view of Teague and his colleagues, nonprofits had done an admirable job on almost all counts. "There is little question," they emphasized, that nonprofit "colleges and universities of this country have rendered outstanding services in educating veterans and have performed their task under many adverse conditions." The problems Teague and his circle did find with these institutions emerged as a result of "regulations governing payment of tuition." But the committee was quick to recognize nonprofits for having a ready solution, one that the committee favored: revamping the system by making payments "directly to the veteran" and allowing veterans to pay tuition, fees, and other charges on the same basis as nonveterans. In other words, they recommended taking educational institutions out of the money business.[44]

Based on the documentation produced by the 1952 Teague report, it's unclear which nonprofit institutions committee members turned to for advice. They had surveyed and interviewed thousands of individuals across the country about problems at for-profits as well as challenges at traditional colleges and universities. But if they had reached out to the University of Michigan, Teague would no doubt have heard an earful from one of the era's most ardent critics of FPCUs: James Bartlett Edmonson.[45]

Just as Teague arrived in Congress and started his GI Bill investigations, James Edmonson had begun his final few years as the University of Michigan's dean of the School of Education. They were at different stages of their careers between the mid-1940s and the early 1950s, and they came at their assignments from different angles. But their commitments and priorities almost perfectly overlapped. While Teague worked on FPCUs at the national and political levels, Dean Edmonson took on the same at the academic and state policy levels.[46]

Edmonson's reading of the GI Bill was prescient. Long before state and federal lawmakers knew what hit them, Edmonson had accurately anticipated an unprecedented and controversial increase (later calculated at 300 percent) in for-profits as a result of the bill. He warned, through his professional and popular writings, that "G.I. Joe" must be protected against being "gypped" by "low-grade colleges." His earliest warnings came out in February 1945, a mere eight months after President Roosevelt signed the Servicemen's Readjustment Act into law. From his bully pulpit in Ann Arbor, Edmonson came out against "so-called higher institutions" that "lacked any adequate accreditation" and hoped to "flourish through the enrollment of veterans under the G.I. Bill of Rights." He chided states for having been "lax in past years in the control of higher education" and warned of an "underworld" of predatory institutions offering little to no value to students. Adding federal funding without adequate safeguards, he imagined, would result in predictable behavior by "sheepskinners." These individuals "issue credits and diplomas which are not accepted as proper qualification for the certificates and licenses required for nursing, teaching, pharmacy, and other professions." He also predicted these low-grade colleges would turn to advertising in ways considered inappropriate or downright exploitative by the nonprofit sector. They would "doubtless make misleading, but attractive inducements to the returning veterans." Edmonson called on states to send "clean" lists of colleges and universities for VA approval, lists free of sheepskinners. "Any state that fails to protect veterans against being 'gypped' in their future education," he added, "should be subjected to severe criticism from both educators and veterans." Edmonson placed ultimate responsibility for controlling for-profit fraud in the hands of state legislators. But he lacked confidence in their assessment of what they needed to do and how soon they'd respond to problems likely to emerge.[47]

Edmonson's academic and popular works spoke to audiences who were likely unaware of for-profit abuses occurring across the country. He gave advice on how to select a reputable institution by consulting local employers about proprietary trade and vocational schools. He walked readers through recent reports of scandals and fraud. And he shared with them the kinds of claims and practices that should raise flags for prospective students. "The fraudulent trade schools have many deceptive tricks," he warned, "such as 'short cuts' and the promise of an attractive position for which few persons could qualify. Others offer short cuts for certificates and misrepresent the opportunities for employment. In general, any trade school that promises short cuts or employment for prospective students should be viewed with suspicion." As a leading critic of FPCUs in the early fifties, Edmonson also asked readers for help in tracking down "gyp" institutions. It was a public call to action and it came with instructions on how to assist in bringing these problems to light.[48]

Edmonson's sounding of alarm bells over for-profits earned him a leadership role in the National Education Association. As chair of the NEA's Committee on Fraudulent Schools and Colleges beginning in 1949, he went after "diploma mills" run by "shysters" and "unscrupulous persons." Fraud in education, for these "racketeers," had proved to be "profitable business." He blamed "lax" state laws, as he had years earlier, and the willingness of men and women to buy "fraudulent degrees and certificates." At the same time, Edmonson lamented that his peers in "reputable schools and colleges have frequently ignored the existence of the 'underworld' in American education." To begin solving the FPCU problem, he conducted a nationwide survey of state boards of education to learn what they knew about for-profits, what they wanted to know about them, and what they needed in order to respond to these institutions in their states. What he and his NEA colleagues found was a situation much worse than anticipated: nineteen states required no charter or license to operate a college or university; twenty-one state boards of education didn't believe or were uncertain they had adequate laws and regulations for closing "low-grade institutions"; thirty-two states didn't require nonaccredited institutions to file documents (e.g., catalogs, degree offerings, or course requirements) with state authorities; ten states acknowledged a problem with these institutions within their borders; twenty-two wanted more information about known "diploma mills"; twenty-eight wanted plans from others states on how to eliminate these schools; and twenty-nine asked for suggestions on proposing effective legislation to give state boards or other state agencies more regulatory control over the sector.[49]

That last finding from the NEA survey really got to Edmonson and ended up dominating a significant portion of his time as chair of the fraud committee. The widespread desire for model legislation inspired a collaboration between Edmonson and William Pencke, a trial attorney with the US Federal Trade Commission. Together, they drafted a template bill for lawmakers to sponsor at the state level. It proposed stricter state laws and regulations governing this sector, particularly with for-profit licensing, chartering, and advertising. Edmonson wanted these new laws to demand evidence of the "value" of nonaccredited colleges and universities and to produce a political culture willing to shame "diploma mills." But he believed none of these solutions would work without one final recommendation: increased and aggressive state-level prosecution of owners and operators of "fraudulent institutions." It all hinged on whether states would put "sheepskinners" and "shysters" behind bars.[50]

As soon as he had a draft bill in hand, Edmonson circulated it to friends, colleagues, and potential critics. For M. A. Nash, chancellor of the Oklahoma State Regents for Higher Education, the draft arrived at just the right time. Nash not only thanked Edmonson for his "high contribution to education in the United States," but also sent him a proposal under consideration in Oklahoma to get his feedback. Edmonson wrote back, pushing Nash to "define a penalty for a violation" and to require FPCUs to "file with your office full information regarding programs and degree requirements" in order to monitor the institutions. Officials at the American Council on Education (ACE) also celebrated Edmonson's "concrete advice" on how to eliminate "fake colleges." And the National Association and Council of Business Schools went on record expressing "very hearty accord with the general objective," despite hard feelings among its members at not having been consulted on earlier versions of the bill.[51]

Colleagues and supporters, however, warned Edmonson that his sharpest critics would come from the ranks of religiously affiliated organizations and institutions. Homer Kempfer, director of the National Home Study Council, shared Edmonson's concern for raising standards, but had no rosy outlook on the challenge ahead. The "diploma mills, fly-by-night schools, and other unethical outfits" would be difficult to root out, Kempfer cautioned, because many "associated with off-brand religious denominations" and sought "refuge in their constitutional rights of religious freedom when attacked in the courts." Even those within the religious community who were sympathetic to the idea of clamping down on fraudulent FPCUs knew great resistance would come from their own camp. Charles Lynn Platt, dean and Old Testament professor at Kentucky's College of the Bible, had "sincere appreciation" for Edmonson's work, but worried about saboteurs putting up "a smoke screen or something of that sort" if they caught wind of the draft bill. "This would, of course," Platt followed, "be very true in the matter of 'religious schools.' This is a case not of liberty but of separation of church and state, in the name of which so many crimes are committed." Despite Platt's attempts to reach out to colleagues in the world of religious education, Edmonson's bill got a cold reception with this group.[52]

Fort Wayne Bible College, later called Summit Bible College and ultimately sold to Taylor University, followed precisely the path Kempfer and Platt had anticipated. While Fort Wayne's president S. A. Witmer considered "diploma mills" a source of "embarrassment" in "Biblical education," he disagreed with Edmonson's proposals to prosecute owners and managers of for-profits who were guilty of defrauding students and taxpayers. The bill, as written, was "too restrictive" and not conducive to the "right of propagating religious faith." Witmer appealed to "freedoms inherent in our democracy" as the reason for his resistance to penalties against and supervision of religiously affiliated for-profits. Edmonson took seriously Witmer's "criticisms," particularly those having to do with the amount of power the draft bill placed in the hands of state superintendents of education. Witmer thought a single state official shouldn't have final say—as the bill proposed—on matters better handled by committee. Edmonson responded favorably to the comment and changed it accordingly, making state school boards rather than the superintendent the executive authority. Yet the two of them never met eye to eye. Witmer knew his freedom-of-religion argument protected "racketeering," but called Edmonson's bill "un-American and undemocratic" at a time when US senator Joseph McCarthy had turned such buzzwords into weapons of character assassination. Witmer also attempted to taint the proposal by describing it as "more characteristically European than American." Edmonson shot back, repeating to all who would listen that "no other major country is as lax as the United States in permitting shyster schools and diploma mills to sell certificates and degrees." The religious liberties claims, as his circle of colleagues had warned, created a powerful cover for fraudulent institutions and a defense against attempts to eliminate them.[53]

Edmonson's academic, public, and policy campaigns against for-profits generated a great deal of national attention. According to Arthur Adams, president of the American Council on Education, Edmonson had "aroused" the public's interest in "the danger of this vicious 'racket.'" A flood of correspondence directed at the Michigan dean's desk in Ann Arbor came from professors, college administrators, state officials, regional accreditors, military officers, journal editors, and agents of philanthropic organizations across the country. For the most part, they wrote asking about specific suspected "diploma mills" or, more generally, about any lists he had of fraudulent institutions. These individuals wanted to know if their local institution, often a Bible college or religiously affiliated FPCU, was worthy of the name "college" or "university." Or they wanted a complete, nationwide accounting of fraudulent institutions so they could identify those located in their state and region. Or they simply wanted to show their support for his work and join him in the "effort to curb such institutions," as some expressed it. At the time, none of these individuals and organizations had anyone else to turn to for this information. And that was Edmonson's point. The problem—the absence of any formal, current, and comprehensive data about untrustworthy for-profits—struck a nerve for him, and his writings did the same for many people across the United States.[54]

The national attention Edmonson received for speaking out against problem for-profits won him a splash of international recognition. European observers, in particular, found the wide variety of American colleges and universities confusing and some called on Edmonson to clarify the matter. The title of "university," to the European mind, conjured notions of tradition and distinction as well as expectations of rigor and excellence supported most often by state regulation. For these reasons, Edmonson wasn't surprised when German official Walter Wienert reached out to him asking for an explanation of what a degree from a US institution meant. "Judicial Courts and Police Offices of the Federal Republic often submit to me diplomas," wrote the official, "asking whether the conferring institutions belong to the so-called 'diploma mills' in the United States. I would ask whether you have a complete list of these diploma mills. If so, I should feel much obliged if you would kindly let me have a copy of it." Edmonson had no such list. And even if he did, the rapid turnover—the way for-profits opened, closed, and then reopened under a different name—made it pointless to compile such lists. By the time Edmonson responded to Wienert's request in the early fifties, the number of for-profits that had received VA approval hovered around 9,000. A full two-thirds of these had been established as a result of the GI Bill during the five-year period after its passage. With American higher education awash in for-profits, he continued to call for stricter state-level regulations so that students and government agencies didn't need such lists.[55]

Edmonson—in his seventies, still in full gear, and ready to take on the for-profit sector—died in 1954. With him went a "one-man crusade," as Adams of ACE put it. "Since his death," stated Adams, "the [NEA fraud] Committee has languished." Plans to complete grant applications to fund for-profit fraud studies, lobby states to pass legislation, conduct national and international policy work on for-profits—all of these plans fizzled, faded, and ultimately became a forgotten chapter in the FPCU story after Edmonson's death. He did live long enough, though, to see many of his predictions realized. These included the call for state laws, the kind of fraud consuming time, energy, and resources at the federal level, and the rise of exploitative practices among FPCUs. What Edmonson couldn't have predicted, and what he didn't live to see, was a groundbreaking debate Congress had a decade later. It was over legislation that fundamentally transformed how all American colleges and universities operated. This legislation, at first silent on the matter of for-profits, would ultimately become the single most significant economic boon for FPCUs in American history.[56]

CHAPTER FOUR

Crisis

W ITHOUT THE HIGHER EDUCATION ACT OF 1965 (HEA) and
its subsequent reauthorizations in the 1970s, the FPCU industry would likely have followed the course many had predicted
for it: extinction for the vast majority of these institutions as soon
as GI Bill funds ran dry. The HEA completely changed how this
prediction played out. FPCUs, as they appeared after 1965, tapped
into a vast source of federal aid giving the sector new life, means of
expansion, and avenues for making industrial-sized profits.[1]

This, of course, wasn't the original intent of HEA. President Lyndon B. Johnson, a former schoolteacher, had a different goal in
mind: increasing access to community colleges as well as public and
nonprofit colleges and universities. As part of his Great Society
campaign—which included the Civil Rights Act, Voting Rights Act,
Economic Opportunity Act, Elementary and Secondary Education
Act, and Medicare—Johnson took great interest in the passage of
legislation designed to move US higher education toward providing
opportunities for students of all social and economic backgrounds.
"The important role of the federal government," he said, "is some-
how to do something for the people who are down and out, and
that's where its major energy in education ought to go." To that end,
HEA launched and extended programs for student scholarships,
grants, loans, and work-study through HEA's Title IV Student Assistance Act. One of the signature features of this assistance was the
Educational Opportunity Grant (later, Supplemental Educational
Opportunity Grant) that went directly to institutions rather than
students. The grant created an exchange between the US government and individual institutions receiving funds on behalf of eligible

students. Another feature involved banks as mediators of Federally Guaranteed Student Loans or what became known as the FGSL program (later, Federal Family Education Loan Program). The loan program gave students eligibility for private bank loans without requiring them to present income history or declare collateral. Bankers and financiers showed interest in participating in the program because the federal government acted as cosigner to the loans and guaranteed banks repayment in cases of loan default.[2]

Subsequent reauthorization of and amendments to HEA made federal student aid programs increasingly palatable to bankers and increasingly accessible to the FPCU sector. The 1968 reauthorization permitted a rise in interest rates for federally guaranteed student loans, ensuring banks higher returns with zero risk. This policy caused an exponential increase in private lending. The expansion continued for two decades, at which time lawmakers—stunned by inflated fees and expenses incurred when guaranteeing loans through the private sector—turned to government direct lending that, by some estimates, cut lending expenses in half. The 1972 reauthorization introduced the Basic Educational Opportunity Grant (later, the Pell Grant). It standardized the definition of student need across institutions and the amount of grant aid students received. Pell also increased the level of grant aid to disadvantaged students in order to reduce access barriers to higher education.[3]

The most significant change for FPCUs in the second reauthorization, however, had to do with the redefinition of higher education. HEA had previously defined an institution of higher education in exclusively "public" or "private non-profit" terms. With the 1972 amendments, Congress inserted language about "proprietary" institutions and used the new language as a proxy for profit-seeking trade, career, and vocational institutions. The change came with a stipulation requiring for-profits to offer programs only to students "who can benefit" from postsecondary instruction.[4]

Redefining higher education in this way was anything but trivial. Congress, through the 1972 HEA amendments, essentially waved a $200 million appropriation in front of the FPCU sector. For-profit

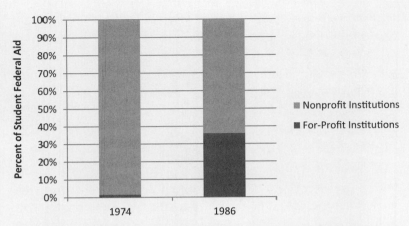

FIGURE 4.1. US Postsecondary Student Federal Aid Distribution. *Sources:* Statistics drawn from Joseph Berger, "Changes in Welfare a Boon to Trade Schools," *New York Times* (August 6, 1988); Michael Winerip, "Billions for School Are Lost in Waste, Fraud, and Abuse," *New York Times* (February 2, 1994).

operators noticed and took advantage of every subsequent expansion of federal student aid programs, such as the 85 percent increase in guaranteed student loan awards and the 58 percent increase in Basic Educational Opportunity Grant awards that occurred from 1976 to 1978. FPCUs played a significant role in this dramatic expansion of federal student aid. At first, in 1974, FPCUs consumed a mere 1.5 percent ($3 million) of all student aid. Four years later, nearly the same amount went to just one for-profit institution—Lacaze-Gardner School, with its nine hundred students. Eight years after that, for-profits had captured $785 million, or roughly 36 percent of the entire guaranteed loan budget, even though approximately 2 percent of all postsecondary students attended FPCUs (Figures 4.1 and 4.2).[5]

The rapid entry and expansion of for-profits into federal student aid programs inspired an investigation by the US comptroller general in 1980. At the time, 1,725 proprietary institutions received more than $275 million in Pell Grants alone. Based on its study of

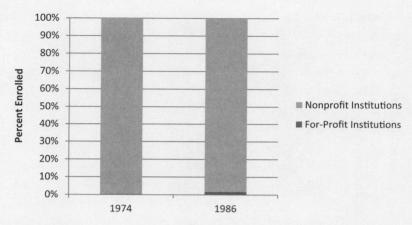

FIGURE 4.2. US Postsecondary Student Distribution. *Sources:* US Department of Education, National Center for Education Statistics, Higher Education General Information Survey (HEGIS), "Fall Enrollment in Colleges and Universities" surveys, 1970 through 1985; Integrated Postsecondary Education Data System (IPEDS), "Institutional Characteristics Survey" (IPEDS-IC: 86–99).

how these FPCUs managed federal funds, the comptroller's office concluded that "many proprietary schools do not comply with [the] Department of Education's Pell Grant requirements." Fieldwork gathered from a random sample of thirty-five institutions across fifteen states showed for-profits engaged in practices that were "not in the best interest of students" and did "not comply with the program requirements." Some of the practices included admitting unqualified students who dropped out at a rate of 74 percent and allowing students to continue in programs without making academic progress (e.g., no limit on absenteeism). Other practices involved providing "misleading" information to prospective students about placement rates and scholarships and disbursing Pell Grant funds in a manner rife with error and false calculations. The comptroller investigation, had it been published, would have sounded an alarm. But the results didn't come to light until congressional leaders began reading about for-profits in news reports, asking questions, and demanding information.[6]

A series of high-profile scandals in the early to mid-eighties spurred on those questions and demands, revealing widespread problems with both for-profit institutions and the government agencies keeping them in business. In New York City, six for-profit institutions consumed almost $20 million in state tuition assistance funding alone—half the entire state's program budget, not including federal subsidies—during the period. High failure rates discovered by investigators raised suspicions about whether the schools were little more than schemes designed to defraud state and federal student aid programs. More than 12,000 students attended these six schools, but 70 percent of those receiving aid dropped out. More tellingly, 60 percent of these dropouts failed to finish even half of their program. Since the for-profit schools received government funding regardless of whether students failed or succeeded, they had great incentive to persuade students to attend. Once students enrolled and became indebted, the institutions had little incentive to provide meaningful educational experiences. Reports pointed to these kinds of abuses indicating that "many of the trade schools did not provide advertised courses or hours of instruction, used unlicensed teachers and had overcrowded classrooms." By the time New York State officials discovered these schemes, the schools had come and gone, leaving a trail of debt, confused students, and false hopes in their wake. Edward V. Regan, New York's comptroller at the time, found these fly-by-night institutions hard to track down and punish. "Recovery of these taxpayers dollars," he stated, has been "seriously hampered because many schools go out of business."[7]

Major urban centers like New York weren't the only ones affected by FPCU fraud. Reports on such scandals began bubbling up in the country's heartland as well. Indiana-based Continental Training Services (also known as Superior Training Services), one of the four largest for-profit educational institutions of the early 1980s, ran a chain of correspondence schools for truck driving. Two-thirds of the driving "instruction" was conducted by mail. This company followed the same path as other for-profits in recognizing that aid programs would continue to pay despite, in this case, having a student loan default rate of 57 percent. By the mid-1980s, Continental's annual revenue reached $100 million in subsidized federal student aid and guaranteed loans. The company received virtually no revenue from sources outside government aid programs. Unlike most of his competitors, Continental's owner, Gary Eyler, maintained strong connections with officials in Washington. According to travel logs, his corporate jet flew politicians around the country—including US senators Dan Quayle, Edward Kennedy, and Bob Dole, all contenders for the White House at the time—during Continental's most aggressive growth period. Eyler regularly hosted fundraisers for political figures he counted on to assist his company when it came under fire for fraud, false student loan applications, and other illegal revenue generating activities. For a time, Quayle and Kennedy came to Eyler's aid when officials in Indiana attempted to clamp down on Continental. But the egregiousness of the fraud perpetrated on both students and federal student aid programs ultimately overwhelmed their efforts. Eyler's connections failed to prevent a $366 million lawsuit filed by the US Department of Education in 1988 for falsified documents and several other counts of fraud at his schools.[8]

Joining Continental among the country's largest for-profits were two more scandal-plagued schools: the Wilfred American Educational Corporation and Robert Fiance Beauty Schools. Wilfred, a Manhattan-based company, operated a nationwide network of beauty and business schools and, throughout the 1980s, received more than $400 million in student aid and guaranteed loans. Toward the end of the decade, reports began to surface that the school had fraudulently applied for Pell Grants and guaranteed student loans on behalf of students. Justice Department attorneys uncovered $117 million in falsified student documents, and Wilfred employees were ultimately found guilty on nine counts of fraud, theft, and racketeering. Fiance, meanwhile, owned and operated schools in the state of Florida, with branches in Tampa and Miami. In the mid-1980s, the school received $65 million annually in federal student aid, but was hit late in the decade with a $10 million US Department of Education fine for falsified records and documents. Although it survived the fine and setback, the school had great difficulty recovering from its lost eligibility for federal aid programs as a result of these charges.[9]

Well over $1 billion of federal student aid and guaranteed loans went to scandal-plagued, for-profit institutions during the early to mid-1980s. Fines against these institutions escalated into the hundreds of millions of dollars. The exponential FPCU growth rate, meanwhile, suggested there was no end in sight to the problems these institutions posed for federal and state agencies. HEA began with an annual appropriation of $200 million when it invited FPCUs to participate. By the mid-1980s, the US Department of Education distributed nearly $250 million annually to the three least trustworthy FPCUs—Continental, Wilfred, and Fiance—despite headlines indicating civil and criminal misconduct.[10]

The FPCU scandals of the seventies and eighties reached a boiling point in 1988. That year, in addition to intense public scrutiny of the sector, US secretary of education Bill Bennett came out swinging against for-profits. Bennett, a conservative pundit and later an advocate and owner of a for-profit educational organization, found FPCUs to be engaged in "exploitative and deceitful practices" that "characterize too many proprietary institutions." With the secretary pulling no punches, his agency rang in a new era of federal investigations into FPCU activities yielding headline-worthy discoveries and revelations. Three key investigations dug up what was known, what wasn't known, and what was known about what wasn't known by Congress and the US Department of Education about the for-profit industry: the Bennett investigations of 1987–1988 and the Sam Nunn investigations of 1990 and 1995.[11]

The Bennett investigations came at the tail end of his tenure as secretary of education. His department had issued fines and charges of fraud, but the explosion of FPCU growth was no match for the understaffed agency. As such, Bennett became both a beneficiary and casualty of the Reagan revolution marked by efforts to shrink the size of government and, in particular, attempts to defund and even close the US Department of Education (or what Reagan called "President Carter's new bureaucratic boondoggle"). Bennett received his first federal appointments during the Reagan years, starting as head of the National Endowment of the Humanities (1981–1985) and continuing with his selection as education secretary (1985–1988). His conservative political and economic beliefs typically aligned with policies coming from the White House, but the secretary and the president parted ways on the matter of defunding the Department of Education.[12]

Reagan government budget cuts of the early 1980s directly affected Bennett. His agency didn't have the staff to investigate the avalanche of federal student aid paperwork coming from for-profit institutions. The Education Department had to reduce spot checks of grant and loan paperwork by 50 percent because of reductions in personnel. As the federal student aid scandals began to make front-page news, Bennett turned to Pelavin Associates, a private consulting firm, to investigate what his agency had little time to explore—the extent of the FPCU problem. Pelavin provided Bennett a way to learn about for-profits and get a handle on what was going on in the sector.[13]

The report Bennett received from Pelavin changed the course of FPCU history. It made its debut in 1988 during a clash with US senator Edward Kennedy, a supporter of Eyler's correspondence truck-driving school. Bennett claimed the for-profit industry was riddled with fraud and deception and that the problem was system wide rather than the work of a few isolated institutions. Kennedy responded to Bennett's statements by demanding to see evidence: "If you've got some . . . let's have it. Mr. Secretary, let's have it right now." In February of that year, Bennett sent Kennedy a dossier filled with reports, statistics, and findings from Pelavin and the Education Department's inspector general. After reviewing the evidence,

Kennedy backpedaled his support for Eyler and the industry in general, stating that Bennett's dossier "documents serious abuses in federal student aid. The situation requires urgent action by both Congress and the Department of Education to end the abuses while preserving the essential role of these programs in helping needy students." From that point forward, Congress took off the kid gloves and went after for-profits, launching investigations into their policies, practices, and profits.[14]

The Pelavin report set Congress on a warpath because of the statistics it contained. The numbers showed that FPCUs had expanded at a much faster rate than congressional leaders had anticipated. The report also linked almost all of this growth to the federal student grant and loan programs. Pelavin researchers established that enrollments at FPCUs rose by 60 percent between 1976 and 1982. By 1985, individual "proprietary" schools made up more than half of all postsecondary institutions. Then came the more difficult news. During the period between 1974 and 1986, the share of Pell Grants received by proprietary schools climbed from 7 percent ($3.5 million) to 21 percent ($783.5 million) or, as analysts put it, a "200-fold increase in dollars." This spike meant that the rate of increase in grant funding far outstripped enrollment numbers, since proprietary students constituted fewer than 5 percent of the overall postsecondary student population. What's more, the institution-to-institution comparisons highlighted another potential problem of imbalance and disproportionality. During the first half of the 1980s, Pell Grant funding rose by 51 percent at public two-year colleges and 36 percent at public four-year colleges. During the same period, proprietary school Pell Grant funding increased at a rate of 192 percent. Pelavin researchers found similar rates when it came to federal guaranteed loan programs. The statistics could have been read by policymakers as a dramatic effort at poverty reduction, given the many for-profits working with disadvantaged communities and populations. But when discussing the Pelavin statistics, Bennett emphasized that 85 percent of high loan default institutions were FPCUs and more than six hundred for-profits had a default rate greater than 50 percent. Rather than offering a few isolated case studies, the Pelavin report showed that hundreds of for-profit institutions, with tens of thousands of students, had suspiciously high rates of failure and distributed outsized debt to those least likely to achieve means of loan repayment.[15]

The statistics alone alerted members of Congress to the need for more careful scrutiny of FPCUs. But the report's qualitative evidence provoked a debate among lawmakers about whether to end federal subsidies to FPCUs altogether. "The pattern of abuses revealed in these documents," said Bennett, "is an outrage perpetrated not only upon the American taxpayer but, more tragically, upon some of the most disadvantaged, and most vulnerable, members of our society." Pelavin researchers uncovered the abuses by analyzing the marketing materials of 160 institutions; interviewing state attorneys general; collecting data from consumer complaint agencies in all fifty states; interviewing local, state, federal, and private accrediting agency officials; and conducting nine site visits in four states (California, Illinois, Ohio, and Texas), among other data-collection strategies and methods. When Bennett talked of a "pattern of abuses," he was referring to the Pelavin report's careful documentation of strategies used by FPCUs to increase revenue.[16]

For the most part, the strategies these institutions relied on had to do with recruitment practices, or the problem of false advertising. According to the report, "state and institutional staff members in all states indicated that violation of standards was common at proprietary institutions." Standards came from state and federal law as well as regulations imposed by accreditation agencies that, when violated, should have triggered a revocation of license to practice. Without accreditation, institutions would lose eligibility to participate in federal student aid programs. Despite potentially costly penalties and outcomes, investigators found widespread violations among FPCUs.[17]

For-profits violated laws and regulations aimed expressly at preventing four kinds of exploitative recruitment practices economists now describe as "asymmetric" information relationships between institutions and, in this case, prospective students. The report depicts the first as "canvassing" unemployment and welfare lines for prospective students. During the eighties, some states, like New York, considered passing laws whereby those on public assistance might lose their eligibility for state support if they didn't apply for work or employment training. "Canvassing" for students experiencing emotional distress due to the threat of lost subsidies struck lawmakers as exploitative in that for-profits capitalized on captive populations waiting in line and unaware of far less expensive public or nonprofit training options. These alternatives often came at no cost or a small fraction of for-profit rates. Because public and non-profit institutions refused to engage in canvassing, prospective students failed to learn, as in one case, that a for-profit might charge $10,000 for the same cosmetology course offered at a public institution for $276. According to "numerous current and former proprietary vocational-technical school recruiters . . . a wide range of prohibited practices were common." These included deceptive practices intended to take advantage of those without the knowledge or training to question these practices in the first place.[18] A whistleblower in Texas reported that recruiters often

> use employment or welfare lines extensively or go door-to-door
> in the poor parts of town. They tell people who are living in
> run-down subsidized housing that they can get them a nice
> apartment out of town and put money in their pockets if they
> sign the [application and student aid] forms. They tell them that
> they will only have to go to school a few times and will not have
> to attend class regularly. [The recruiter] may have to go back
> a half dozen times to get the $100 deposit, but they get their
> commission whether the student drops out in a month or not.[19]

Paying recruiters by such commission structures violated accreditation standards, but that didn't prevent the increasingly common practice of contracting freelance recruiters to canvass populations facing hardship. FPCUs could skirt these standards by claiming no permanent employment relationship with freelancers. This strategy gave for-profits the advantages of aggressive, predatory recruitment practices without running afoul of government student federal aid regulations.

Along with canvassing, FPCUs recruited students by printing false or misleading advertising in local papers and periodicals. Proprietary schools often marketed themselves under the employment sections of newspapers. Nineteen student accounts from California indicated that such "employment" advertising resulted in only an "admissions interview." This put those without basic skills and in need of a job in front of trained "admissions" recruiters who were known to promise cash payments for signing federal student grant and loan documents. For-profits used similar strategies with self-published marketing information. Pelavin researchers analyzed the materials produced by 160 accredited institutions in California, Illinois, Massachusetts, New York, Pennsylvania, Texas, and Vermont. The report called the materials "inadequate in terms of the presence of information" necessary for making informed decisions. Only 25 percent of these accredited institutions provided placement data. None of the materials contained completion rates, success rates on licensing exams, wage rates, or loan default rates. More than 25 percent "made no mention of admissions requirement." Without fail, however, investigators found that "all materials mentioned the availability of Federal student aid." The disproportionate emphasis on aid support, without adequate information on basic program expectations, opened the schools to charges of predatory lending and predatory recruiting practices.[20]

In addition to problems with canvassing and advertising, FPCUs engaged in the practice of targeting children. Investigators found minors, among the most vulnerable in any asymmetrical information relationship, on the receiving end of for-profit recruitment efforts. Evidence of trafficking in children's signatures and documentation was found, despite regulations classifying this age group as categorically ineligible to qualify for any federal loan programs. This included Guaranteed Student Loans, Supplemental Loans to Students, and Parent Loans for Undergraduate Students. According to HEA requirements, only those students who had graduated or left elementary or secondary school could apply for federal student aid programs. State investigations, nevertheless, discovered for-profits had enrolled minors and submitted loan and grant applications on their behalf. The institutions lured children as young as fifteen into the practice of "admitting high school students" through phony concurrent enrollment in FPCUs. As distributors of loan programs, these for-profits increased their revenue stream by having children illegally sign promissory notes guaranteeing loan repayment before they had reached legal adulthood.[21]

A final strategy used by FPCUs, as documented by the Pelavin report, involved setting tuition rates to the maximum allowable by grant and loan packages. "State agency staff," the report announced, "indicated that serious structural and aid management problems and regulatory violations exist at some proprietary institutions." The basic structural problems included rate setting according to availability of funds rather than "true program cost," disregarding a federally required needs analysis. FPCUs that failed to provide adequate needs analyses came under fire for falsified expense and income reporting on loan applications. As a result, the report's multistate study found a nationwide explosion in "unrealistically high costs" and recent "large [fee] increases" at FPCUs, fueled by the expansion of aid availability as well as document manipulation and fraud. Investigations in Illinois showed institutions charging "extremely high costs, $10,000 to $12,000 [approximately $20,000 to $24,000 in current dollars], for essentially one-year programs." When inspectors pressed institutions for an itemized breakdown of charges, for-profits would invariably "drop the costs." Pelavin investigators showed how disadvantaged students seeking basic literacy and employment skills stood little chance of contending with industry-wide manipulation of tuition and unexplained expense rates.[22]

In the end, the report identified canvassing, advertising, targeting, and rate setting as strategies used by FPCUs to gain an unfair advantage as a result of information asymmetry. Interviews with state agency officials and former FPCU staff members described the student-institution relationship as a lucrative imbalance of knowledge and information generating subsidized profits at the expense of disadvantaged populations. As one California official put it, "These kids definitely don't have enough information. They don't know how many kids drop out of programs, can't get jobs, and default on loans." Another official in Illinois corroborated this view, noting that "kids either aren't getting enough information or are getting inaccurate information. Many kids who we speak to about their defaulted loans say they were told they would get jobs. Others say they were told they could earn far in excess of what they are [actually] earning—near minimum wage—which is why they are having difficulty paying their loans." The report exposed these problems in a year when analysts expected guaranteed student loan defaults from FPCUs alone to reach $1 billion annually. For-profits turned these defaults into revenue and left the US government with an expanding liability on its balance sheet.[23]

The Pelavin report gave congressional leaders the quantitative and qualitative firepower to launch two subsequent investigations led by US senator Sam Nunn of Georgia. The first of these began two years after Bennett made public the findings from his investigation. It also began after several of the largest for-profits faced criminal indictments, suspension of funds, or federal civil suits. At the time, the annual combined share of federal aid distributed to the sector's three biggest institutions alone had reached approximately $250 million. And with FPCU student loan defaults hitting the $1 billion mark, Congress had no option but to respond.[24]

Outraged by the continuing stream of federal funding into the coffers of scandal-tainted FPCUs, Nunn led an eight-day congressional hearing in September 1990. What his committee ultimately turned up produced shocking headlines. Fifty current and former FPCU students, recruiters, operators, and investigators testified before Congress on the systemic, structural, and pervasive problems in the for-profit industry. Their testimony, reported on by news outlets across the country, described a culinary school that operated out of the cafeteria of a sewage treatment plant, a school that hired actors to fill classrooms and "pose as students" when accreditation inspections took place, a truck-driving school that stuffed six students into a cab with their limbs hanging out the window, and a nursing school that, according to one report, "consisted of a bed, a desk and a classroom accessible through a hole in the drywall of an X-rated videotape store." The hearings fanned flames already directed at FPCUs that were now spreading toward the US Department of Education. Nunn and fellow members on the Permanent Subcommittee on Investigations wanted to know what the new secretary of education, Lauro Cavazos, was doing about the problem. Cavazos, anticipating the mood of Congress, had already drafted a statement comparing Bennett's record with that of the agency's new leadership. Despite accusing FPCUs of "exploitative and deceitful" practices, Bennett only managed to finish 372 investigations of the 7,000 or so for-profits in 1987. Cavazos, by contrast, could report to Congress on the 1,200 investigations his agency had launched in 1990. Meanwhile, the US General Accounting Office had discovered a group of 135 FPCUs responsible for 54 percent of all student loan defaults. While startling to Nunn and his committee, Education Department officials weren't surprised. FPCUs took up three-fourths of the agency's enforcement activity, they noted, even though the sector, largely dominated by enrollments at the two-year level (Figure 4.3), had only 5 percent of the overall total student population.[25]

The 1990 Nunn investigation presented a picture of a broken system desperately in need of action, and with plenty of blame to go around. "I used to buy the rhetoric that there were just a few bad apples," testified the president of the Massachusetts Higher Education Assistance Corporation, "but then I discovered there were orchards of bad apples." A consumer law specialist from South Brooklyn Legal Services agreed, saying that "there are more than a 'few bad apples'; the system is so fundamentally rotten that it simply does not—and perhaps cannot—keep up with uncovering all the bad actors." What Nunn learned from the parade of witnesses and whistleblowers coming forward was that state agencies were "woefully undermanned" to handle basic inspections

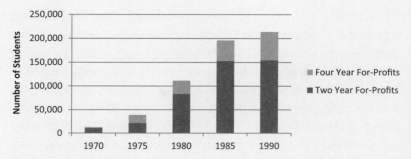

FIGURE 4.3. For-Profit Enrollments in US, 1970–1990. *Sources:* US Department of Education, National Center for Education Statistics, Higher Education General Information Survey (HEGIS), "Fall Enrollment in Colleges and Universities" surveys, 1970 through 1985; Integrated Postsecondary Education Data System (IPEDS), "Fall Enrollment Survey" (IPEDS-EF: 90–99).

and investigations. The hearings also taught him about how accreditation could be "bought" and that the Education Department had a "dismal record" of indifference to the abuses. The three-part system of checks and balances—state agencies, private accreditation organizations, and the US Department of Education—had failed to adequately uncover and prosecute for-profit abuses in the federal aid program.[26]

Two attention-grabbing cases from the 1990 Nunn hearings highlighted this breakdown in checks and balances. The American Career Training Corporation (ACT), the first case, represented problems having to do with rapid growth and industrial-sized fraud in the sector. During a three-year period (1985–1988), ACT's guaranteed student loan volume increased virtually tenfold—from $4.7 million to $45.5 million. By the end of the decade, the institution had received $153.3 million in revenue from guaranteed student loans. The huge expansion of loan receipts at this one institution didn't necessarily present a problem, but its interests and operating culture did. According to one whistleblower, "There is no way to escape being a slave to the quarterly reports. Quality education and higher earnings are two masters. You can't serve both." Former

ACT employees described the way their institution focused on recruitment and ignored instructional quality, retention, or placement of graduates. The institution provided perks, rewards, and incentives to increase recruitment and enrollment numbers, but the same wasn't provided for the other ACT divisions. A former financial aid administrator described feeling "a little strange that the instructors never had a contest, or that the placement office never was rewarded if they placed a high number of graduates." Resources at ACT went toward increasing revenue at the expense of operations. In the late 1980s, instructor pay increased 1.4 percent while advertising and marketing increased by 33.8 percent. Classroom resources, meanwhile, declined from 0.4 percent to 0.3 percent during the same period. The institution also practiced what industry experts called "front-end-loaded" tuition. Under this system, students took out loans and grants to pay for the bulk of tuition payments up front, with the expectation that most would drop out. Up-front payment maximized ACT's returns and minimized its losses in instructional expenses. With this increased revenue, witnesses contended, FPCUs could purchase their credibility from one of a number of accreditation agencies. The seven largest agencies doubled their combined revenue from $8.5 million to $17 million through membership dues during the late 1980s. Accrediting organizations depended on members for their survival. Competition for members between agencies was fierce and ultimately lowered standards as FPCUs could go "shopping" around until they found one willing to accredit them.[27]

ACT had also succeeded in increasing its own bottom line through fraud. Investigators discovered truckloads of documentation with student financial aid paperwork containing such phony addresses as "403 Cant Read, Pritchard, Alabama." These documents lacked signatures and verification of whether such students ever existed. Despite the evidence and years of investigation, it became clear to Rebekah Poston, ACT's former attorney, that the US Department of Education was outmatched and without the staff necessary to adequately address the company's violations. "It was

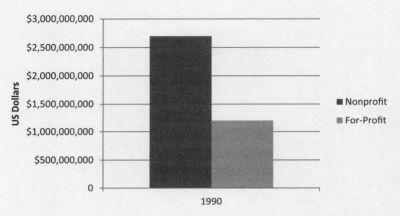

FIGURE 4.4. US Postsecondary Student Loan Default Distribution, 1990. *Source: Abuses in Federal Student Aid Programs: Report Made by the Permanent Subcommittee on Investigations of the Committee on Governmental Affairs, US Senate* (Washington, DC: GPO, 1991), 2.

not the amount of manpower I would have expected," she later stated.[28]

The second attention-getting case study came from a former owner and operator of a for-profit who had been convicted of defrauding the Government Student Loan Program. He began his career in the industry as a recruiter for Delaware's North American Training Academy, a truck-driving school with a history of perpetrating fraud against students and the government. "In the proprietary school business," he explained to Congress, "what you sell is 'dreams,' and so ninety-nine percent of the sales were made in . . . poor black areas . . . [in] welfare offices and unemployment lines, and in housing projects." Recruiters cared only whether the prospective student could "breathe, scribble his name, had a drivers license, and was over 18 years of age." If candidates met these conditions, they would be enrolled in the federal student aid program. What's more, the academy's owners encouraged and approved these tactics, including, among other things, "making the down payment for the prospect (the amount of which would be reimbursed to me

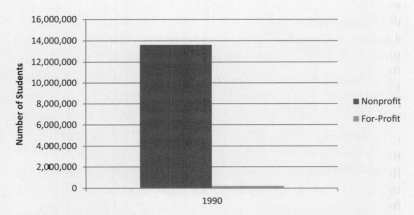

FIGURE 4.5. US Postsecondary Student Population Distribution, 1990.
Source: US Department of Education, National Center for Education
Statistics, Integrated Postsecondary Education Data System (IPEDS),
"Fall Enrollment Survey" (IPEDS-EF: 90–99).

out of the financial aid proceeds) and . . . going so far as to accom-
pany the prospect to a pawn shop in order for him to obtain enough
money for it." These were hardly isolated actions on his part. Testimony after testimony piled on evidence of widespread use of misleading strategies by FPCU employees, owners, accreditors, and
bankers. After eight days of hearings, Nunn depicted the system
as "plagued with fraud and abuse at every level." Exasperated by
the pervasiveness of misconduct among for-profits, the committee
turned from listening to testimony to compiling and preparing a
report.[29]

By the time Nunn's committee published the results of their 1990
investigation, US student loan defaults had climbed to $2.7 billion.
The investigation concluded that at least 44 percent of this amount
($1.2 billion) came from FPCUs, even though they continued to en-
roll only 2 percent of the overall student population (Figures 4.4
and 4.5). For a brief period after the hearings, Nunn and the rest of
Congress attempted to sort out FPCU issues through the 1992 HEA
reauthorization. The reauthorization gave them an opportunity to
address for-profit fraud and misappropriations through amendments

to HEA. Congressional leaders also used the momentum from the hearings and reauthorization to propose new regulations requiring institutions to demonstrate compliance with an 85-15 rule. Under the rule, institutions had to secure 15 percent of their funding from sources other than the federal student aid program. This new mandate became a bone of contention for FPCUs in the decade ahead and, through strategic, persistent, and concerted lobbying, the for-profit industry ultimately managed to water it down to a 90-10 rule. But in the immediate aftermath of the 1990 Nunn hearings and 1992 HEA reauthorization, it didn't take long for observers to see the changes hadn't gone far enough.[30]

Scandals soon resurfaced, triggering another look at the problem in 1995 by Nunn and the Permanent Subcommittee on Investigations. They followed in the footsteps of earlier federal investigations by Bennett and Nunn that gave rise to a cottage industry of independent investigations, reports, and attempts at regulating the for-profit industry at state and federal levels. All this attention kept FPCUs squarely in the public eye during the early 1990s. Bart Gordon, a US representative from Tennessee, teamed up with NBC news to go undercover, carrying a video camera to document fraud at FPCUs in his state. "If we don't trust schools to handle loan dollars responsibly," Gordon reported while briefly in the for-profit-scandal limelight, "we shouldn't trust them to do any better with grant funds." Calls to close legislative loopholes and pass stiffer penalties to fight FPCU fraud intensified just as scandals continued to take up a greater share of the headlines. In the lead-up to Nunn's 1995 investigation, congressional leaders looked into a collection of fly-by-night, religiously affiliated schools claiming tax-exempt status. What they found was a multi-hundred-million-dollar Pell Grant fraud modeled after abuses common to the FPCU industry. "We are being beaten at every turn," an Education Department official told Congress. "The crooks open one school, run thousands of students through their program, close their school, and retire as millionaires before they were even scheduled for a program review." Such schools paid students a "stipend" to enroll and apply for Pell

Grants—with some students receiving payments for seventeen years—regardless of whether they attended or intended to complete a course of studies.[31]

With these developments in mind, Nunn brought seven witnesses to testify before the Permanent Subcommittee on Investigations in July 1995. The principal witnesses included congressional investigator Alan Edelman, the Education Department's inspector general John P. Higgins, and assistant secretary for postsecondary education David Longanecker. Unlike previous hearings, these witnesses all came prepared to testify about the single biggest and most sensational case of FPCU fraud to date: the IADE American School.[32]

Located in Los Angeles, the IADE American School caught the attention of Nunn's committee in 1995 when it was discovered that the owners, Abraham Stofenmacher and his two brothers, ran a $58 million Pell Grant scam. Evidence showed a "blatant and intentional" scheme to defraud the US government. Two of the Stofenmachers abruptly left the country for somewhere in Latin America just as their scheme began to collapse. Investigators, meanwhile, were left sorting through the rubble of fraud, bankruptcy, and embezzlement. The school ostensibly served a predominantly Latin American population, with courses in auto repair, computer technology, and basic English, but the Education Department became suspicious when it found that IADE was funded almost exclusively by Pell Grants. Witnesses testified that the Pell program operated "essentially on the honor system," without student signatures and without substantive monitoring of the use of these funds. Testimony also indicated that the owners led lavish lifestyles, spending Pell funds on a house in Beverly Hills, Club Med vacations, luxury cars, and lingerie. They kept the flow of federal aid dollars coming to the school by creating "ghost" students. According to the school's language instructor, Lourdes Galvan, they would have "students listed on our rolls who had never come, and when we would go to the office to tell someone, they would always say to just keep them on the list." What's more, a team of investigators found a "widespread pattern of altering student financial aid files" as well as "forgery of student signatures" and "falsification of information on course attendance and grade sheets." Together, these revenue-making strategies gave IADE the ability to extract tens of millions of dollars in student financial aid at virtually no instructional cost to the school.[33]

Ken Williams, IADE's chief financial aid officer, at first turned a blind eye to the schemes perpetrated by the Stofenmachers. In recorded testimony, as presented to the Nunn committee, he claimed that he chose "to remain ignorant of these activities" and had no reason to report them "to any authority." But that wasn't the whole story. Williams warned the owners in a confidential memo that they owed millions of dollars in non-refunded Pell Grant monies. Knowing the school had become little more than a "Pell Grant mill," as the hearings dubbed it, Williams understood how "relaxing previously existing procedures allows IADE to significantly increase cash flow in the short run." But in the long run, the financial aid officer's memo explained, over 1,600 students "should never have received Pell Grants at all" and, as a result, "IADE's senior management could face criminal prosecution." Well aware of the implications of their scheme, the Stofenmachers had little interest in the memo that became the smoking gun in the case. Interviews with a former instructor at the school revealed that the "owners intended to make as much money as they could in 1 or 2 years and then sell the school." What Williams and instructors might not have known is how far the Stofenmachers had gone to "fool" investigators who participated in more than ten site inspections. They unplugged fax machines at IADE and directed employees to use those lines to pretend to be business owners who employed IADE graduates, deceiving inspectors charged with verifying placement rates. They went to the courthouse to find businesses that had recently filed bankruptcy to add to their placement employer list. This allowed IADE to claim they had placed students at local businesses before they went bankrupt while making it virtually impossible for investigators to verify these claims. They also enrolled students who merely requested information about IADE, but who never signed up. Very little was as it appeared at IADE. The owners succeeded in preying on the ignorance of prospective students, enrolled students, accreditors, auditors, and government inspectors.[34]

Congressional leaders turned to witnesses Edelman, Higgins, and Longanecker to find out how to stop FPCUs like IADE. Edelman, counsel and investigator to the committee, reviewed the procedures and systems already in place and found it "outrageous" that reports from one investigation found no "credible allegations of criminal wrongdoing." While identifying a breakdown in the investigative process, Edelman warned Nunn's 1995 committee that the inspector general's office at the Education Department had "a very heavy caseload" and cited "understaffing at the Department" as a critical reason for lackluster oversight performance. What they needed was more investigators on the ground conducting more thorough studies of FPCUs because "most of the problems" came from these institutions. Inspector General Higgins followed with specifics. While his office had approximately 350 staff members, he anticipated a reduction in staff to 300 as a result of budget cuts. To handle the hundreds of cases in backlog, Higgins told the committee he needed at least 640 investigators. The entire Pell Grant program's honor system, he argued, made site inspections imperative. Nunn agreed and described the program as "an open purse" with an oversight procedure akin to "leaving the back door open and removing the guards" or "an open bank with no security guards and no tellers."[35]

Nunn reserved some of his harshest tongue-lashing, however, for Longanecker, the agency's assistant secretary for postsecondary education. Evidence from testimony and reports revealed that Longanecker had reassigned investigators after telling them they had been "too aggressive" in their investigations and had taken "this oversight stuff too seriously." Longanecker replied by admitting some mistakes, but also by describing new initiatives and investigations aimed at tracking down for-profit fraud. "Your assurances today," Nunn hit back, "I have heard everybody make before." Nunn questioned the assistant secretary's reason for optimism, given the industrial-sized fraud coming from operations like IADE. Moreover, he told Longanecker that, although there was much talk of improvements, "your default rates belie that and your placement rates belie that." The committee also questioned the official's ability to lead an underfunded, understaffed agency facing seam-busting caseloads as well as pressure from congressional leaders with FPCUs in their states and districts.[36]

The IADE scandal, as far as the 1995 Nunn investigation was concerned, had analogs in every state, highlighting the problem of known unknowns—FPCU problem hotspots that the US Department of Education had reason to investigate, but had little or no resources to devote to a full-fledged investigation. "We throw a dart at the board, go out and investigate," said Nunn, "and, bang, you find a huge scandal." To his mind, these weren't anomalies and aberrations. Rather, Nunn had seen enough in the way of testimony and case studies to believe "there is a real pattern here." But the budget-cutting mood of Congress and the American public suggested little possibility of relief. With such government cuts, Nunn said, "you save $100 by cutting a person and waste $1,000 in programs." The hearings ended in 1995 with warnings about how FPCU fraud and predatory practices, if left to continue, threatened the entire student financial aid program.[37]

CHAPTER FIVE

Capital

SENATOR SAM NUNN'S CLOSING REMARKS about for-profits in the mid-nineties were several years ahead of their time. When his hearings ended, with warnings about how the financial gaming and maneuvering of FPCUs threatened the entire federal student aid program, the idea of systemic economic risks hadn't yet become the subject of dinner-table conversations.

Aside from the stock market crash of 1987 and the tech bubble that burst at the turn of the millennium, the last two decades of the twentieth century signaled little other than unprecedented growth for Wall Street. Blinded by success, brokers, investment bankers, hedge fund managers, and CEOs worried more about wealth creation than system-wide market risks. Deregulation during the eighties and nineties unleashed market energies that led to the financialization of the economy, where finance became the tail wagging the dog. Nonfinancial institutions like General Electric and General Motors went big into the world of finance during this period, developing loan divisions that quickly outpaced their other divisions in revenue production. Aggressive investment banks and private equity firms, meanwhile, scooped up industries they viewed as markets to financialize, asset strip, load up with debt, and sell off quickly for a fee. Industry—actually making things—was out, especially given the outsourcing of production work to Asian countries. Debt swept in and the era of big finance, with its short-term, quarterly report–driven thinking, took center stage. Creative financial instruments turned debts, particularly in the mortgage industry, into highly speculative bets, and the age of systemic economic risk threatening the entire global economy was born.[1]

Just as all this financialization fervor began to take off, executives at a handful of for-profit colleges and universities began to wonder if they too should go big and financialize what they had to sell. They wondered if the era of the big for-profit had arrived. Despite the scandals, lawsuits, and backlash from the Bennett and Nunn investigations, the number of FPCU institutions increased 266 percent and their enrollments increased 59 percent between 1989 and 1999. This remarkable rate of expansion dwarfed the 7 percent rise in traditional higher education during the same period. The principal reason for this for-profit growth had to do with the allies FPCU operators cultivated in Washington and on Wall Street.[2]

Early innovators in the financialization of big for-profits owe much to the successful reorganization and marketing efforts of Stephen Blair and his circle of Washington lobbyists. Blair, described by observers as "flamboyant" and given to wearing "silk scarves and derby hats," began his career in the US Department of Education, serving for thirteen years in the agency's financial aid division before the Pelavin report made its debut. When Pelavin began making headlines, Blair, by then president of the National Association of Trade and Technical Schools (NATTS), had gone through the well-used revolving door leading from public service to private lobbying firms. He saw the writing on the wall when the Bennett and first Nunn hearings took place. In response, Blair launched the most ambitious FPCU lobbying campaign to date, beginning in 1989 and running its course through the mid-1990s. He started this campaign by attempting to convince 2,200 FPCUs to pay NATTS membership dues. His goal was to fund a $1 million per year public relations blitz to manage the political fallout after the Bennett investigation.[3]

The pitch worked. Institutions paid their dues, and he used those funds to hire top-paid consultants to recast the FPCU image. Blair drew from both sides of the political spectrum. He brought people like Bob Beckel of Walter Mondale's campaign and Haley Barbour of the Reagan White House into the FPCU fold.[4]

During the lead-up to the 1992 HEA reauthorization, Blair knew the mood on Capitol Hill had soured toward FPCUs, especially after Nunn's first for-profit hearing. To Blair's mind, Nunn had declared war on for-profits, and Blair intended to win it by gathering a massive dues-funded war chest and assembling a circle of influential advisers. The NATTS fund paid for an increasingly sophisticated lobbying machine that involved courting congressional leaders and their aides, making campaign contributions to key members of the US House and Senate, and arranging for politicians and regulators to visit model FPCUs. It also paid staff to fabricate a grassroots telephone and postcard campaign from ostensibly outraged students demanding that federal aid requirements to attend for-profits remain unchanged. The money even helped broker a merger between NATTS and the Association of Independent Colleges and Schools to create the Career College Association (CCA). The name change came out of discussions with a rebranding consulting firm that helped Blair tap into the expectations of the American public. Consultants told Blair that "people think that what you do after high school is college, so call yourself colleges." He liked the "logic" and "flow" and "what it declared us to be," although Nunn's circle of critics likely found the rebranding a distraction from the substantive, scandal-producing problems within the industry.[5]

On the eve of the 1992 reauthorization, Blair could boast to his funders about how "members of Congress are beginning to feel the heat." The lobbying blitz and its questionable tactics, however, didn't sit well with all FPCUs. According to Sharon Parrott, vice president for government relations at Illinois-based DeVry, Blair had crossed the line. She acknowledged widespread problems in the for-profit sector existed and suggested that ignoring the fraud and malfeasance spreading throughout the system invited future problems for the entire FPCU industry. To Parrott, the lobbying "looked a little slick" for her comfort.[6]

The heat Blair placed on Congress, nevertheless, translated into several substantive victories over Nunn and other FPCU critics. After the passage of the 1992 reauthorization, Blair celebrated having "won the war." The rest, he claimed, were "minor skirmishes" posing no serious threat to his core FPCU members. Victories included altering right-to-know legislation that would have required FPCUs to publish graduation and placement rates. They won the right to challenge government publication of loan default rates and to contest the rates presented to the public even after publication. They also won the delay of implementation of right-to-know legislation as well as the 85-15 rule that would've required at least 15 percent of student funding to come from sources other than government aid programs. The CCA lobbying efforts aimed at managing the reauthorization outcome came with a $1.9 million price tag. But their investment, or what Blair called "democracy at work," yielded big returns. They succeeded in eliminating or delaying transparency requirements and weakening the ability of the Education Department to root out fraud and predatory practices.[7]

By the mid- to late 1990s, Blair had a finely tuned lobbying machine ready for damage control whenever impending legislation or investigations posed a threat to the FPCU industry. And he found plenty to keep the machine busy. Former industry lobbyist and consultant Patty Sullivan estimated institution-based fraud throughout the industry at "35–40" percent of all FPCUs. Federal audits year after year showed for-profits failed to make hundreds of millions of dollars in legally required refunds to the government. Regulators identified 20 percent of the $20 billion spent on federal aid as lost each year to fraud. Approximately half of that portion came from for-profits enrolling 5 to 6 percent of the total student population in American higher education. Orlando US attorney Larry Colleton reported a "naive presumption of honesty on the Government's part" when describing FPCU cases he'd investigated. "When Congress opened the doors of opportunity to benefit students," he continued, "it really opened the door for cons. . . . The Government's being had. And the public doesn't understand what's going on." US Department of Education inspector general James B. Thomas saw matters differently. He had hundreds of institution-level FPCU fraud cases to inspect but lacked the resources and inspection teams to bring the cases to completion. These were known unknowns that remained in the dark corners of the Education Department's archives. The inspector general's successor, Thomas B. Bloom, found shoddy record keeping throughout the agency in the mid-1990s, complicating basic organizational matters such as sorting, filing, and consolidating records. The confusion worked against the government's ability to monitor and investigate.[8]

Whatever the difficulties in regulatory oversight, one thing was clear for the sector as a whole: the mechanisms preventing greater transparency in for-profit reporting had arrived with Blair's lobbying machine. Each time Congress or the Education Department attempted to respond to problem areas with legislation and regulation, the CCA stepped up their efforts. "All of our people are up on the Hill right now, lobbying," said Tony Calandro, vice president for government affairs at CCA, when asked about the perennial fight over the 85-15 rule and attempts to delay its passage. US senator Tom Harkin privately caved to their demands for delay after receiving a $1,000 campaign contribution from FPCU lobbyists, while publicly telling them they had to "get their house in order or else." The message fell on deaf ears.

Harkin was one of many lawmakers who fell to the lobbying blitz across the nineties due to the lack of pushback from campaign-contributing constituents on the other side of the issue. Lobbyists flexed their muscles again in 1998 and got lawmakers to water down the 85-15 rule to 90-10. This lowered the bar for FPCU operators, only requiring them to demonstrate that 10 percent or more of their revenues came from sources other than government student aid programs. Harkin came back to this very issue a dozen years later in the most comprehensive FPCU investigation in for-profit history, making the Bennett and Nunn investigations look mild by comparison. But he did so only after for-profits had become the darlings of Wall Street.[9]

Of all the people to forge a connection between higher education and Wall Street, John Sperling, founder of the University of Phoenix, was the least likely candidate for the job. That he became one of the first among for-profit operators to create alliances with New York financiers and to put his company on the stock exchange should have surprised just about anyone who knew his past.[10]

Sperling's background, before his University of Phoenix days, appeared fitted for a life critical of investors and the moneyed class. From an early age, Sperling identified as a Depression-era socialist. After a stint at sea with the Merchant Marines, where he developed friendships with many "socialists and a sprinkling of communists," he studied at a range of institutions of higher education—two year, four year, and research intensive—and, in the end, graduated with a PhD in history from Cambridge University. He gained a reputation as a radical tenured professor at San Jose State, where he organized a faculty union and led a strike in the late sixties. Sperling's unpopularity on campus for his collectivist organizing drove him out of the ivory tower and into Sunnyvale, California's working-class neighborhoods. Through a federal grant in the 1970s, he worked with adult learners—mostly teachers and police officers—who wanted to pursue college studies but found few traditional colleges and universities willing to accommodate their work schedules. Inspired by their desire to study, Sperling decided to open the University of Phoenix with eight students in 1976. The university later added online programs, created parent company Apollo Group, and expanded enrollments to approximately 25,000 before becoming a publicly traded corporation in 1994. Sperling turned to Wall Street to see how far and how big he could take the for-profit.[11]

When Sperling's Apollo went public in the mid-nineties, most didn't know much about the FPCU sector beyond its history of bad publicity. Investors decided to test the waters with the University of Phoenix and a few other companies making their way onto the stock exchange. It didn't take long for interest in the new market to spread like wildfire. The last few years of the twentieth century gave rise to the tech stock frenzy. The mania directed piles of cash from venture firms eager to "go public" with startups brandishing mere concepts alone. Stark imbalances in the US economy, ones decades in the making, created an overaccumulation of capital among wealthy investors that helped inflate the dot-com bubble between 1997 and 2000. Sperling's Apollo and the rest of his sector ballooned along with it. When the bubble burst, redirecting overaccumulated capital from virtual concepts to such tangible assets as real estate, for-profits managed to survive. FPCUs offered a defined and stable source of revenue. They offered a sure thing attractive to investors no other moneymaking opportunity could provide: income derived from federal student aid. And there was lots of it.[12]

The multi-billion-dollar federal student aid program, made accessible to financial markets through FPCUs, gave a subsidized refuge to "free enterprise" traders during the opening decade of the twenty-first century. Market analysts like Chas Edelstein of Credit Suisse pointed to subsidies as the reason why "it's not hard to make a profit" in the FPCU sector. Investors still smarting from the dot-com collapse had no qualms about tapping income from these subsidies. Easy money through FPCUs represented the kind of principle around which Hank Greenberg, CEO of American International Group (AIG), defined his career in big finance: "All I want in life is an unfair advantage." Pressure from investors to expand on the FPCU advantage meant getting as many students into subsidized profit-making colleges and universities as possible. From 2000 to 2003, postsecondary education stock prices reflected this eagerness to expand, with increases of more than 460 percent. Apollo maintained annual federally subsidized profits of more than $100 million and broke the $1 billion revenue mark in 2003. In that year, over 750,000 students nationwide attended FPCUs. By 2007, the University of Phoenix had well over 125,000 students of its own at its 116 locations. DeVry had more than 55,000 students at its 70 branches. Strayer had at least 14,000 students at 20 sites. During the final years of the first decade of the twenty-first century, FPCUs continued to receive $4.3 billion in Pell Grants and process $19.6 billion in federally subsidized student loans annually. What's more, $1.65 billion in 9/11 GI Bill funds—allocated for veterans of Afghanistan and Iraq—was also flowing to FPCUs, much of it to help cover the

"10" part of the 90-10 rule. With such moves, sixteen of the largest for-profits began making a combined $2.7 billion anually, with profit margins in the 33 to 37 percent range.[13]

Enticed by the rapid growth and guaranteed student dollars, private equity firms jumped into the market during this period, setting a new precedent and marking an important turn in FPCU history. These firms, typically organized around a limited partnership with a ten-year life span, earned the dubious distinction of producing a culture of short-term thinking and, worse, ringing in the era of the leveraged buyout. The most notorious of the bunch would gather outside investors, purchase companies, slash benefits, raid pensions, and load up their targets with debt. The loans paid for sky-high fees, fund manager salaries, and unsustainable but speciously attractive expansion plans—all of which supported the goal of then selling off the "hollowed out" company to less-informed buyers. *Leveraged buyouts* and *asset stripping* entered the business lexicon of the late twentieth century, in part, to describe private equity practices. At the very start of the twenty-first century, these firms turned their attention to for-profit colleges and universities and participated in 3 percent of all transactions involving changes in college ownership. Six years later, that number had risen to 37 percent. During the same period, private equities accounted for an average of 107 college company ownership changes per year. The short-term mentality these takeovers brought with them created a palpable churning in the market.[14]

During the opening years of the twenty-first century, big finance firms approached for-profits as another market to financialize for a quick return. The private equity fund Huron Capital Partners bought Delta Educational Systems in 2001, acquiring its five campuses throughout the southeast—in Louisiana, North Carolina, South Carolina, Tennessee, and Virginia—for $10 million. Huron took over the company's management, expanded the number of campuses to sixteen, and sold it for $117 million five years later to Gryphon Investors, a private equity firm based in San Francisco. TA Associates, an investor fund out of Boston, paid $53 million for Florida Career College's four campuses and its 2,500 students in 2004. Fund managers added three more campuses, expanded enrollments to 4,000 students, and sold the company in under three years. Over one hundred other comparable private equity transactions occurred annually during the first decade of the twenty-first century. And these exchanges involved crucial educational decisions—about student enrollments, campus expansion, faculty and staff quality, and federal subsidies—made by fund managers under the gun to turn a handsome profit in the shortest possible time.[15]

The purchase that turned the most heads was made by Goldman Sachs Group and Providence Equity Partners. Goldman, described by one critic as "a great vampire squid wrapped around the face of humanity, relentlessly jamming its blood funnel into anything that smells like money," had by then made one of its many fortunes by manipulating tech stock prices in an illegal practice called "laddering" just before the dot-com crash. The investment company settled its tech stock manipulation suit for $40 million in 2005. Goldman treated the settlement as a small fee for doing business relative to outsized profits made and, the following year, teamed up with Providence to purchase Educational Management Corporation (EMC) for $3.4 billion. At the time, this was the single largest purchase in FPCU history. It turned a publicly traded for-profit into a privately held corporation run by private equity managers. John R. McKernan Jr., EMC's chief executive officer and former Maine governor, celebrated the deal as a victory for its colleges and universities. He suggested that the quality of for-profit higher education suffered under the publicly traded corporate model with shareholders clamoring for higher returns each quarter. What FPCUs needed, he argued, was "patient capital," and he placed his hopes in the private equity ownership model. McKernan believed he'd found investors with the "longterm strategic horizon" necessary for running an institution of higher education.[16]

The deal lasted eighteen months. Goldman and Providence flipped EMC after loading the company up with a startling amount of debt over the year-and-a-half-long relationship. Despite McKernan's original quality concerns, EMC went back to being a publicly traded company. They did so in order to raise $500 million to pay debts owed to its two former investors.[17]

These financial positions taken by Huron, Gryphon, TA, Goldman, and Providence represented a broader for-profit buyout fever that struck Wall Street halfway through the first decade of the twenty-first century. Some market movements involved takeovers of struggling nonprofits willing to sell off their accreditation status; others looked to consolidate existing for-profits. Generation Partners bought Post University in Connecticut in 2004. Bridgepoint Education bought Franciscan University of the Prairies in 2005 and renamed it Ashford University. DeVry bought Deaconess College of Nursing and recast it as Chamberlain College of Nursing in 2006. That year, Lincoln Educational Services Corporation bought the New England Institute of Technology (now Lincoln College of Technology), the New York private equity firm Liberty Partners bought Concorde Career Colleges with its twelve campuses in seven states, and the online Capella University became publicly traded under the Capella Education Company umbrella. While these purchases involved tens or hundreds of millions of dollars each, the next giant buyout to shake the sector involved ten "financial players," including Kohlberg Kravis Roberts and Company and Citigroup Private Equity in 2007. For $3.8 billion, this investor consortium took over Laureate Education with its more than 240,000 online and campus-based students in the United States, Latin America, Europe, and Asia.[18]

The Laureate purchase in 2007 heralded an FPCU trend toward expanding abroad at a time when these companies were also buying for-profit high schools and marketing businesses. That year, Bridgepoint Education joined forces with Kaplan to establish a footing in the United Kingdom. British-based BPP Professional Education, recently approved to become the first degree-awarding for-profit in England, had caught their attention. Through Kaplan Higher Education International, the US companies applied for degree-granting authority in the country. The fanfare surrounding the move came with official statements applauding recent cuts to publicly supported British higher education. Bridgepoint and Kaplan saw the cuts as having "leveled the playing field" for their comparatively more expensive degree programs. Laureate, meanwhile, looked eastward in a move into China. The company's venture won support and financial backing from Microsoft's Paul Allen and global investor George Soros. In a bid to shore up their global credentials, DeVry and Apollo made similar moves. DeVry hired Sergio Abramovich, the general director of La Fundación Universitaria Iberoamericana (FUNIBER), an online education consortium of Spanish universities. The new hire telegraphed DeVry's interest in overseas expansion. Apollo, around the same time, signed a $1 billion agreement with Carlyle Group to purchase or create for-profits abroad. Their first target was a Chilean university with 3,000 students.[19]

By 2007, the rush of money into FPCUs had created a problem industry officials attempted to solve by moving into for-profit high schools and Web-based advertising companies. Overaccumulated investor capital had saturated the for-profit sector and, as Washington attorney and FPCU buyout broker Neil Lefkowitz put it, "after a while, there's not a lot left to consolidate." To fill seats in their for-profit colleges, Apollo bought Insight Schools. As they saw it, the Portland-based online high school company would create a feeder school for Apollo's virtual two-year Axia College. The reasoning was simple: capture students online before they leave high school and roll them over into the first two years of college. The trend continued at two other FPCUs. Kaplan bought Sagemont Virtual and DeVry took over Advanced Academics—both for the same feeder school strategy. With increasing competition in the FPCU markets, recruitment and advertising played as important a role as the virtual and for-profit high school education companies. The movement of capital into this FPCU-related market created a $500 million to $1 billion industry in the last few years of the decade. Of all the companies operating in this market, lead companies received the most attention. Designed to produce leads on potential college students, these advertising outfits created Web pages intended to extract information from visitors. The information was then used to create databases for sale to for-profit as well as nonprofit colleges and universities. Dozens of Internet-based recruitment and marketing firms appeared to fill this and allied niches, such as Course Advisor, QuinStreet, and Education Dynamics. The Washington Post, owner of Kaplan and its $2 billion per year revenue-creating FPCUs, purchased lead company Course Advisor to increase enrollments. Apollo executives had the same goal in mind when they paid $48 million for Aptimus to use its online marketing and recruiting tools.[20]

By the time Apollo purchased Aptimus in 2007, the company had long shed any resemblance to what John Sperling had created in the seventies and took to Wall Street in the nineties. Getting investors, shareholders, private equity firms, and financial managers involved in FPCUs radically changed how the for-profit made and spent its money. Apollo showed it had transformed into something else when it outspent Apple Corporation in advertising following the Aptimus purchase. Analysts estimated that Apollo's marketing and recruitment efforts had reached $1 billion at the start of the next decade. Skyrocketing advertising expenditures far outstripped instructional ones, making these institutions first and foremost about attracting rather than teaching students. Studies of the industry showed that, on average, thirty leading FPCUs spent 23 percent of their revenues on marketing and 17 percent on instruction. Put another way, these institutions paid out 250 percent more on profits and advertising combined than on instruction.[21]

Heavy emphasis on advertising to meet revenue projections generated unwelcome publicity, and Apollo responded by allocating a portion of its profits to create the Nexus Research and Policy Center (NRPC), a nonprofit "think tank," in 2008. Headed by Jorge Klor de Alva, the NRPC's first publication—"For-Profit Colleges and Universities: America's Least Costly and Most Efficient System of Higher Education" (2010)—cast a pall over the center. It set a polemical rather than a research tone, calling traditional colleges "studies in inefficiency" while hailing the virtues of for-profits. Even de Alva, a former faculty member at the University of California at Berkeley and at Princeton University, apologetically acknowledged concern over whether the white paper would tarnish the nonprofit's credibility. "We've got a lot of things going," he assured observers, "that won't sound as sharp." Despite claims of impartiality, the organization assisted for-profits in generating a "cookbook" for creating an alternate, more favorable-looking graduation rate than the one used by the US Department of Education. Controversy continued to dog NRPC, as researchers identified basic flaws in later reports. The center produced "careless" and "grossly misleading" work that, as one scholar stated, failed to conform to the norms of "traditional academic studies, in which the methodology is generally clearly articulated and the reader can judge for himself the quality of the study." Brushing aside criticism, NRPC continued to advocate on behalf of the for-profit sector and its focus on revenues, significant budgets for advertising, and strategies for expansion.[22]

The FPCU's emphasis on marketing and recruitment as *the* core function of higher education—based on how the sector spent its resources—put extraordinary pressure on nonprofit colleges and universities between 2005 and 2010. Nonprofits, most of which traditionally budgeted a mere 1–2 percent for these areas, began to devote increasing attention to lead companies and other Web-based advertisers. Indiana University's business school opened its purse for "search engine optimization" to put their MBA programs at the top of Google search results. George Washington University's College of Professional Studies hired Educational Sales Management (ESM), a call-center company, to handle two hundred leads per month. ESM reported on the trend as their business with nonprofits shot up from 5 percent to 25 percent over two years during this period. Pressure to keep pace with advertising quantity rather than instructional quality became a growing concern for traditional nonprofit institutions, a concern threatening the core function, purpose, and mission of higher education.[23]

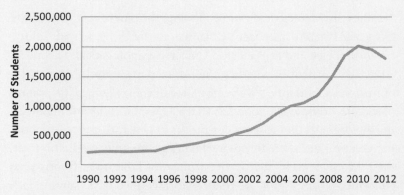

FIGURE 5.1. Enrollment at Degree-Granting For-Profits, 1990–2012.
Sources: US Department of Education, National Center for Education
Statistics, Integrated Postsecondary Education Data System (IPEDS), "Fall
Enrollment Survey" (IPEDS-EF: 90–99), and spring 2001 through spring
2013, enrollment component.

If Wall Street indicators provide any measure, the threats were
real and imminent. For-profit executives cheered as their stock prices
soared across the first decade of the twenty-first century. The prices
mirrored the sector's stunning enrollment increases of more than
300 percent between the late nineties and late 2008 (Figure 5.1).
Even in the weakest performing years in terms of yields throughout
this period, the FPCU sector continued to book between 4 and
20 percent profit margins for its investors. Robert W. Wrubel, executive vice president of marketing and product development at
Apollo's University of Phoenix, recalled the especially celebratory
mood about their stock price at the end of 2009. But in the background, something didn't sit well. As he described it, they all had the
same feeling, one "in the pit of everyone's stomach: That felt too
good." Nagging doubts about the sustainability of Apollo's business
practices came about after executives had extracted significant
profits and after they knew they could no longer ignore litigation
nipping at their heels. The sinking feeling likely emerged from persistent, long-standing suits over fraud, the misappropriation of funds,

and violations of the False Claims Act against Apollo and the rest of the industry.[24]

Large-scale claims against the shiny new line of publicly traded and private-equity-owned FPCUs began to surface in 2000. These claims continued to multiply, intensify, and mar the industry across the decade and a half that followed. The most troubling ones came from those who knew the industry best—students and whistleblowers. But many other cases came forward, resulting in wave after wave of legal, legislative, and regulatory activity at state and federal levels during the period.[25]

Students from a subsidiary of Whitman Education Group, a medium-sized player among FPCUs, kicked off one series of lawsuits involving for-profits at the turn of the twenty-first century. They filed a class action representing a total of 5,300 students against the company's Ultrasound Diagnostic Schools located along the coast from New York to Florida. After hearing the case, Judge Anita Brody called the program a "complete sham." She was shocked to find students had "experienced virtually all of the abuses" characteristic of FPCU fraud. These included admission without "requisite credentials," enrollment without the necessary "entrance exam," graduation despite having "failed the clinical portion," and indebtedness after being "unable to find a job." Given the thousands of students affected and the sweeping evidence of predatory practices, Whitman had little choice but to settle the lawsuit in 2000 for $7.3 million.[26]

Whistleblowers, meanwhile, launched another series of suits, although they generally faced lengthier, more challenging court battles with big for-profits. Few, if any, reached resolution within a year. What's more, the first whistleblowers received no support from the US Department of Justice for their initial claims. During most of President George W. Bush's two terms and President Barack Obama's first, litigants had difficulty getting prosecutors at Justice to move on white collar crime. Testimony and evidence indicating large-scale fraud and systemic violations of taxpayer-supported federal student aid programs received a yawn.[27]

Mary Hendow and Julie Albertson Behn, two former recruiters at Apollo's University of Phoenix, discovered this apathy at the federal level when they first came forward in 2003. The institution, they argued, had perpetrated fraud against government student aid programs by claiming to be in compliance with the prohibition against commission-based recruitment. The case didn't look good for the company. The year before, Apollo had agreed to pay a $490,000 fine to the US Department of Education for violating the law when it outsourced some of its recruiting to a third party that received a portion of tuition paid by each new enrollee. In the months leading up to the 2003 suit, however, executives at the company had reason to think they had dodged a bullet when the Bush administration made two key appointments: Sally Stroup, Apollo's chief lobbyist, to assistant secretary of postsecondary education and Jeffrey Andrade, consultant to the Career College Association lobby, to deputy assistant secretary of postsecondary education. These appointments fueled accusations that the administration was "stacking the deck" in favor of for-profits. When Stroup and Andrade moved quickly to propose "safe harbor rules" for the FPCU sector, critics had evidence to support their claims. The new rules softened the ban on incentive pay for recruiters at for-profits. They also allowed companies to increase recruiter pay two times per year, but indicated that the adjustments couldn't be based "solely" on the number of students recruited.[28]

Hendow and Behn's 2003 whistleblower complaint against Apollo claimed the company came nowhere close to following the spirit or letter of the law. For six years, the company fought Hendow and Behn, eventually appealing to the US Supreme Court to prevent the case from going to trial. Justice Department prosecutors joined the case in time to help broker a deal between the parties. In the end, Apollo opted to settle the case for $78.5 million, avoiding a potentially larger penalty for fraudulently acquiring billions in federal student aid subsidies.[29]

Suits and settlements against Apollo continued to pile up in the following years. In 2004, the company agreed to pay another fine—this time a $9.8 million penalty—to the US Department of Education for violating the ban on commission-based recruiting. Investigators interviewed over sixty current and former Apollo employees and found that the company knowingly rewarded recruiters based on who put the most "asses in classes." Recruiters who performed below aggressive expectations were harassed and shamed by supervisors. Apollo executives withheld from shareholders a scathing report by the Education Department about recruitment abuses resulting in the multi-million-dollar penalty. By failing to release the report to investors, Apollo broke securities laws and potentially caused hundreds of millions of dollars in investor stock losses. In October 2004, shareholders sued, the case went to trial, and the plaintiffs won a $145 million settlement with the company. In 2006, Apollo faced another shareholder suit over fraudulent data used to award stock option compensation to company executives and managers. "Backdating," stated the complaint, "allowed the option recipients to reap a windfall when the Company looked back in time and chose option issue dates when the stock was trading at lower prices, thereby allowing recipients to make even more money when they exercised the options on the spread between the artificially depressed option price and the later exercise price." The settlement awarded to the shareholders came in the form of 413,000 repriced stock options used to compensate executives and managers, a restructuring of the compensation board, and $13.1 million in damages.[30]

Whitman and Apollo were anything but isolated cases of FPCUs engaged in fraud for private gain. Kaplan adopted similar practices between 2000 and 2006, according to two former career and student advisers. Whistleblowers Dolores A. Howland-Justice and Victoria G. Gatsiopoulos claimed Kaplan willfully violated the ban on commission-based recruiting. Their complaint described a compensation system "based solely and directly on their enrollment success." In addition, they outlined the Washington Post subsidiary's violations of the False Claims Act. Kaplan's overall placement rates of 83 to 92 percent, they indicated, were designed to deliberately and systematically mislead prospective students. The plaintiffs argued that Kaplan regularly inflated the numbers with complete fabrications.[31] Examples involved instances where Kaplan claimed "a graduated student who secured employment as a Sales Associate at Wal-Mart as working in the related field of Accounting Management; a graduated student who worked as a Telemarketer for Dial America as working in the related field of Business Administrative Fashion Merchandising; and a graduated student who worked as a McDonald's Crew Leader as working in the related field of Criminal Justice."[32] Howland-Justice and Gatsiopoulos also recounted a culture of fear and intimidation directed at faculty who held rigorous academic standards. If they graded too harshly, faculty knew they wouldn't last at the company. Loss of students meant loss of revenue for Kaplan, and faculty who failed students translated into lost students. To preserve the flow of federal aid funds, Kaplan routinely overrode faculty decisions. Administrators were "encouraged to change students' grades to falsely elevate students' cumulative grade point average" to meet minimum academic progress requirements for federal funding eligibility.[33]

With brand-name for-profits exposed by litigation, cases against other giants like Career Education Corporation (CEC) began to come forward, indicating an industry-wide pattern of fraud. CEC marketed itself to students at their culinary school in San Francisco as having a 97 percent placement rate from 2003 to 2008. Students sued when they discovered the company had grossly and illegally misrepresented these rates. Among the placements the institution could verify were graduates who waited tables, served as baristas, and otherwise held jobs that didn't require a degree from the school. Students filed a class-action lawsuit and ultimately won a $40 million settlement. During and after the period of culinary school litigation, CEC continued to mislead students at its New York subsidiaries. They did so with inflated placement rates, suggesting the company interpreted litigation as a fee for doing business rather than a fine, penalty, or punishment for fraud and violation of the False Claims Act. Beginning in 2009, CEC subsidiaries in New York advertised placement rates ranging from 55 to 80 percent, when actual rates ranged from 24 to 64 percent. The fraud cost CEC $10.25 million in a settlement with students and the state of New York.[34]

The largest suit in FPCU history involved Educational Management Corporation and the same kinds of claims landing other for-profits in court. It began with a whistleblower suit in 2007 and later expanded in size and scope when additional plaintiffs, including the US Justice Department and four states, joined the case in 2011. This was one of the first whistleblower actions against a for-profit to receive coordinated backing from multiple government agencies. Two former employees filed the original complaint: Lynntoya Washington and Michael T. Mahoney. Washington had served as an EMC assistant director of admissions and Mahoney had worked as an EMC director of training. Together, they provided evidence of a detailed performance-based pay system focused on "quality factors" assigned for each new enrollment. EMC paid "commission[s], bonus[es], or other incentive payment[s]," knowingly and systematically in violation of the federal ban. EMC's violation of the False Claims Act, according to prosecutors, made the institution retroactively ineligible to receive $11 billion in federal student aid subsidies. Since frauds perpetrated against the US government can, in such cases, result in penalties of up to three times the amount defrauded, EMC faced a potential $33 billion fine for falsely claiming eligibility. In late-2015, after years of vigorous attempts to have the case dismissed, EMC settled for $200 million in loan forgiveness and civil penalties.[35]

All of the settlements and lawsuits won by whistleblowers, shareholders, and government agencies energized the work of others tracking illegal activities within the FPCU sector. State-level lawmakers, state attorneys general, and a wide range of regulators reexamined their roles in reining in for-profits. They took a harder look at what they could do to control the repeated, predictable problems these institutions created in a heavily subsidized market.

California set the pace for other states in its crackdown on FPCU abuses. It began a three-year investigation of Corinthian Colleges in 2004, focusing on how the company misled students about job placements and career prospects. Edmund G. "Jerry" Brown, state attorney general (later California governor), filed suit on behalf of students who'd fallen prey to false claims. Upon investigation, noted Brown, "Corinthian's records even list non-existent businesses as the students' places of employment." Some of the "placements" included "businesses" created as part of class projects to design business cards. Brown's suit yielded a $6.5 million settlement, most of which went to students affected by the scam. California also went after ITT in 2005 for falsifying grades and submitting fraudulent paperwork on behalf of academically ineligible students in order to tap into the state's Cal Grants aid program. The state recovered $725,000 in a settlement over this scheme. A few years later, midway through Arnold Schwarzenegger's tenure as governor of California, for-profit industry officials assumed positions in the state's regulatory arm charged with overseeing FPCUs. Regulatory capture became unmistakable with Schwarzenegger's appointment of Barbara Ward, a former University of Phoenix employee, as head of California's Bureau of Private Postsecondary and Vocational Education. Cuts to the agency followed, and so too did a pattern of inaction. Elena H. Ackel, senior lawyer at the Legal Aid Foundation of Los Angeles, represented scammed students and kept close tabs on the changes. "Since 1998," she said in 2006, "there has been no enforcement of the law. The bureau does absolutely nothing regarding investigation of student complaints, which they are required to investigate under the law." California lawmakers responded to part of the problem in subsequent years by linking default and graduation rates to Cal Grant funding.[36]

New York made a definitive move against FPCU fraud by cracking down on Interboro Institute at the end of 2005. According to state investigators, the company used predatory recruiting practices to attract their 2,600 enrolled students, 80 percent of whom had neither a high school diploma nor a GED. An audit conducted by the state's comptroller also found $2.4 million worth of government aid processed by the institution for students who had "not matriculated" or were "not in full-time attendance." To keep state and federal aid flowing to the company, the institute kept students on their books by manipulating their sky-high dropout rates, especially the records of students who failed to complete a single semester. Documents showed that out of one hundred sample students, only two finished in the period the company advertised it would take to complete their programs. EVCI Career Colleges Holding Corporation, Interboro's parent company, spent the next two years attempting to find a buyer for its New York campuses. The search failed, even after hiring an investment bank to help with the sale, and Interboro closed its multi-million-dollar operation in 2007.[37]

With these and a multitude of other cases making headlines, ten state attorneys general gathered in spring 2011 to coordinate their efforts against for-profits. They shared common experiences dealing with FPCU fraud and abuse: predatory admissions practices, unacceptably low completion rates, disproportionate loan defaults, fabricated placement practices and reporting, and patent violations of state and federal law. Led by Kentucky attorney general Jack Conway, the group of ten agreed to conduct investigations in their respective states. By 2013, the group had expanded to thirteen, all of whom signed an open letter to Congress calling for legislation prohibiting the use of federal student aid dollars for FPCU advertising and marketing.[38] Attorneys general, they noted, "strongly support higher education as a way to improve the standard of living for Americans and help them reach their financial goals. However, federal taxpayers should not be asked to foot the bill for aggressive recruiting and deceptive sales tactics of colleges that have placed profits ahead of ensuring student success."[39] The group of thirteen wanted congressional leaders to work with them against companies that had "violated our state consumer protection laws" and warranted further legal action.[40]

In January 2014, the attorneys general pooled their resources and collectively hit ITT, EMC, CEC, and Corinthian with a flurry of subpoenas and civil investigation demands. Securities and Exchange Commission (SEC) filings by the companies described the massive scope of the investigation and documentation under action. From ITT, they wanted all documents related to "marketing and advertising, recruitment, financial aid, academic advising, career services, admissions, programs, licensure exam pass rates, accreditation, student retention, graduation rates and job placement rates, as well as many other aspects of the Company's business." From EMC and CEC, the list included anything on "recruitment of students, graduate placement statistics, graduate certification and licensing results, and student lending activities, among other matters." And Corinthian, then experiencing one of its worst public relations slumps, faced the longest list of demands. In its case, thirteen state attorneys general collaborated to demand "documents and answers to interrogatories related to the students recruited from the various states; organizational information; tuition, loan and scholarship information; lead generation activities; enrollment qualifications for students; complaints; accreditation; completion and placement statistics; graduate certification and licensing results; and student lending activities, among other matters." The era of state inaction had come to a close.[41]

The for-profits these attorneys general moved against were born out of an age of big finance. In the last quarter of the twentieth century and well into the first decade and a half of the present century, the American economy finished shifting from one that produced tangible products to one heavily dependent on risky financial instruments. Forty percent of all profits in the United States during the period between 2007 and 2008, when the global economy collapsed, went to the financial sector. For-profit colleges and universities partnered with big finance before and after this period to create institutions driven by the same aggressive, predatory practices scholars now identify with systemic financial risk. Defenders of big FPCUs, like David Salisbury, director of the Cato Institute's Center for Educational Freedom, have argued that students have a right to attend any school they wish. To his mind, it shouldn't matter what kind of information institutions provide prospective students. "My gut feeling on diploma mills," Salisbury stated, "is the whole idea of having to regulate this is the denial of intelligence of consumer and marketplace. If people want to waste their money buying a diploma from a diploma mill, let them do so." State attorneys general disagreed, especially when it came to taxpayer-subsidized grants and loans spent fruitlessly on predatory programs. According to Tom Dresslar of the California attorney general's office, for-profits marketed misinformation and profited from the misinformed. From the student's viewpoint, said Dresslar, "you're out there, you want to improve your life, and you see this advertisement, with these great numbers. You sign up, and to complete the course you need a student loan, which can get into the tens of thousands of dollars. You graduate and you find out they lied, and you can't get a decent job. So now you're in a situation where you have enormous debt." From the FPCU's point of view, student loan debt accounted for 80 to 90 percent of the tremendous growth in for-profit stock valuation since the start of the twenty-first century.[42]

For over a decade, whistleblowers, shareholders, and states attempted to stop the redistribution of wealth from taxpayers to FPCU investors and executives through fraudulently acquired student aid processed by big for-profits. But the massive revenues and lobbying power backing the $35 billion FPCU industry steamrolled past the fines, penalties, and settlements. FPCUs used this leverage to fight student suits in courts and, by defending arbitration clauses in student enrollment contracts, won a victory over students' rights to even sue. The US Supreme Court effectively sided with for-profits in 2011 when ruling in favor of "arb clauses." This allowed the sector to require students to waive their right to a jury trial. These "customers" now had to submit to arbitration firms with financial ties to for-profits. Knowing constituents across the country had become weary of the willful and deliberate disregard for the law, the erosion of consumer rights, and the cycle of false promises, student debt, and joblessness created by these institutions, congressional leaders began to speak out. Some focused on the crimes and injustices committed against students and taxpayers. Others responded by demanding the largest investigation in for-profit college and university history. Out of this uproar, Senator Tom Harkin stepped forward and promised to offer HELP.[43]

Conclusion

A T FIRST BLUSH, it might have passed for instructions to a game. The one-page document had illustrations of a funnel, a puzzle, and procedures on how to get from one end to the other. But peppered all over the page—as revealed by US senator Tom Harkin, chair of the Housing, Education, Labor, and Pension (HELP) committee—was the word "pain."[1]

Those who read the document learned of four levels of pain that could be inflicted on others through a series of strategically worded, open-ended questions. These questions dropped unsuspecting prospective for-profit college students into a funnel of emotional manipulation. At the end of the funnel, prospects were left with a puzzle that, if presented effectively, had only one possible solution: signing federal student aid agreements and enrolling in a for-profit college. Harkin and the rest of the HELP committee, startled by what they found, saw nothing amusing in these and other "find the pain" for-profit recruiter training materials collected during their investigation of FPCUs from 2010 to 2012.[2]

Had members of the HELP committee dug into the basic contours of for-profit college and university history, none of this would have surprised them. Rather, they might have seen the profitable use of pain as the logical extension of a long-standing breakdown in checks and balances regulating exchanges between those with the greatest interests at stake: disadvantaged students, understaffed regulators, FPCU operators, and private investors. Instead, Harkin's HELP committee received lessons largely derived from the recent past, despite having launched the most comprehensive investigation of any in the sector's history. It missed an opportunity to consider the long view.

HELP's lessons came from people like money manager Steve Eisman, known for anticipating the 2008 global economic meltdown. Eisman compared FPCUs to the recently failed mortgage industry and described for-profits as "marketing machines masquerading as universities." Expense reports corroborated Eisman's claim by showing that large-scale FPCUs typically spent twice as much on advertisement as on faculty. Committee members also learned about the students who went to these institutions. FPCUs enrolled between 10 and 12 percent of the overall postsecondary student population, received a quarter of the total student federal aid disbursements, and were responsible for 44 percent of all loan defaults. With nearly half of all loan defaults coming from the FPCU sector, the HELP committee listened carefully to what Katheleen Tighe had to say. As the US Department of Education's inspector general, Tighe had found "recurring areas of fraud and abuse" in the FPCU industry. For-profits, at the time, consumed approximately 75 percent of Education's criminal investigation activity. The inspector described the challenges her agency faced when dealing with widespread falsification of federal aid eligibility documents from students at for-profits who never attended sessions, physically or virtually, and never completed assignments. Her lesson about the recent past spoke to the improbable task of monitoring the activities of fourteen institutions with their 1.4 million FPCU student population.[3]

The Harkin committee also echoed much of what previous investigations had discovered, while adding a few novel undercover flourishes of its own. HELP members held hearings about the practices used by thirty of the country's biggest FPCUs over the previous decade. They relearned patterns from the past: for-profits employed more than twice as many recruiters as support staff, focused on revenue creation rather than high-quality instruction, violated the False Claims Act, and even sent recruiters to military hospitals. Stories of hospital bedside recruitment came to light, especially after the case of US Marine corporal James Long. The veteran recalled an FPCU agent visiting him in a brain trauma ward and enrolling him in a program at for-profit Ashford University.

But, when asked, Long couldn't remember what classes he was taking. The Harkin lessons continued, with a wide range of additional anecdotes, charts, and graphs. Some depicted wildly disproportionate tuition rates at for-profits when compared with similar programs at public institutions, reliance on 80 to 90 percent part-time instructional faculty, and multi-million-dollar FPCU executive salaries. Others showed dependency on federal student aid for 80 to 90 percent of FPCU revenue, 50 percent dropout rates after a median of four months in for-profit programs, online programs—such as the University of Phoenix's—with graduation rates as low as 5 percent, and so on. The list of grievances from the recent past and present was long. But some of the most provocative and novel findings came from an undercover investigation conducted by the Government Accountability Office (GAO). The GAO sent undercover applicants to secretly record conversations with admissions officers at fifteen for-profits. All fifteen "made deceptive or otherwise questionable statements" and four "encouraged fraudulent practices" including falsification of financial aid forms.[4]

In the end, Harkin's HELP committee did more than just construct a recent history of for-profit colleges and universities. It also armed state and federal agencies with plenty of data to support their active claims against for-profits. In 2013, California's state attorney general filed suit against Corinthian for falsely reporting placement rates. Evidence suggested the company engaged in "unlawful, unfair, and fraudulent practices in connection with the sale of programs." Corinthian claimed placements rates "at times as high as 100 percent," none of which could be substantiated when investigators requested documentation. That same year, Massachusetts' attorney general filed a similar lawsuit against Sullivan and Cogliano Training Centers. The state ultimately recovered hundreds of thousands of dollars in tuition and fee payments on behalf of students who were "induced" to enroll as a result of "unfair or deceptive acts or practices." The practices included falsely announcing that "virtually all students" obtain jobs in their field of training. Career Education Corporation, likewise, came under scrutiny and, in 2013, paid a $27.5 million settlement to investors misled by the institution's falsely reported placement rates.[5]

At the federal level, the HELP committee's history lessons aided the US Consumer Financial Protection Bureau (CFPB). The bureau was then engaged in some of the farthest reaching efforts to protect taxpayer-funded student aid programs. The CFPB took special interest in newly-created private loan departments at several big for-profits. These loan divisions mirrored financialization moves increasingly common among other nonfinancial institutions, but they had an added benefit for FPCUs. They allowed for-profits to charge inflated tuition costs, receive the maximum in federal student aid, and remain in compliance with regulations like the 90-10 rule. In 2014, the CFPB sued two of the country's largest for-profits—ITT and Corinthian, with a combined enrollment of 125,000—for predatory lending that closely resembled practices leading to the subprime mortgage crisis. ITT sold nine-month teaser loans with 0 percent interest to entering students. The financial product called "Temporary Credit" covered tuition costs at times exceeding $44,000 for an associate's degree that students could get for $6,520, on average, at community colleges.[6] Without warning, ITT then "coerced" students "into paying off their Temporary Credit amounts with high-interest, high-fee private loans payable over ten years. At the same time, to cover the tuition gaps for the upcoming year, students were coerced into taking out additional private student loans. If students were unable to pay off the Temporary Credit and pay the second-year tuition gap, and they refused the private loans, they were threatened with expulsion."[7] By ITT's own projections, more than 60 percent of the private loans were bound to default. But the for-profit continued to offer these financial products, as highlighted in the CFPB complaint, in order to "enhance its financial statements and appearance to investors" at the expense of students facing debt ruination.

The CFPB, meanwhile, sued Corinthian for a similar private loan program affecting nearly 130,000 students and involving more than $500 million in debt. To cover tuition costs equivalent to ITT's, Corinthian developed "Genesis" loans with a third-party lender.

Together, they sold complex financial instruments to students who lacked basic skills training and were uninformed about loan options. Corinthian's financial aid staff used coercive, high-pressure sales tactics to "close the deal" on over half a billion dollars in loans in under three years. The loans came with interest rates of about 15 percent and an origination fee of 6 percent at a time when federal student loans ranged from 3 to 7 percent with low or no origination fees. More than 60 percent of borrowers defaulted on these loans in three years or less.[8] The court ultimately sided with the CFPB and, in 2015, delivered a $500 million judgment for "ill-gotten gains" against the company.

Collectively, HELP's lessons about the for-profit's recent past—coupled with the state and federal lawsuits of the mid-2010s—began to outline the extent of FPCU fraud. The investigations and suits, involving at least twenty-seven states and five federal agencies, showed the impact this fraud had on students, taxpayers, and investors across the country. The lessons also highlighted a trend in the blending of big finance and big for-profits. FPCU private loan programs shared much in common with predatory strategies used by the mortgage industry in the lead-up to the 2007–2008 global economic meltdown. After the housing bubble burst, the practices reappeared in for-profit loan divisions. Along with them, not surprisingly, came extreme volatility. Corinthian, one the country's largest for-profit, filed for bankruptcy in May 2015, giving observers reason to wonder if the FPCU bubble had finally begun to pop.[9]

The HELP committee's hearings, the recent history lessons they offered, and the suits that followed have all provided useful points of reference for current debates over the merits of for-profit colleges and universities. But the long view, the broader historical perspective on FPCUs, has largely been absent from discussions about how to move forward. Much of what has appeared as new and scandalous in the sector is, in reality, old wine in new bottles. Too often students, investigators, lawmakers, and taxpayers have had to spend valuable resources to relearn and reinvestigate the for-profit's perennial problems. What this book's brief exploration of FPCU history can offer are a few fixed stars to help illuminate potential paths forward, or at least point out a few messes to avoid stepping in along the way.

For-profits claim to do more than they can and promise more than they should. The profit motive puts pressure on FPCU managers and operators to make inflated claims about the services they provide. Early American shopkeepers advertised lessons on everything imaginable, from astronomy to writing. Nineteenth-century proprietary business colleges promised any takers a "sure road to success" in "the greatest educational enterprise in the world." For-profit medical schools at the turn of the twentieth century falsely claimed to have facilities they couldn't afford. Congressional investigations of the mid- to late twentieth century turned up more than their fair share of misleading advertising, which continues to the present and has left a trail of overindebted students and defrauded public coffers. Without the long view, we tend to forget past abuses, and our charitable tendency is to dismiss the most recent news of damaging practices as the work of "a few bad apples." But the voices and concerns expressed in this FPCU history paint a different picture. Disadvantaged students, it turns out, have consistently been no match against an industry willing to spend astonishing sums in order to expand market share. In the nineteenth century, one business college alone spent more than the annual salary of Harvard's president for a single full-page newspaper advertisement. More recently, Apollo spent more than the multi-hundred-million-dollar annual marketing budget of Apple Corporation to attract customers. These kinds of tactics have appeared throughout the nation's history, among institutions of every size and variety, and have most recently taken the form of sky-high placement rate claims or promises of guaranteed employment coming from big for-profits. With such vast resources, the imbalance will always leave students—particularly those facing economic hardship and without basic reading, writing, and critical-thinking skills—vulnerable to the kinds of claims the well educated and well off can easily dismiss and ignore.[10]

Stanford business school instructor Samuel C. Wood has described the problem of FPCUs' inflated claims as the "gym" model of profit seeking. "They are going to spend the money on getting you," his research indicates, "and a little bit on keeping you around. Once you've acquired a student, it's like you've acquired an annuity." Treating students like annuities creates an imbalanced exchange. Something has to give and, historically, the givers have been unemployed, underqualified graduates saddled with billions of dollars in debt at the expense of the public's trust and treasury.[11]

For-profits deliver less than they could. While the profit motive conflicts with making reasonable claims about what FPCUs can do and provide, it also works against student-centered postsecondary practices. Nineteenth-century British observers of American for-profits understood this without missing a beat. As soon as profit-seekers discovered "there was 'money in it,'" stated a report to British Parliament, the proprietary business college industry changed. The introduction of the profit motive resulted in "unprincipled exploitation" and "disgrace and discredit [to] an honorable profession." Early twentieth-century citizen groups found the same when they learned how much more for-profits spent on competing with one another than on quality instruction and qualified instructors. As Chicago's City Club discovered, for-profits had a tendency of "employing teachers who lack training." In the 1950s, President Truman wrung his hands at the way for-profits "blemished" the GI Bill and gave "less than acceptable quality" instruction to veterans. Similar discontent swept over the general public when it came to the biggest for-profits from the 1980s to the recent past, particularly with their bare minimum instructional budgets and overemphasis on noninstructional expenses. On average, the thirty leading FPCUs in 2009 spent 17 percent of their budget on instruction and 42 percent on getting students to enroll and making payments to investors. For-profits have shown time and again their preference for spending on advertising and dividends over instruction. This market tendency is profit driven, rather than a reflection of what's best for American higher education.[12]

The profit motive's never-ending search for efficiencies ultimately leads to shortcuts, and the easiest cuts to disguise come in the form of instruction. All indicators suggest, however, that postsecondary instruction has always been and will likely always be an expensive endeavor. This means the aggressive quest for efficiency found in for-profits creates environments less than adequate to meet student needs. For-profits, at bottom, are fundamentally incapable of serving the challenging postsecondary student demographics they often target while also producing record profits demanded by executives and shareholders. Expenses for supporting disadvantaged students—those for programs and initiatives commonly found at nonprofits—are at odds with the production of profits in an FPCU context. Retention programs, remedial courses, loan reduction initiatives, mental health services, and the promotion of financial literacy all have a relevant purpose at nonprofits, given their mission, but they conflict with the central goal of FPCUs. Programs eat into profits. This is why the University of Phoenix decided to abandon almost all of its associate's degree offerings in 2015. Officials at the institution described the move as "cost cutting" and acknowledged failing to solve retention issues among high-needs students. As one 1990s whistleblower reminds us, "Quality education and higher earnings are two masters. You can't serve both." To date, FPCUs have erred disproportionately on the side of maximizing returns and there's no indication this will change anytime soon.[13]

For-profits have strong incentives to water down academic standards. The professions have traditionally been in charge of defining academic standards through research, publication outlets, professional organizations, and annual meetings. Out of nineteenth-century professionalization movements came standards dictating what counts as quality instruction and content and what doesn't. For-profit colleges and universities came under fire in the early twentieth century for failing to live up to the standards demanded by professions like medicine and law. Organizations representing both of these professions published clear, unequivocal statements about the corrosive effect of for-profits in the maintenance of professional standards. In 1907, the chair of the Council on Medical Education flatly rejected for-profit medical schools, calling them a "menace" and forcefully encouraging the profession to rid itself of this class of institution. Fifteen years later, the American Bar Association and the Association of American Law Schools officially came out against law schools "operated as commercial enterprises." They viewed institutions dependent on "the fees received" as antithetical to the maintenance of standards.[14]

The clash between for-profits and standards has beaten a clear path to the present. Administrative whistleblowers and former instructors have come forward to describe the way for-profits override faculty decisions or exert systemic pressure to reduce content and course requirements below minimum standards practiced at nonprofits. According to a former FPCU instructor,

> The integrity of the institution, the development of individual scholarship, the implicit promise made to students that college provides meaningful and legitimate learning experiences—all of the things that have historically been of value in higher education—have no place in the world of for-profit colleges. . . . Faculty members at these colleges need to stand up and expose the lie about opportunity that is at the heart of the for-profit model. They need to remind the parent corporations just exactly what education is supposed to be and who is qualified to assess student work.[15]

For-profit history is shot through with examples of institutions across the spectrum—from small-scale proprietary enterprises to publicly traded and private-equity-run multinationals—that have a different metric for evaluating "quality," one centered on the profit motive rather than the professional imperative. Medicine and law gave up on FPCUs for reasons having to do with an inexorable downward pressure on academic standards created by profit motives. The same pressure can be seen in recent revelations indicting for-profits for rock-bottom standards that excuse plagiarism, poor attendance, and administrative interference with academic quality decisions made by faculty.[16]

For-profits resist transparency and too often fail to operate within the law. Transparency and law-abiding behavior are expensive and cut into profit margins. For these reasons, for-profits have often worked aggressively against attempts to gather information on their practices and to rein in criminal behavior within the industry. Citizen groups of the early twentieth century spent countless hours campaigning for greater regulations and transparency. New York's Bertha Stevens conducted research for one such group. Based on several years' worth of interviews and document collection, she concluded that the state needed to demand transparency from for-profits the way it required medical schools to reveal their practices. The Veterans' Affairs (VA) agency of the 1940s fought a collection of lawsuits against disclosure when the agency attempted to collect data about FPCU activities. After overcoming the challenge, VA inspectors exposed an industry brimming with fraud and reclaimed millions of dollars on behalf of taxpayers. The for-profit lobby of the 1990s and onward has become a fixture on Capitol Hill, ready to block transparency initiatives (e.g., right-to-know regulations) and legislation holding for-profits accountable for misdeeds (e.g., commission-based recruitment).[17]

By the time of the HELP committee hearings, the FPCU lobbying arm had again rebranded itself and went by a new name: the Association of Private Sector Colleges and Universities (APSCU). They represented a $35 billion industry showing few signs of slowing down. APSCU spent $16 million on a lobbying blitz in 2013 after the US Department of Education announced its intention to impose stricter transparency regulations. The department's proposed rules would have required publication of dropout and loan default rates. But the blitz worked, only a single year after the Harkin investigation. For-profits were, as higher education scholar and Michigan State University's College of Education dean Don Heller noted, "successful in that they got the regulations weakened. The Department of Education really bent to the lobbying push." The regulatory and lobbying victory, as in previous campaigns, meant prospective FPCU students would be denied access to clear, accurate data with which to make informed decisions about their postsecondary options.[18]

The fixed stars—about what for-profits claim, promise, deliver, water down, resist, and violate—complicate the most common arguments made by partisans engaged in debating the future of FPCUs. For those on the left, *Diploma Mills* challenges some easy assumptions about the potential these institutions have for improving social mobility. It shows how for-profits have historically neither served the poor and disadvantaged well nor tended to improve their lot in life. This isn't to say for-profits have failed all students. Rather, any intellectually responsible assessment of history and statistical probability would indicate that for-profits privilege earnings to the detriment of learning, especially in light of the costs and debts students typically incur. In searching for ways to break cycles of poverty, it makes little sense to advocate for a $44,000 two-year program when community colleges offer the same for under $7,000. For those on the right, particularly those concerned about taxes, morality, and law and order, *Diploma Mills* presents a different challenge. It shows how the biggest and therefore most influential for-profits have generally failed to win the public's trust in terms of resource usage, ethical practices, and lawful behavior. This was certainly the case in the first decade and a half of the twenty-first century, but American history is punctuated with widespread, notable instances of the same, as surveyed in this book. Most on the right side of the political ledger would agree that the drive to capture market share and increasing rates of revenue, a drive at the center of market activity, shouldn't translate into misleading students, injuring investors, and defrauding the public. But it has—and far too frequently and systemically to represent the work of just a few bad apples. Given the challenges of monitoring and enforcement, it's likely the vast majority of criminal FPCU behavior has gone undetected. When for-profit crimes have been detected and penalized, settlements too often appear to the industry as a cost of doing business rather than a punishment for unethical practices and violations of law.[19]

For-profit college and university history bears out the pattern. It offers for both sides of the political debate a set of constants drowned out by the clamor and outrage over the scandals HELP and other investigations have unearthed. Profit motives produce institutions fundamentally at odds with the core, historical mission of higher education. These institutions aren't simply traditional colleges and universities with a different funding stream, leaving the original functions untouched. The "bottom line" creates palpable pressure to change what it means to talk about serving disadvantaged students, creating a faculty body, maintaining academic standards, cultivating law-abiding behavior, and providing access to the American dream.[20]

Recent studies and economic observations have produced insights useful for understanding what *Diploma Mills* might mean for the FPCU's past, present, and potential future. Researchers now point to the collapse of the Soviet Union in the late twentieth century as generating an unbridled, deregulated confidence in market forces that blurred important distinctions between market economies and market societies. Market economies use the tools of economic reasoning to produce efficiencies, in terms of price signals and the flow of other information, to produce certain goods and services. Market societies apply economic reasoning to almost any facet of life. But not all goods and services lend themselves well to market-based models of efficiency, or at least they don't play out well for most members of society or are repugnant to social norms.[21]

A critical misstep occurs, for instance, when companies provide compensation packages to FPCU executives bearing no resemblance to those given to leaders of nonprofit colleges and universities. It distorts the core mission of all higher education. The move to integrate the world of finance with the world of higher education over the past quarter century has produced what researchers call "excess relative wages." This kind of executive compensation "cannot be explained by difference in education" or "job security" or "individual ability." But it can, they note, be traced back to "deregulation" allowing corporate boards to set executive pay at virtually any level they wish. Such deregulated environments incentivize cost cutting (e.g., eliminating programs for high-needs students) and illegal behavior (e.g., recruitment at any cost) at the highest level to meet quarterly earnings projections, otherworldly bonuses, and golden parachutes—all examples of market values crowding out nonmarket norms.[22]

When the 2009 compensation of Robert Silberman, chief executive officer of for-profit Strayer Education, reached $42 million, the company's compensation board sent an unmistakable message: keep privileging shareholder gains over student gains. That year, Strayer spent $1,329 per student on instruction and $6,968 per student on marketing and profit—or, in other words, they valued marketing and profit well over 500 percent more than instruction. Such distortions in the purpose of higher education offer the only valid reason why *one* for-profit university executive could earn more than the *combined* 2009 salaries of the presidents of Harvard ($800,000), Yale ($1,627,649), Princeton ($910,626), Stanford ($985,569), Columbia ($1,527,217), New York University ($1,513,723), Boston University ($1,142,307), Swarthmore ($1,756,293), University of Pennsylvania ($1,321,040), Massachusetts Institute of Technology ($931,603), Rensselaer Polytechnic Institute ($1,771,877), Johns Hopkins ($3,821,886), Vanderbilt ($1,890,274), Ohio State ($1,576,825), University of Washington ($905,004), University of Delaware ($810,603), University of Texas System ($787,258), University of Michigan System ($783,850), University of Virginia ($773,648), University of Colorado at Denver and Health Sciences Center ($753,115), Virginia Tech ($732,064), Auburn ($727,761), Arizona State ($709,196), Kentucky Community and Technical College System ($532,907), Delaware Technical and Community College ($450,066), Valencia Community College ($439,135), Virginia Community College System ($434,654), Hillsboro Community College ($381,295), Cuyahoga Community College ($377,748), Virginia Commonwealth University ($549,846), Texas A&M at College Station ($551,960), University of Oregon ($636,445), University of Cincinnati ($653,223), University of Chicago ($1,276,950), Northwestern ($2,240,775), and Drexel ($4,912,127). Given trends in FPCU history, it's highly unlikely Strayer awarded Silberman's salary—*more* than the combined total given to thirty-six of the country's best and brightest leaders in nonprofit postsecondary education—for adhering to student-centered practices or following just, ethical, and lawful business strategies.[23]

Higher education has historically been about the advancement and diffusion of knowledge yielding social, cultural, political, technical, vocational, and intellectual enrichment, rather than returns for shareholders and outsized compensation for executives. For-profit owners and operators come at the postsecondary world with values derived from the latest market movements and quarterly reports. Behaviors that circumvent codes, laws, and regulations, if they generate industrial-sized profits, are rewarded handsomely at the highest levels of executive compensation. The rewards dwarf or eclipse just about any other concern. The profit motive replaces a centuries-old culture of academic trust with a focus on quarterly statements, a strong legal department, and clever rebranding and marketing campaigns.[24]

Current FPCU practices have too often been found to be neither sustainable nor socially responsible. The simplest and most effective response, based on the intractable patterns outlined in this book, is to end public subsidies in all forms to for-profit colleges and universities.

Regulations won't do. Lobbyists too easily undo them, or capture the agencies that can revise them, or advocate for operators with very deep pockets who can afford to ignore them. Even Senator Harkin likely fell to lobbyist influence in 2014 when he quietly slipped a $303 million cut into Pell Grant legislation to provide a windfall for large companies charged with servicing student loans. When regulations aren't undone, undermined, or unheeded, they still produce bureaucratic "red tape," leaving dissatisfaction among stakeholders across the political spectrum. The US Department of Education's recently proposed "gainful employment rules," aimed at curbing for-profit placement fraud, have the potential to spill over into the nonprofit world and move all postsecondary education toward workforce preparation. This would have grave consequences for the many other social, cultural, and intellectual purposes of American higher education. Taking for-profits out of the federal student aid programs—by eliminating reference to the sector in the next Higher Education Act reauthorization—would put a halt to the fraud as well as the spread of for-profit regulations.[25]

FPCU advocates have argued that we can't afford to live without for-profits. Costs to the states of California, New York, Ohio, and Texas for receiving current for-profit students, they suggests, would run into the billions. What these advocates tend to ignore, however, are the tremendous costs currently absorbed by students through outsized loan debt and disproportionate postgraduation unemployment, by state and federal governments though loan defaults, and by taxpayers through litigation over multi-billion-dollar fraud schemes. The argument also elides the systemic economic risks posed by the $1.2 trillion student loan bubble, almost half of which comes from for-profit students. But even when taken on its own terms, the FPCU's value to states appears increasingly suspect as for-profits go bankrupt (e.g., Corinthian) or abandon associate's degree programs (e.g., University of Phoenix). If FPCUs are worth keeping around, free-market principles would suggest they should be able to find a niche in the free, rather than subsidized, marketplace. Innovators are already experimenting in such spaces with low-profit limited liability companies (L3Cs), also known as benefit corporations, and for-profit universities organized around the "freemium" model that charge tuition so low as to make federal student aid irrelevant.[26]

Despite significant and recurring patterns of for-profit abuses, recent debates over the sector's path forward continue to overlook the long view. This comes at a great but unnecessary cost. The investigations, legislation, and reorganization central to this past offer valuable lessons and more than a few warnings. They highlight the kinds of violations, predatory behavior, government aid abuse, and poverty profiteering we're likely to see in the years ahead.

Without substantive changes like the ending of public subsidies to FPCUs, litigants will continue to come forward and battle over these now forseeable patterns and outcomes. Past performance, in this case, has turned out to be a good indicator of future results. What this past tells us is that traditional institutions of higher education have long operated on the ideal of the advancement and diffusion of knowledge. For-profits, by contrast, have established a different tradition. If balance sheets are any guide, they have organized around the advancement and diffusion of advertising—or, as researchers in the field of agnotology might put it, "ignorance production"—to secure profits.[27]

Whatever the direction of future debates, FPCU history sheds light on the fundamental conflicts of interest that arise when profit motives privilege owners, shareholders, and quarterly profits at the expense of students, faculty, and long-term objectives. If we can come to terms with the limitations of market motives, a tall order in the current political climate, there's hope for achieving a future different from this past and a way around the problems experienced by those stiffed by American for-profit colleges and universities.

ACKNOWLEDGMENTS

During the first decade and a half of the twenty-first century, media coverage of for-profits—the good, the bad, and the ugly—was hard to miss. Public releases told of massive enrollments and record profits, while news outlets exposed a steady stream of scandals. Then came the stunning trove of documents assembled by congressional investigations into for-profits between 2010 and 2012. What most caught my attention at the time was the way media and political debates over the value of these institutions had virtually no grounding in history. I could hardly blame these pundits and politicians, since nothing in my own reading in higher-education history had provided much insight. I found plenty from political scientists, sociologists, legal scholars, and economists, but little more than silence from historians. The existing research either overlooked this history entirely or gave very brief summaries that raised far more questions than they answered. I wrote *Diploma Mills* because I wanted to fill gaps in my own understanding about where this dynamic, complex, and provocative industry had come from. I also wanted to consider what the long view could contribute to policy discussions about the road ahead for this sector of postsecondary education.

Throughout the research and writing process, I racked up a number of outsized debts to those who made this project both a possibility and a pleasure to complete. First and foremost are the ones I owe my parents, Alberto Elias Angulo and Cristina Rionda. This book is dedicated to them for many reasons. A few include their bold decision to immigrate to the United States during the Vietnam War, their unwavering belief in higher education's transformative power, and their lifelong commitment to justice. I'm grateful for the values they shared with me that have inspired a number of themes in my program of research. Their support has been critical in making this program a possibility. I'm indebted to them in more ways than words can convey.

I'm also indebted to several who helped me gather and organize the pieces to this for-profit history puzzle. Ashley Burnside, my longtime graduate assistant, overcame more than a few obstacles in the hunt for US Department of Education data and assisted with the logistics of manuscript preparation. She has set an unreasonably high bar for my future assistants. Thomas Underwood of Boston University carefully read the final draft of the manuscript. I'm always grateful to have his collegial support, encouragement, and expert feedback. Acorn Angulo read the book from start to finish just before its final submission. She offered wise suggestions that pushed me to expand certain sections of the manuscript and clarify others. Jackie McFadden assisted with the search for government documents at Winthrop University's Dacus Library. She found precisely what I was looking for and did so with remarkable speed and a sunny disposition. Archivist Vakil Smallen helped track down National Education Association papers housed at George Washington University's Special Collections Library. He gave generously of his time and was patient with my many questions about this large archival collection. I'm also grateful to Malgosia Myc of the University of Michigan's Bentley Historical Library. She directed me to key sources, and her handling of my requests kept the project moving forward.

Special thanks go to Greg Britton, editorial director at Johns Hopkins University Press. Anyone who's had the pleasure of working with Britton knows he has a limber mind that moves lightning fast from the small details to the big picture, improving everything along the way. The field of higher education is lucky to have his energy and talents at Johns Hopkins. Britton's assistant, Catherine Goldstead, spent countless hours paving the way toward a smooth manuscript submission. She's one of the unspoken heroes in the book publishing process. I also wish to thank Julie McCarthy, Hilary S. Jacqmin, Ashley Moore, and Debbie Masi for their direct and indirect support behind the scenes at the press.

Closer to home, I wish to acknowledge my great debt to Winthrop University's Mark Dewalt and Gregory Crider. They generously accommodate my teaching schedule every semester, allowing me to carve out time for writing and reflection. Without their support, I wouldn't have been able to start, much less finish, the project. Pansy Phillips deserves praise for her outstanding administrative assistance over the years. All of us fortunate enough to work with her know there isn't a soul who could fill her shoes.

And, last but not least, I thank Kaitlyn Herthel. She's been there for me every step of the way. She's seen this and other projects develop from a glimmer in my eye right through to manuscript completion. I couldn't be more grateful to have her in my corner and to derive inspiration from her impressive career.

NOTES

Preface

1. Joseph Whitaker, "Lacaze Teachers in District Fired; U.S. Aid Halted; Lacaze Downtown Faculty Is Fired," *Washington Post* (November 14, 1978).

2. Joseph Whitaker, "Students Accuse School of Financial Manipulations; Lacaze-Gardner Students Accuse School of Financial Manipulation," *Washington Post* (November 13, 1978).

3. Ibid.; Whitaker, "Lacaze Teachers." Industry insider and consultant Patty Sullivan estimated that "35 or 40 percent" of for-profit institutions engaged in fraud. See Jason DeParle, "Trade Schools Near Success as They Lobby for Survival," *New York Times* (March 25, 1992). US Bureau of Labor Statistics, CPI Inflation Calculator, http://data.bls.gov/cgi-bin/cpicalc.pl.

4. Eli Leher, "Subprime Borrowers: Not Innocents," *Businessweek* (December 11, 2007); Michael Lewis, *The Big Short: Inside the Doomsday Machine* (New York: W. W. Norton, 2011); Simon Johnson and James Kwak, *Thirteen Bankers: The Wall Street Takeover and the Next Financial Meltdown* (New York: Vintage, 2011); Matt Taibbi, "The Last Mystery of the Financial Crisis," *Rolling Stone* (June 19, 2013); Matt Taibbi, "'You F—ked Up, You Trusted Us!': Talking Ratings Agencies with Chris Hayes," *Rolling Stone* (June 21, 2013); Glen Harlan Reynolds, *The Higher Education Bubble* (Jackson, TN: Encounter Books, 2012); Steve Eisman, "Subprime Goes to College," testimony at hearings before the US Senate, Health, Education, Pensions, and Labor Committee (June 24, 2010); *For Profit Higher Education: The Failure to Safeguard the Federal Investment and Ensure Student Success, Prepared by the Committee on Health, Education, Labor, and Pensions, United States Senate*, 4 vols. (Washington, DC: Government Printing Office, 2012), I: 92–101 (hereafter, *HELP*); Editor, "For-Profit Schools Major in Harvesting Federal Money," *USA Today* (July 31, 2012); Jonathan Marino, "Some on Wall Street Say $1.2 Trillion

in Student Debt Could Trigger the Next Market Crash," *Business Insider* (April 29, 2015), www.businessinsider.com/student-debt-crisis-could-trigger -crash-2015-4; Chris Kirkham, "U.S. Targets For-Profit Colleges That Saddle Students with High Debt," *LA Times* (October 31, 2014).

5. David Breneman, Brian Pusser, and Sarah E. Turner, eds., *Earning from Learning: The Rise of For-Profit Universities* (Albany: SUNY Press, 2006); Kevin Kinser, *From Main Street to Wall Street: The Transformation of For-Profit Higher Education* (Hoboken, NJ: Wiley Periodicals, 2006); Jared L. Bleak, *When For-Profit Meets Nonprofit: Educating through the Market* (New York: Routledge, 2005); Sheila Slaughter and Gary Rhoades, *Academic Capitalism and the New Economy: Markets, State, and Higher Education* (Baltimore: Johns Hopkins University Press, 2004); Derek Bok, *Universities in the Marketplace: The Commercialization of Higher Education* (Princeton, NJ: Princeton University Press, 2003); Richard S. Ruch, *Higher Ed, Inc.: The Rise of the For-Profit University* (Baltimore: Johns Hopkins University Press, 2001); Sheila Slaughter and Larry Leslie, *Academic Capitalism: Politics, Policies, and the Entrepreneurial University* (Baltimore: Johns Hopkins University Press, 1997). Historians have begun to note the current trend away from narrow case studies and toward the long view of specific topics. See, for instance, Jo Guldi and David Armitage, *The History Manifesto* (New York: Cambridge University Press, 2014).

6. See, for instance, congressional investigations from 2010 through 2012 that resulted in *HELP*. Tamar Lewin, "For-Profit College Group Sued as US Lays Out Wide Fraud," *New York Times* (August 8, 2011); United States ex rel. Washington et al. v. Education Management Corp. et al., Civil No. 07-461 (W.D. Pa. 2011); Gretchen Morgenson, "Inspecting a Student Loan Spigot," *New York Times* (January 18, 2014); Tom Harkin, "For-Profit Colleges and the Threat of a New Bubble," *LA Times* (July 13, 2010).

7. The most recent data from the National Center for Education Statistics confirm a long-standing pattern established by the research community: two-year for-profit programs have significantly higher completion rates than traditional nonprofit community colleges (63 percent vs. 20 percent, respectively). It also confirms an inversion of this pattern when comparing four-year for-profits to four-year nonprofits (32 percent vs. 58 percent, respectively). See National Center for Education Statistics, "Institutional Retention and Graduation Rates for Undergraduate Students," in *The Condition of Education, 2015* (Washington, DC: US Department of

Education, 2015), https://nces.ed.gov/programs/coe/pdf/coe_cva.pdf. At the same time, questions continue to emerge over what graduates actually receive when they earn a diploma from a for-profit. For a sampling of this literature, see the following studies: Thomas Baily, Norena Badway, and Patricia Gumport, "For-Profit Higher Education and Community Colleges," NCPI Working Paper (Stanford, CA: National Center for Postsecondary Improvement, 2003), http://ccrc.tc.columbia.edu/media/k2/attachments/for -profit-higher-education-community-colleges.pdf; Yuen Ting Liu and Clive Belfield, "The Labor Market Returns to For-Profit Education: Evidence for Transfer Students," CAPSEE Working Paper (New York: Center for Analysis of Postsecondary Education and Employment, 2014), http://ccrc .tc.columbia.edu/media/k2/attachments/labor-market-returns-to-for-profit -higher-education.pdf; Yuen Ting Liu and Clive Belfield, "Evaluating For-Profit Higher Education: Evidence from the Education Longitudinal Study," CAPSEE Working Paper (New York: Center for Analysis of Postsecondary Education and Employment, 2014), http://ccrc.tc.columbia.edu/media/k2 /attachments/capsee-evaluating-for-profit-els.pdf.

8. As of 2014, for-profits received $32 billion in taxpayer funding alone. See *HELP*. The following classic and contemporary histories of American higher education make no mention of proprietary postsecondary institutions in their indexes or elsewhere: Frederick Rudolph, *The American College and University: A History* (New York: Knopf, 1962); Lawrence Veysey, *The Emergence of the American University* (Chicago: University of Chicago Press, 1965); Frederick Rudolph, *Curriculum: A History of the American Undergraduate Course of Study since 1636* (San Francisco: Jossey-Bass, 1977); Christopher J. Lucas, *American Higher Education: A History* (New York: St. Martin's Press, 1994); Julie Reuben, *The Making of the Modern University: Intellectual Transformation and the Marginalization of Morality* (Chicago: University of Chicago Press, 1996); Roger Geiger, ed., *The American College in the Nineteenth Century* (Nashville: Vanderbilt University Press, 2000); John R. Thelin, *A History of American Higher Education* (Baltimore: Johns Hopkins University Press, 2004). Thelin's second edition of 2011 and Roger L. Geiger's *The History of American Higher Education: Learning and Culture from the Founding to World War II* (Princeton, NJ: Princeton University Press, 2014) stand out as exceptions to this rule. In these works, Thelin offers brief reflections on recent for-profit developments and Geiger discusses nineteenth-century

proprietary medical and law schools in relation to mainstream higher education.

On the *Dartmouth* case, see Jane F. Green, "'An Opinion of Our Own': Education, Politics, and the Struggle for Adulthood at Dartmouth College, 1814–1819," *History of Education Quarterly* 52 (May 2012): 173–195; Elizabeth B. Monroe, "The Influence of the Dartmouth College Case on the American Law of Educational Charities," *Journal of Supreme Court History* 32 (2007): 1–21; Jürgen Herbst, "How to Think about the Dartmouth College Case," *History of Education Quarterly* 26 (1986): 342–349.

9. For a history of college and university rankings, see J. Salmi and A. Saroyan, "League Tables as Policy Instruments: Uses and Misuses," *Higher Education Management and Policy* 19 (2007): 31–68. Contemporary discussion about the international ranking system can be found in Andrejs Rauhvargers, *Global University Rankings and the Impact: EUA Report on Rankings* (Brussels: European University Association, 2011); Ernest Boyer, *Scholarship Reconsidered: Priorities of the Professoriate* (Princeton, NJ: Carnegie Foundation for the Advancement of Teaching, 1990); Charles Glassick, Mary Taylor Huber, and Gene I. Maeroff, *Scholarship Assessed: Evaluation of the Professoriate* (San Francisco: Jossey-Bass, 1997); Pat Hutchings, Mary Taylor Huber, and Anthony Ciccone, *The Scholarship of Teaching and Learning Reconsidered: Institutional Integration and Impact* (San Francisco: Jossey-Bass, 2011); Devon Haynie, "Number of International College Students Continues to Climb," *US News and World Report* (November 17, 2014).

10. See *HELP*.

11. Recent coverage about the FPCU–Black Caucus nexus has brought about scrutiny and criticism from across the political spectrum. See James Rucker, "Congressional Black Caucus Staffer: Members Are 'Actively Shilling' for For-Profit Colleges," *Huffington Post* (May 25, 2011). Frank Newport and Brandon Busteed, "Americans Still See College Education as Very Important," *Gallup* (December 17, 2013), http://www.gallup.com/poll/166490/americans -college-education-important.aspx; "60 Minutes/Vanity Fair Poll: The American Dream," *CBS News* (April 6, 2015), http://www.cbsnews.com/news/60 -minutesvanity-fair-poll-the-american-dream; "The American Dream," *The Atlantic Politics* (June 1, 2015), https://www.scribd.com/doc/270133740 /The-American Dream?secret_password=1Rj95jqAHMgw9Cddc7Jq.

12. Amanda Terkel, "Mitch McConnell's Solution to Soaring Student Debt: Less Yale, More For-Profit Schools," *Huffington Post* (July 14, 2014).

13. "Edupreneurs" discussed in Kenneth Saltman, *The Edison Schools: Corporate Schooling and the Assault on Public Education* (New York: Routledge, 2005). Milton Friedman, *Bright Promises, Dismal Performance: An Economist's Protest* (San Diego: Harcourt Brace Jovanovich, 1983), 74.

14. James B. Edmonson, "'Gypped!': G.I. Joe Must Be Protected against Low-Grade Colleges," *The Nation's Schools* 35 (February 1945): 25; James B. Edmonson, "Some Policies of States Governing the Granting of College Charters and Related Problems," Association of Higher Education, National Education Association, 1953, in box 1, folder "Fraudulent Schools," James B. Edmonson Papers, Bentley Historical Library, University of Michigan. "Gypped" is a pejorative term and its usage is now considered controversial; see Janaki Challa, "Why Being 'Gypped' Hurts the Roma More than It Hurts You," *Code Switch* (December 30, 2013), www.npr.org /sections/codeswitch/2013/12/30/242429836/why-being-gypped-hurts-the -roma-more-than-it-hurts-you; Robert Louis Stevenson and Lloyd Osbourne, "The Wrecker," *Scribner's Magazine* 10 (August 1891): 177–179; Osamudia R. James, "Predatory Ed: The Conflict between Public Good and For-Profit Higher Education," *Journal of College and University Law* 38 (2011): 45–105.

Chapter One: Commerce

1. See "New England's First Fruits" (1643), in Samuel Eliot Morison, *Founding of Harvard College,* 2nd ed. (Cambridge, MA: Harvard University Press, 1968), for an example of the colonial uses of the traditional college. On the scope and development of institutional forms, see Jurgen Herbst, *From Crisis to Crisis: American College Government, 1636–1819* (Cambridge, MA: Harvard University Press, 1982).

2. Howard Gordon, *The History and Growth of Vocational Education in America* (Boston: Allyn and Bacon, 1999), 5–6; J. V. Erden, "Linking Past and Present, Students and Jobs," *Vocational Education Journal* 66 (1991): 30; Craig Honnick, "The Story behind Proprietary Education in the United States," in *Community Colleges and Proprietary Schools: Conflict or Convergence?,* ed. Darrel Clowes and Elizabeth Hawthorne (San Francisco: Jossey-Bass, 1995), 29.

3. William Johnson, *Schooled Lawyers: A Study in the Clash of Professional Cultures* (New York: New York University Press, 1978), 10–11; Robert Stevens, *Law School: Legal Education in America from the 1850s to the 1980s* (Chapel Hill: University of North Carolina Press, 1983), 17.

4. Martin Kaufman, "American Medical Education," in *The Education of American Physicians: Historical Essays*, ed. Ronald Numbers (Berkeley: University of California Press, 1980), 8–9.

5. Tamara Plakins Thornton, *Handwriting in America: A Cultural History* (New Haven, CT: Yale University Press, 1996); Alan Houston, ed., *Franklin: The Autobiography and Other Writings on Politics, Economics, and Virtue* (Cambridge: Cambridge University Press, 2004), 203–214.

6. See the following for statistics on early American institutions and student populations: D. G. Tewksbury, *The Founding of American Colleges and Universities before the Civil War* (New York: Teachers College Press, 1932); R. Collins, *The Credential Society: An Historical Sociology of Education and Stratification* (New York: Academic Press, 1979); Colin Burke, *American Collegiate Populations: A Test of the Traditional View* (New York: New York University Press, 1982).

7. *Report of the [US] Commissioner of Education for the Year 1878* (Washington, DC: Government Printing Office, 1880), 367–377; Cheesman Herrick, *Meaning and Practice of Commercial Education* (London: Macmillan, 1904), 206. For related statistics, see also Benjamin Haynes and Harry Jackson, *A History of Business Education in the United States* (Cincinnati: South-Western, 1935), 37–38.

8. "Original Papers in Relation to a Course of Liberal Education," *American Journal of Science and Arts* 25 (1829): 297–351; Michael S. Pak, "The Yale Report of 1828: A New Reading and New Implications," *History of Education Quarterly* 48 (2008): 30–57; David Potts, *Liberal Education in a Land of Colleges: Yale's "Reports" of 1828* (New York: Palgrave, 2010).

9. Discussions of this well-established trajectory for the nineteenth-century college and university can be found in the following works: Julie Reuben, *The Making of the Modern University: Intellectual Transformation and the Marginalization of Morality* (Chicago: University of Chicago Press, 1996); Roger Geiger, ed., *The American College in the Nineteenth Century* (Nashville: Vanderbilt University Press, 2000); John R. Thelin, *A History of American Higher Education* (Baltimore: Johns Hopkins University Press, 2004); Roger L. Geiger, *The History of American Higher Educa-*

tion: Learning and Culture from the Founding to World War II (Princeton, NJ: Princeton University Press, 2014).

10. On the multiversity and other blended institutional configurations, see Geiger, *American College in the Nineteenth Century*.

11. David D. Corey, *Sophists in Plato's Dialogues* (Albany: SUNY Press, 2015). See also James Fredal, "Why Shouldn't the Sophists Charge Fees?," *Rhetoric Society Quarterly* 38 (2008): 148–170; Keith Crome, "Plato's Criticism of Sophistry," *Richmond Journal of Philosophy* 9 (2005): 11–16.

12. On money's dodgy reception in the West, see Niall Ferguson, *The Ascent of Money: A Financial History of the World* (New York: Penguin, 2008); Knud Haakonssen, ed., *Adam Smith: The Theory of Moral Sentiments* (Cambridge: Cambridge University Press, 2002), 173; Adam Smith, *Wealth of Nations: Representative Selections* (1776; New York: Dover, 2003), 108.

13. "Business Colleges. Packard's Business College," *Scientific American* 43 (December 18, 1880): 388.

14. Board of Education, *Special Reports on Educational Subjects*, vol. 2, *Education in the United States of America, Part 2* (London: Wyman and Sons, 1902), 235.

15. Notre Dame and Wake Forest are discussed in *Report of the [US] Commissioner, 1878*, 368, 370; Sebastian A. Erbacher, *Catholic Higher Education for Men in the United States, 1850s–1866* (Washington, DC: Catholic University of America, 1931), 87; Rakesh Khurana, *From Higher Aims to Hired Hands: The Social Transformation of American Business Schools and the Unfulfilled Promise of Management as a Profession* (Princeton, NJ: Princeton University Press, 2007), 81. James Dunwoody Brownson De Bow is sometimes credited with establishing a short-lived school of commerce at the University of Louisiana between 1851 and 1857 where courses on political economy and commerce were offered. See Haynes and Jackson, *History of Business Education*, 83–84.

16. Herrick, *Meaning and Practice*, 182–188.

17. Ibid., 182, 186–187.

18. H. Colman, "Colman National Business College," *Scribner's* 3 (June 1888): A025; Hamilton Child, *Gazetteer and Business Directory of Cortland County, New York, for 1869* (Syracuse: Journal Office, 1869), R001. Quill-based penmanship was considered a professional art form

until steel pens appeared in the late 1840s and typewriters made their commercial debut in the 1870s. For more on the impact of these innovations, see Thornton, *Handwriting in America*.

19. Herrick, *Meaning and Practice*, 189–190, 195; Harvard University, "Treasurer's Statement" (Cambridge, MA: Harvard University, 1858–1859); see Harvard's "Treasurer's Statement" (Cambridge, MA: Harvard University Archives) of the 1850s and 1860s for salaries, archived at http://hul.harvard .edu/lib/archives/refshelf/AnnualReportsSearch.htm; Carrington C. Gaines, "Eastman Business College," *Century* 52 (October 1896): A031; Bryant and Stratton, "Home Study," *Harper's* 97 (November 1898): G050.

20. J. W. McClung, *Minnesota as It Is in 1870* (St. Paul, MN: Press Printing, 1870), 10. Famed Swiss naturalist Louis Agassiz complained as a faculty member at mid-nineteenth-century Harvard College that his institution resembled a "high school" when compared with European universities. See A. J. Angulo, *William Barton Rogers and the Idea of MIT* (Baltimore: Johns Hopkins University Press, 2009), 111.

21. H. B. Bryant, H. D. Stratton, and S. S. Packard, *Bryant and Stratton's Counting House Book-Keeping* (New York: Ivison, Phinney, Blakeman, and Co., 1865), 6.

22. Thomas Dilworth's *The Young Bookkeeper's Assistant* (London: H. Kent, 1765) makes a similar claim: "Some (few) Instructors of Youth propose to teach Book-keeping in six weeks, some in a month, and some in twenty-four Hours, and all of them, in their own proposed Times, engage to make their Pupils compleat Masters of the Art: But whatever their Pretensions may be, this Treatise (though inferior to none of them) has none such. . . . All this can't be done in six Weeks, much less in twenty-four Hours. Such hasty Performances in Book-keeping, or in any other Branch of Literature, being more likely to produce a crazy tottering Building, subject to fall at every Blast, if not wholly undermine it, rather than make it firm and lasting" (iv–v).

23. William H. Rideing, "The Progress of a Clerk," *Scribner's* 22 (September 1881): 790; Clifford L. Snowden, "The Amour Institute of Technology," *New England Magazine* 22 (May 1897): 354; Philip Quilibet [George Pond], "Degrees," *Galaxy* 16 (July 1873): 129–130; Alfred Holbrook, *School Management* (Lebanon, OH: Josiah Holbrook, 1871), 110. Pond sometimes, as in the case above, wrote under the assumed name Philip Quilibet.

24. *A History of Education in Ohio: Centennial Volume* (Columbus, OH: The Gazette Printing House, 1876), 298; J. H. Goodwin, "The Book-Keeper," *Century* 45 (April 1893): A090.

25. Quilibet, "Degrees," 129.

26. Robert Louis Stevenson and Lloyd Osbourne, "The Wrecker," *Scribner's* 10 (August 1891): 177–178. Quotes from serialized version of the complete novel: Robert Louis Stevenson and Lloyd Osbourne, *The Wrecker* (New York: Charles Scribner's Sons, 1900).

27. Ibid., 178–179.

28. Henry Clews, *Fifty Years in Wall Street* (New York: Irving, 1908); Henry Clews, *The Wall Street Point of View* (New York: Silver, Burdett and Company, 1900), 50–51, 54, 56.

29. For background on James Hodges, see the biographical summary, "James Hodges (1822–1895)," MSA SC 3520-12479, Maryland State Archives, Baltimore, Maryland, http://msa.maryland.gov/megafile/msa/speccol/sc3500/sc3520/012400/012479/html/12479collect.htm.

30. Ibid.; Wilbur F. Coyle, *The Mayors of Baltimore* (Baltimore: Baltimore Municipal Journal, 1919), 129–138.

31. James Hodges, "Finance and Commerce," in *Public Opinion: A Comprehensive Summary of the Press throughout the World on All Important Current Topics,* vol. 8 (New York: Public Opinion, 1889–1890), 270.

32. Ibid.

33. Ibid.; James Hodges, "Commercial Education," *North American Review* 144 (May 1887): 464–465, 467.

34. Hodges, "Commercial Education," 470; Khurana, *From Higher Aims,* 74, 89.

35. Charles Robson, ed., *The Biographical Encyclopædia of Pennsylvania of the Nineteenth Century* (Philadelphia: Galaxy, 1874), 623; Erasmus Briggs, *History of the Original Town of Concord* (Rochester, NY: Union and Advertiser Company's Print, 1883), 927, 902.

36. Robson, *Biographical Encyclopædia,* 638; J. E. Homans, ed., *The Cyclopædia of American Biography,* vol. 10 (New York: The Press Association Compilers, 1924), 10; Michigan Pioneer and Historical Society, *Michigan Historical Collections,* vol. 35 (Lansing, MI: Wynkoop, Hallenbeck, and Crawford, 1907), 721–724; James Smart, *The Indiana Schools and the Men Who Have Worked in Them* (Cincinnati: Wilson, Hinkle, and Co.,

1876), 110–111; Isaac N. Demmon, ed., *History of the University of Michigan* (Ann Arbor: University of Michigan Press, 1906), 215–216.

37. Caitlyn Rosenthal, "The Long and Controversial History of For-Profit Colleges," *Bloomberg* (October 25, 2012). Harvey Firestone also attended Folsom's. See Chancellor University, http://206.180.165.169/history .html; J. E. Homans and L. E. Dearborn, eds., *The Cyclopædia of American Biography*, vol. 7 (New York: The Press Association Compilers, 1926), 286; James Sullivan, ed., *History of New York State, 1523–1927*, vol. 6 (New York: Lewis Historical, 1927), 414; Robert B. Ross and George B. Catlin, *Landmarks of Wayne County and Detroit* (Detroit: Evening News Association, 1898), 124, 126; B. Franklin, "After Petroleum," *Harper's* 30 (December 1864): 57. See Thomas Picketty's *Capital in the Twenty-First Century* (Cambridge: Harvard University Press, 2014) for an analysis of wealth creation since the eighteenth century and, by extension, the role of luck in the making of these storied American industrialists.

38. James W. Sheahan, *The Great Conflagration, Chicago: Its Past, Present and Future* (Chicago: Union, 1872), 348–349; Albert E. Cowles, *Past and Present of the City of Lansing and Ingham County, Michigan* (Lansing: Michigan Historical Publishing Association, 1905), 236–237.

39. Charles R. Tuttle, *General History of the State of Michigan* (Detroit: R. D. S. Tyler and Co., 1873), 585–588. Ira Mayhew, *The Means and Ends of Universal Education* (New York: A. S. Barnes and Burr, 1860). Mayhew also served as the inaugural president of the Business Educator's Association of America. See Frank Passic's description: "Ira Mayhew," www.findagrave.com/cgi-bin/fg.cgi?page=gr&GRid=9074750.

40. See the following on patterns of nineteenth-century professionalization: Thomas Haskell, *The Emergence of Professional Social Science: The American Social Science Association and the Nineteenth-Century Crisis of Authority* (Urbana: University of Illinois Press, 1977); Sally Kohlstedt, *The Formation of the American Scientific Community: The American Association for the Advancement of Science, 1846–1860* (Urbana: University of Illinois Press, 1976); A. Hunter Dupree, *Science in the Federal Government: A History of Policies and Activities* (Baltimore: Johns Hopkins University Press, 1986); Robert V. Bruce, *The Launching of American Science, 1846–1876* (New York: Knopf, 1987); Paul Starr, *The Social Transformation of American Medicine: The Rise of a Sovereign Profession and the Making of a Vast Industry* (New York: Basic Books, 1984); Stevens, *Law School;*

Monte Calvert, *The Mechanical Engineer in America, 1830–1910* (Baltimore: Johns Hopkins University Press, 1967).

41. See "The Professionalization of Management" in Alfred Chandler's classic *The Visible Hand: The Managerial Revolution in American Business* (Cambridge, MA: Harvard University Press, 1977), 464–468.

42. "The Education Required for Business," *The Manufacturer and Builder* 5 (November 1873): 258.

43. Ibid.

44. James Stanley Grimes, *Geonomy: A Theory of Ocean Currents and Their Agency in the Formation of Continents* (Boston: Samuel L. Nichols, 1866), RA02, RA07.

45. For more on the turbulent 1850s, see Kenneth M. Stampp, *America in 1857: A Nation on the Brink* (New York: Oxford University Press, 1990).

46. "Editorial," *Debow's Review* 5 (August 1858): 783.

47. For an introduction to the subject of women in higher education during this period, see Barbara Miller Solomon, *In the Company of Educated Women: A History of Women and Higher Education* (New Haven, CT: Yale University Press, 1986), and Margaret Nash, *Women's Education in the United States, 1780–1840* (New York: Palgrave, 2005).

48. Edward Clarke, *Sex in Education: or, A Fair Chance for the Girls* (Boston: J. R. Osgood and Co., 1873); Sue Zschoche, "Dr. Clarke Revisited: Science, True Womanhood, and Female Collegiate Education," *History of Education Quarterly* 29 (1989): 545–569; Nash, *Women's Education.*

49. Grimes, *Geonomy,* RA05; Virginia Penny, *The Employments of Women: A Cyclopaedia of Woman's Work* (Boston: Walker, Wise, and Co., 1863), 39.

50. Penny, *The Employments of Women,* 40.

51. Ibid.

52. Francis Stites, *Private Interest and Public Gain: The Dartmouth College Case, 1819* (Amherst: University of Massachusetts Press, 1972); Aaron Brenner, Benjamin Day, and Immanuel Ness, eds., *The Encyclopedia of Strikes in American History* (New York: Routledge, 2009).

53. Charles Barnard, "Some Experiments on Co-operation," *Scribner's* 12 (May 1876): 99, 105.

54. Angela G. Ray, *The Lyceum and Public Culture in the Nineteenth-Century United States* (Lansing: Michigan State University Press, 2005);

Tom F. Wright, *The Cosmopolitan Lyceum: Lecture Culture and the Globe in Nineteenth-Century America* (Amherst: University of Massachusetts Press, 2013); Bruce Sinclair, *Philadelphia's Philosopher Mechanics: A History of the Franklin Institute, 1824–1865* (Baltimore: Johns Hopkins University Press, 1974); David Armstrong, *The History of Gallaudet University: 150 Years of a Deaf American Institution* (Washington, DC: Gallaudet University Press, 2014); Beverly Bower and Kimberly Hardy, "From Correspondence to Cyberspace: Changes and Challenges in Distance Education," in *From Distance Education to E-Learning: Lessons along the Way,* ed. Beverly Bower and Kimberly Hardy (San Francisco: Jossey-Bass, 2005), 5–12; Joseph F. Kett, *The Pursuit of Knowledge under Difficulties: From Self-Improvement to Adult Education in America, 1750–1990* (Stanford, CA: Stanford University Press, 1994), 235–242; Todd Savitt, "Four African-American Proprietary Medical Colleges: 1888–1923," *Journal of the History of Medicine and Allied Sciences* 55 (July 2000): 203–255; Arthur B. Moler, *Standardized Barber's Manual* (1911); see also the National Barber Museum, www.nationalbarbermuseum.org. Correspondence schools (e.g., Chautauqua and International Correspondence Schools of Scranton, Pennsylvania) were among the most successful FPCUs in terms of revenue, but their educational impact is difficult to determine. Tens of thousands of students enrolled in the late nineteenth century and millions took correspondence courses in the early twentieth century. At the same time, dropout estimates hovered around 90 percent. See Malcolm S. Knowles, *A History of the Adult Education Movement in the United States,* rev. ed. (Malabar, FL: Robert E. Krieger, 1977), 40.

Chapter Two: Competition

1. For a sampling of Progressive Era trends affecting FPCUs, see Rakesh Khurana, *From Higher Aims to Hired Hands: The Social Transformation of American Business Schools and the Unfulfilled Promise of Management as a Profession* (Princeton, NJ: Princeton University Press, 2007); William G. Rothstein, *American Medical Schools and the Practice of Medicine: A History* (New York: Oxford University Press, 1987); Robert Bocking Stevens, *Law School: Legal Education in America from the 1850s to the 1980s* (Chapel Hill, NC: University of North Carolina Press, 1983); Steven G. Brint and Jerome Karabel, *The Diverted Dream: Community Colleges and the Promise of Educational Opportunity in America, 1900–1985* (New

York: Oxford University Press, 1989); James D. Anderson, Harvey A. Kantor, and David B. Tyack, eds., *Work, Youth, and Schooling: Historical Perspectives on Vocationalism in American Education* (Stanford, CA: Stanford University Press, 1982).

2. For a general introduction to the Progressive Era, see Nell Irvin Painter, *Standing at Armageddon: The United States, 1877–1919,* rev. ed. (New York: W. W. Norton, 2008).

3. On the origin and development of professional law organizations, see William Johnson, *Schooled Lawyers: A Study in the Clash of Professional Cultures* (New York: New York University Press, 1978), 10–11; Stevens, *Law School.*

4. Alfred Z. Reed, *Present-Day Law Schools in the United States and Canada* (New York: Carnegie Foundation for the Advancement of Teaching, 1928), 100.

5. Johnson, *Schooled Lawyers,* xiv–xv.

6. Ibid., 133.

7. Stevens, *Law School,* 76.

8. Ibid., 76, 108.

9. Ibid., 174–177.

10. Ibid., 205–206.

11. Khurana, *From Higher Aims,* 23–86.

12. Alfred D. Chandler Jr., *The Visible Hand: The Managerial Revolution in American Business* (Cambridge, MA: Harvard University Press, 1999), 464–467.

13. In response to real and perceived threats, the first business school associations appeared. Twenty-three FPCUs and private nonprofits organized the Association of Independent Colleges and Schools (AICS) in 1912. Four years later, they had a lobbying presence in Washington, DC. Beauty schools followed suit in 1924 with the National Accrediting Commission of Cosmetology Arts and Sciences (NACCAS). See John B. Lee and Jamie P. Merisotis, "Proprietary Schools: Programs, Policies and Prospects," ASHE-ERIC Higher Education Report No. 5 (Washington, DC: George Washington University Press, 1990).

14. Thomas Neville Bonner, *Iconoclast: Abraham Flexner and a Life in Learning* (Baltimore: Johns Hopkins University Press, 2002); Abraham Flexner, *Medical Education in the United States and Canada; A Report to the Carnegie Foundation for the Advancement of Teaching* (Boston: Merrymount

Press, 1910); Martin Kaufman, "American Medical Education," in *The Education of American Physicians: Historical Essays,* ed. Ronald Numbers (Berkeley: University of California Press, 1980), 11.

15. Kaufman, "Medical Education," 14, 19–21.

16. Ibid., 20–21.

17. Todd Savitt, "Four African-American Proprietary Medical Colleges: 1888–1923," *Journal of the History of Medicine and Allied Sciences* 55 (July 2000): 219.

18. Ibid., 220.

19. Ibid., 203–255.

20. Todd L. Savitt, "Abraham Flexner and the Black Medical School," in *Beyond Flexner: Medical Education in the Twentieth Century,* ed. Barbara M. Barzansky and Norman Gevitz (Westport, CT: Greenwood Press, 1992), 69–70.

21. Kaufman, "Medical Education," 20.

22. See Brint and Karabel, *The Diverted Dream;* George A. Baker III, ed., *A Handbook on the Community College in America: Its History, Mission, and Management* (Westport, CT: Greenwood Press, 1994); Leverett S. Lyon, "Education for Business and the Junior College," *Journal of Business of the University of Chicago* 4 (1931): 283–298.

23. Brint and Karabel, *The Diverted Dream,* 25–26.

24. George F. Zook, "The Junior College," *The School Review* 30 (October 1922): 578; George F. Zook, *Higher Education for American Democracy: A Report of the President's Commission on Higher Education,* 6 vols. (Washington, DC: Government Printing Office, 1947); Thomas Diener, *Growth of an American Invention: A Documentary History of the Junior and Community College Movement* (Westport, CT: Greenwood Press, 1986), 43–45; *Bradley Polytechnic Institute: The First Decade, 1897–1907* (Peoria, IL, 1908).

25. Brint and Karabel, *The Diverted Dream,* 26–30.

26. George F. Zook, ed., *National Conference of Junior Colleges, 1920, and First Annual Meeting of American Association of Junior Colleges, 1921* (Washington, DC: GPO, 1922), 89.

27. Robert H. Bremner, ed., *Children and Youth in America: A Documentary History,* vol. 3 (Cambridge, MA: Harvard University Press, 1931); James L. Ratcliff, "Seven Streams in the Historical Development of the Modern American Community College," in Baker, *Community College in America,* 18.

28. Sol Cohen, "The Industrial Education Movement, 1906–7," *American Quarterly* 20 (1968): 98–99.

29. Herbert M. Kliebard, *The Struggle for the American Curriculum, 1893–1958* (New York: Routledge, 1995), 8–25; David L. Angus and Jeffrey E. Mirel, *The Failed Promise of the American High School, 1890–1995* (New York: Teacher's College Press, 1999), 18–56, 98, 111–124.

30. Cohen, "Industrial Education," 107–108.

31. The five acts are as follows: Smith-Hughes Act of 1917; George-Reed Act of 1929; George-Ellsey Act of 1934; George-Deen Act of 1937; and George-Barden Act of 1946.

32. Regina Werum, "Sectionalism and Racial Politics: Federal Policies and Programs in the Predesegregation South," *Social Science History* 21 (1997): 414–416.

33. M. D. Mobley, "A Review of Federal Vocational-Education Legislation, 1862–1963," *Theory into Practice* 3 (1964): 167–170; H. M. Hamlin, "National Aid to Agriculture and Vocational Education," *The High School Journal* 45 (1962): 167–175; William C. Reavis, "Federal Aid for Education," *Annals of the American Academy of Political and Social Science* 265 (1949): 56–60.

34. See City Club of Chicago, *A Report on Vocational Training in Chicago and in Other Cities* (Chicago: Henry O. Shepard, 1912); Bertha Stevens, *Private Commercial Schools, Manhattan and the Bronx* (New York: New York Public Education Association, 1918).

35. City Club of Chicago, *Vocational Training,* 2, 10, 241.

36. Ibid., 252.

37. Ibid., 33, 38, 252–256, 266.

38. Ibid., 251, 253–254.

39. Ibid., 254.

40. Ibid., 255.

41. Ibid., 255–256.

42. Ibid., 256.

43. Ibid., 255–257.

44. Ibid., 241.

45. Ibid.

46. Ibid., 143, 40.

47. Stevens, *Private Commercial Schools,* 34.

48. Ibid., 78, 89, 41, 15, 36.

49. Ibid., 36.

50. Ibid., 37

51. Ibid., 78, 37–39.

52. Ibid., 42–43.

53. Ibid., 78.

54. Ibid., 81–82.

55. City Club of Chicago, *Vocational Training,* 4, 40; Stevens, *Private Commercial Schools,* 44, 129.

56. Stevens, *Private Commercial Schools,* 98, 133; City Club of Chicago, *Vocational Training,* 257.

57. "Editorial Comment: Our Orgy of Speculation," *Banker's Magazine* 119 (1929): 907.

Chapter Three: Control

1. Stephen Daggett, "Costs of Major U.S. Wars," US Congressional Research Service RS22926 (June 29, 2010), 2; David M. Kennedy, *The American People in World War II* (New York: Oxford University Press, 1999), 288.

2. August C. Bolino, *Career Education: Contributions to Economic Growth* (New York: Praeger Publishers, 1973), 116–127; Educational Policies Commission of the National Educational Association and the American Association of School Administrators, *The Structure and Administration of Education in American Democracy* (Washington, DC, 1938), 23.

3. David Vacchi and Joseph Berger, "Student Veterans in Higher Education," in *Higher Education: Handbook of Theory and Research,* vol. 29, ed. Michael Paulson (Dordrecht, Netherlands: Springer, 2014), 96–99; Kevin Kinser, "GI Bill," in *Higher Education in the United States: An Encyclopedia,* ed. James Forest and Kevin Kinser (Santa Barbara, CA: ABC-CLIO, 2002), 276–279; V. R. Cardozier, *Colleges and Universities in World War II* (New York: Praeger Publishers, 1993), 211–229. For an introduction to the long-standing debates among economists as to the success of the GI Bill in increasing attainment and completion rates, see the following: Marcus Stanley, "College Education and the Midcentury GI Bills," *Quarterly Journal of Economics* (May 2003): 671–708; John Bound and Sarah Turner, "Going to War and Going to College: Did World War II and the G.I. Bill Increase Educational Attainment for Returning Veterans?," Working Paper No. 7452 (Cambridge, MA: National Bureau of Economic Research, December 1999), www.nber.org/papers/w7452.

4. Vacchi and Berger, "Student Veterans," 96–99; Kinser, "GI Bill," 276–279; Cardozier, *Colleges and Universities*, 211–229. Scholars have also examined the relationship between the GI Bill and such matters as mental health and concerns over psychological maladjustment. For more on this, see Christopher P. Loss, *Between Citizens and the State: The Politics of American Higher Education in the Twentieth Century* (Princeton, NJ: Princeton University Press, 2012), 91–120.

5. House Select Committee to Investigate Educational, Training, and Loan Guaranty Programs under GI Bill, US House Report No. 1375 (Washington, DC: Government Printing Office, 1952), 12 (hereafter, HSC52). This report calculated 1,878 FPCUs in operation on June 22, 1944. After the passage of the GI Bill, that number increased to 5,635, representing a 300 percent increase.

6. *Report on Education and Training under the Servicemen's Readjustment Act, as Amended from the Administrator of Veterans' Affairs* (Washington, DC: GPO, 1950), 5 (hereafter, VA50).

7. Illinois Legislative Council, *Statutory Control of Private Trade Schools* (Springfield, IL: The Council, 1948), 2.

8. Ibid.

9. Ibid., 2–3.

10. Ibid., 26, 32.

11. Ibid., 1–3.

12. Ibid., 38–39.

13. Ibid., 39.

14. Ibid., 40.

15. Ibid.

16. Very little has been written on Olin E. "Tiger" Teague. See, for instance, Alec Philmore Pearson Jr., "Olin E. Teague and the Veterans' Administration" (PhD dissertation, Texas A&M, 1977), and Mitch Bauer, "Oran Nicks and the Evolution of Space Research at Texas A&M," *History of Spaceflight* 18 (2011): 38–44.

17. GI Bill amendment of 1946, Pub. L. No. 79-679, 60 Stat. 934 (1946); GI Bill amendment of 1949, Pub. L. No. 80-862, 62 Stat. 1196 (1949); GI Bill amendment of 1950, Pub. L. No. 81-266, 63 Stat. 631 (1950); GI Bill amendment of 1950, Pub. L. No. 81-610, 64 Stat. 336 (1950).

18. William A. Pencak, ed., *Encyclopedia of the Veteran in America* (Santa Barbara, CA: ABC-CLIO, 2012), 393; Thomas E. Hachey, "American

Profiles on Capitol Hill: A Confidential Study for the British Foreign Office in 1943," *Wisconsin Magazine of History* 57 (Winter 1973–1974): 141–153.

19. *VA50, 50–77*.

20. Ibid., 9, 114.

21. Ibid., 10, 11, 50, 56, 57, 59, 69.

22. Ibid., 72, 74, 77, 71, 114, 162. The "typical examples" of problems with FPCUs included the following: "improper records and vouchering, charges for improper and excessive supplies for use in the training program, fraudulent practices on the part of institutions, excessive charges for training rendered, misrepresentation of costs in the negotiations for tuition rates, adding and extending courses, questionable character of training and equipment, inclusion of excessive administrative costs in the negotiations for tuition rates, and the establishment of separate companies or corporations in connection with institutional operations in order to obtain higher tuition rates or additional profits from the sale of supplies" (114).

23. "Original Sound Intent of the Servicemen's Readjustment Act," Joint Report of the House of Representatives, Doc. No. 466 (February 13, 1950), 2.

24. GI Bill amendment of 1950, Pub. L. No. 81-610, 64 Stat. (1950). The amendment passed on July 13, 1950. See also Barbara McClure, "Veterans' Education Assistance Programs," US Congressional Research Services, Doc. No. 86-537 (January 31, 1986).

25. House Select Committee to Investigate Educational and Training Programs under GI Bill, US House Report No. 3253 (Washington, DC: GPO, 1951; hereafter, HSC51).

26. Ibid., 11, 8, 2; *VA50*, 114. Teague later questioned a portion of the 228 cases in his 1952 committee report (212–215) discussed later in this chapter. The overwhelming evidence presented in both Teague reports and the hundreds of cases of FPCU fraud in the GAO report make this subset a negligible issue.

27. HSC51, 6, 7.

28. Ibid., 8.

29. Ibid., 8.

30. Ibid., 24.

31. Ibid., 16, 14; *VA50*, 160.

32. HSC51, 15, 27.

33. Ibid., 28.

34. General Accounting Office, *Report of Survey—Veterans' Education and Training Program* (Washington, DC: GPO, 1951; hereafter, *GAO51*).

35. Ibid., 7–9.

36. Ibid., 10, 87–88.

37. Ibid., 10–11, 92–93.

38. Ibid., 10–12. US Bureau of Labor Statistics, CPI Inflation Calculator, www.bls.gov/data/inflation_calculator.htm.

39. HSC52.

40. Ibid., 1–4. "The college program," referring to the nonprofit sector, meanwhile, "has been successful" (9).

41. Ibid., 14–16.

42. Ibid., 29, 32–38.

43. Ibid., 41, 167–169.

44. Ibid., 66, 80.

45. James B. Edmonson (1882–1954) graduated with a PhD in education and history from the University of Chicago in 1925. His areas of expertise included secondary and postsecondary administration, policies, and curricula.

46. For more on Edmonson's career, see the James B. Edmonson Papers, Bentley Historical Library, University of Michigan (hereafter, JBEP).

47. James B. Edmonson, " 'Gypped!': G.I. Joe Must Be Protected against Low-Grade Colleges," *The Nation's Schools* 35 (February 1945): 25.

48. James B. Edmonson, "Fraudulent Schools and Colleges," *School and Society* 72 (July 15, 1950): 33–35.

49. James B. Edmonson, "Some Policies of States Governing the Granting of College Charters and Related Problems," Association of Higher Education, National Education Association, 1953, box 1, folder "Fraudulent Schools," JBEP.

50. "Preliminary Draft of a Bill to Provide for Regulatory Licensure of Schools Conducted for Profit in the State of _____ (Purpose: To Eliminate Fraudulent Institutions)," Association of Higher Education, National Education Association, 1953, box 1, folder "Fraudulent Schools," JBEP.

51. M. A. Nash to James B. Edmonson, February 21, 1953, box 1, folder "Fraudulent Schools," JBEP; James B. Edmonson to M. A. Nash, February 27, 1953, ibid.; Arthur S. Adams to James B. Edmonson, July 27, 1953, ibid.; H. D. Hopkins to James B. Edmonson, February 19, 1954, ibid.

52. Homer Kempfer to James B. Edmonson, May 14, 1953, box 1, folder "Fraudulent Schools," JBEP; Charles L. Platt to James B. Edmonson, May 4, 1953, ibid.; Charles L. Platt to Duke McColl and Earl Cranston, April 3, 1953, ibid.

53. S. A. Witmer to James B. Edmonson, May 6, 1953, box 1, folder "Fraudulent Schools," JBEP; James B. Edmonson to S. A. Witmer, May 12, 1953, ibid.; S. A. Witmer to James B. Edmonson, May 26, 1953, ibid.; S. A. Witmer to James B. Edmonson, November 3, 1953, ibid.; Edmonson, "Some Policies of States Governing the Granting of College Charters and Related Problems," ibid.

54. Correspondence included communications from officials of the following organizations: the Ford Foundation, Western College Association, National Catholic Educational Association, National Association of College Deans and Registrars, National Home Study Council, National Association and Council of Business Schools, US Air Force, US Veterans' Affairs, Psychological Corporation, and California Department of Education, as well as from dozens of other individuals and institutions. See letters in box 1, folder "Fraudulent Schools," JBEP. Arthur S. Adams to James B. Edmonson, July 27, 1953, ibid.

55. James B. Edmonson, "The Underworld of Education: Degrees and Diplomas Can Be Bought," *Michigan Alumnus Quarterly Review* 59 (Autumn 1952): 262; Walter Wienert to James B. Edmonson, March 24, 1953, box 1, folder "Fraudulent Schools," JBEP; on FPCU statistics, see General Accounting Office, *Veterans' Education*, 46.

56. Arthur S. Adams to Harlan H. Hatcher, July 23, 1958, box 1, folder "Fraudulent Schools," JBEP; Henry C. Herge to Francis H. Horn, July 20, 1953, ibid.; Francis H. Horn to James B. Edmonson, July 9, 1953, and May 29, 1952, ibid.; James B. Edmonson to Francis H. Horn, May 27, 1952, ibid.; James B. Edmonson to Alvin C. Eurich, May 31, 1952, ibid.; Alvin C. Eurich to James B. Edmonson, June 26, 1952, ibid.; Frank G. Millard to James B. Edmonson, November 19, 1953, ibid.

Chapter Four: Crisis

1. Higher Education Act of 1965, Pub. L. No. 89-329, 79 Stat. 1219 (1965); *Report on Education and Training under the Servicemen's Readjustment Act, as Amended from the Administrator of Veterans' Affairs* (Washington, DC: Government Printing Office, 1950), 9.

2. Patricia Strach, "Making Higher Education Affordable: Policy Design in Postwar America" *Journal of Policy History* 21 (2009): 61–88; Francis Keppel, "The Higher Education Acts Contrasted, 1965–1986: Has Federal Policy Come of Age?" *Harvard Educational Review* 57 (February 1987): 49–67; Harold Howe II, Oral History, October 29, 1968, in Lyndon Baines Johnson (LBJ) Library, Oral History Collection, AC 73-20, tape II, cited in Angelica Cervantes, Marlena Creusere, Robin McMillion, Carla McQueen, Matt Short, Matt Steiner, Jeff Webster, *Opening the Doors to Higher Education: Perspectives on the Higher Education Act 40 Years Later* (Round Rock, TX: TG Research, 2005); Rupert Wilkinson, *Aiding Students, Buying Students: Financial Aid in America* (Nashville, TN: Vanderbilt University Press, 2008). Other useful works on student federal aid programs include Carnegie Commission on Higher Education, *Higher Education: Who Pays? Who Benefits? Who Should Pay?* (New York: McGraw-Hill, 1973); Michael S. McPherson and Morton O. Schapiro, *Keeping College Affordable: Government and Educational Opportunity* (Washington, DC: Brookings Institution Press, 1991); and Michael S. McPherson and Morton O. Schapiro, *The Student Aid Game: Meeting Need and Rewarding Talent in American Higher Education* (Princeton, NJ: Princeton University Press, 1998).

3. See Keppel, "Higher Education Acts Contrasted," for a comparative analysis of the HEA reauthorizations. See also Jesse P. Mendez, "The History of the Pillsbury Doughboy: The Essential Elements of the Federal Pell Grant" (PhD dissertation, Indiana University, 2006).

4. Education Amendments of 1972, Pub. L. No. 92-318, 86 Stat. 235 (1972); Melanie Hirsch, "What's in a Name? The Definition of an Institution of Higher Education and Its Effect on For-Profit Postsecondary Schools," *New York University Journal of Legislation and Public Policy* 9 (2006): 817–832.

5. Cervantes, *Opening the Doors*, 35. For most of the period discussed in this paper, the US Department of Education did not differentiate between FPCU and nonprofit vocational, career, and community colleges. Statistics drawn from the following sources: Joseph Berger, "Changes in Welfare a Boon to Trade Schools," *New York Times* (August 6, 1988); Joseph Whitaker, "Lacaze Teachers in District Fired; U.S. Aid Halted; Lacaze Downtown Faculty Is Fired," *Washington Post* (November 14, 1978); Michael Winerip, "Billions for School Are Lost in Waste, Fraud, and Abuse," *New York Times* (February 2, 1994).

6. *Report by the Comptroller General of the United States: Many Proprietary Schools Do Not Comply with Department of Education's Pell Grant Program Requirements,* GAO/HRD-84-17, August 20, 1984 (Gaithersburg, MD: General Accounting Office, 1984), i, 4, 20, 7, 16. For the 1980–1981 award year, a total of $278 million in Pell Grants went to proprietary institutions.

7. Berger, "Changes in Welfare."

8. Karl Vick, "Trade Schools Accused of Fraud Still Receive Aid," *St. Petersburg Times* (November 20, 1988); Karl Vick, "Politics a Factor in Giving Trade Schools Student Aid," *St. Petersburg Times* (December 11, 1988); Karl Vick, "For-Profit Career Schools Confront Credibility Problem," *St. Petersburg Times* (December 18, 1988).

9. "Education, US Moves on Career Schools," *New York Times* (August 16, 1989); Pat Meisol, "Half of Bad Loans Tied to Trade Schools," *St. Petersburg Times* (February 10, 1988); Vick, "Politics a Factor," "Trade Schools Accused of Fraud," and "For-Profit Career Schools."

10. Estimates based on media reports from the *New York Times*, *St. Petersburg Times*, and *Washington Post* articles cited in this book. See, especially, Vick, "For-Profit Career Schools."

11. Vick, "Trade Schools Accused of Fraud."

12. Edward B. Fiske, "Reagan Record on Education: Mixed Results," *New York Times* (November 14, 1982); "Dr. Bill Bennett Bio," Georgia Chamber of Commerce website, www.gachamber.com/billbennett; Catherine Lugg, *For God and Country: Conservatism and American School Policy* (New York: Peter Lang, 2000).

13. Vick, "For-Profit Career Schools"; Meisol, "Half of Bad Loans"; Keith B. Richburg, "Reagan Upbeat on Education; President Defends Cuts in Aid to College Students," *Washington Post* (March 1, 1985); Barbara Vobejda, "Bennett to Hill: Investigate Trade Schools; Education Secretary Sends Evidence of Abuses in Student Loans, Recruiting, Testing," *Washington Post* (February 10, 1988).

14. Brian Fitzgerald and Lisa Harmon, *Consumer Rights and Accountability in Postsecondary Vocational-Technical Education: An Exploratory Study* (Washington, DC: Office of Planning, Budget, and Evaluation, US Department of Education, 1988); Vick, "Politics a Factor"; Meisol, "Half of Bad Loans." By the time of the Pelavin report, over 84 percent of students at proprietary institutions depended on state and federal aid, compared with

38 percent at public institutions and 65 percent at private, nonprofit institutions. See McPherson and Schapiro, *Keeping College Affordable,* 7.

15. Fitzgerald and Harmon, *Consumer Rights,* 3–5; Vobejda, "Bennett to Hill." For a breakdown of the Pell Grant distribution to FPCU students for the period between 1973 and 1994, see McPherson and Schapiro, *Student Aid Game,* 31.

16. Meisol, "Half of Bad Loans"; Fitzgerald and Harmon, *Consumer Rights,* 9–10.

17. Fitzgerald and Harmon, *Consumer Rights,* 15.

18. Frederick S. Mishkin, "Asymmetric Information and Financial Crises: A Historical Perspective," in *Financial Markets and Financial Crises,* ed. R. Glenn Hubbard (Chicago: University of Chicago Press, 1991), 69–108; David S. Hilzenrath, "Goldman Fined $22M for 'Willfully' Violating Law on Information-Sharing, SEC Says," *Washington Post* (April 12, 2012); Consent Order, Massachusetts v. Goldman Sachs, No. E2009-0079, MA, June 9, 2011; Fitzgerald and Harmon, *Consumer Rights,* 14–15; Berger, "Changes in Welfare"; Vick, "Trade Schools Accused of Fraud."

19. Fitzgerald and Harmon, *Consumer Rights,* 16.

20. Ibid., 15–16, 20–21.

21. Ibid., 16–17.

22. Ibid., 28, 30–31; US Bureau of Labor Statistics, CPI Inflation Calculator, http://data.bls.gov/cgi-bin/cpicalc.pl.

23. Fitzgerald and Harmon, *Consumer Rights,* 21–22; Meisol, "Half of Bad Loans." In the 1987–1988 academic year, there were 6,229 for-profits. See McPherson and Schapiro, *Keeping College Affordable,* 142.

24. Vick, "For-Profit Career Schools"; Meisol, "Half of Bad Loans."

25. *Abuses in Federal Student Aid Programs: Report Made by the Permanent Subcommittee on Investigations of the Committee on Governmental Affairs, US Senate* (Washington, DC: GPO, 1991; hereafter, *AFSAP*); Karl Vick, "Trade Schools under Sustained Fire for Abuses," *St. Petersburg Times* (September 14, 1990); Tamara Henry, "Cavazos Testifies about Student Loan Problems," *Associated Press* (October 10, 1990); Winerip, "Billions for School."

26. *AFSAP,* 9–10; Jason DeParle, "Panel Finds Wide Abuse in Student Loan Program," *New York Times* (May 21, 1991).

27. *AFSAP,* 7–9; Vick, "Politics a Factor."

28. Winerip, "Billions for School."

29. *AFSAP,* 12–13, 33; Jason DeParle, "Trade Schools Near Success as They Lobby for Survival," *New York Times* (March 25, 1992).

30. DeParle, "Panel Finds Wide Abuse." A Department of Education official remarked that during the 1980s student loans "became a mail order business. The school filled out an application . . . sent it to some bank [and] the student had no idea . . . whether [the loan] came . . . from California or otherwise" (*AFSAP,* 22).

31. *Abuses in Federal Student Grant Programs: Proprietary School Abuses, Hearing before the Permanent Subcommittee on Investigations of the Committee on Governmental Affairs, US Senate* (Washington, DC: GPO, 1995), 145 (hereafter, *AFSGP*); Michael Winerip, "Overhauling School Grants: Much Debate but Little Gain," *New York Times* (February 4, 1994); DeParle, "Trade Schools Near Success"; Polly B. Elliott, "Congressman Targets Beauty School Fraud," *States News Service* (October 27, 1993); Winerip, "Billions for School." On the investigation of religiously affiliated schools, see *Abuses in Federal Student Grant Programs: Hearing before the Permanent Subcommittee on Investigations of the Committee on Governmental Affairs, US Senate* (Washington, DC: GPO, 1993), 2, 7. Right-to-know legislation requiring FPCUs to publish default, graduation, and placement rates also made some headway in Congress at this time, but lawmakers stalled its passage for several years and weakened the provisions most sought by regulators and investigators.

32. *AFSGP,* 1.

33. Ibid., 4, 7, 11, 14; Rene Sanchez, "Tuition, Books, Lingerie and Club Med: California Trade School Accused of Scheme to Collect and Misspend Education Grants," *Washington Post* (July 13, 1995).

34. *AFSGP,* 15–16, 24, 72, 74.

35. Ibid., 26–27, 36, 45–48, 88–89.

36. Ibid., 57–58, 94.

37. Ibid., 57; Michael Winerip, "In Managing Federal Money, Education Officials Fall Short," *New York Times* (February 3, 1994).

Chapter Five: Capital

1. Thomas Picketty, *Capital in the Twenty-First Century* (Cambridge, MA: Harvard University Press, 2014); Simon Johnson and James Kwak, *Thirteen Bankers: The Wall Street Takeover and the Next Financial Meltdown* (New York: Vintage, 2011); William Lazonick, "The Financialization

of the U.S. Corporation: What Has Been Lost, and How It Can Be Regained," *Seattle University Law Review* 36 (2013): 857–909; Özgür Orhangazi, "Financialization and Capital Accumulation in the Non-Financial Corporate Sector: A Theoretical and Empirical Investigation of the U.S. Economy: 1973–2003," Working Paper No. 149 (Amherst, MA: Political Economy Research Institute, 2007); Greta R. Krippner, "The Financialization of the American Economy," *Socio-Economic Review* 3 (2005): 173–208; Gerald A. Epstein, *Financialization and the World Economy* (Northampton, MA: Edward Elgar, 2005).

2. Jared L. Bleak, *When For-Profit Meets Nonprofit: Educating through the Market* (New York: Routledge, 2005), 5.

3. Jason DeParle, "Trade Schools Near Success as They Lobby for Survival," *New York Times* (March 25, 1992); Kenneth J. Cooper, "Trade School Revolving Door Worry: Legislator Links Former Education Dept. Officials, High Default Rate," *Washington Post* (September 7, 1990).

4. DeParle, "Trade Schools Near Success"; Cooper, "Trade School Revolving Door."

5. DeParle, "Trade Schools Near Success."

6. Ibid.

7. Ibid.; Michael Winerip, "Overhauling School Grants: Much Debate but Little Gain," *New York Times* (February 4, 1994); Editor, "Crackdown on Student Aid Abuse," *New York Times* (June 21, 1994); Charles R. Babcock, "Loan Abuses by Some Trade Schools Leave Taxpayers with Big Bill," *Washington Post* (October 29, 1997).

8. DeParle, "Trade Schools Near Success"; Michael Winerip, "Billions for School Are Lost in Waste, Fraud, and Abuse," *New York Times* (February 2, 1994); Karl Vick, "Trade Schools under Sustained Fire for Abuses," *St. Petersburg Times* (September 14, 1990); Charles R. Babcock, "Rising Tuitions Fill Loan Firm Coffers: Constellation of Businesses Grows around Education Financing," *Washington Post* (October 27, 1997).

9. Michael Winerip, "House Panel Is Facing Vote on School Aid," *New York Times* (June 19, 1994); Editor, "Another Year to Rip Off Students," *Atlanta Journal and Constitution* (September 23, 1994).

10. John G. Sperling, *Rebel with a Cause: The Entrepreneur Who Created the University of Phoenix and the For-Profit Revolution in Higher Education* (New York: J. Wiley, 2000).

11. Emily Hanford, "The Story of the University of Phoenix," *American Radio Works,* http://americanradioworks.publicradio.org/features/tomorrows-college/phoenix/story-of-university-of-phoenix.html; Robin Wilson, "For-Profit Colleges Change Higher Education's Landscape," *Chronicle of Higher Education* (February 7, 2010).

12. David Harvey, *A Brief History of Neoliberalism* (New York: Oxford University Press, 2007); Roger Lowenstein, *Origins of the Crash: The Great Bubble and Its Undoing* (New York: Penguin, 2004); Jeffrey Selingo, "U. of Phoenix Owes Rapid Growth to Use of Technology, Its President Says," *Chronicle of Higher Education* (June 6, 2005); Kim Strosnider, "For-Profit University Challenges Traditional Colleges," *Chronicle of Higher Education* (June 6, 1997).

13. Goldie Blumenstyk, "Private Equity Juggernaut Rolls through Higher Education," *Chronicle of Higher Education* (August 3, 2007); David Leonard, "All I Want in Life Is an Unfair Advantage," *Fortune* (August 8, 2005); Bleak, *When For-Profit Meets Non-Profit,* 5; Sam Dillon, "Troubles Grow for a University Built on Profits," *New York Times* (February 11, 2007); Tamar Lewin, "Senator Calls for New Rules for For-Profit Colleges," *New York Times* (June 25, 2010); Tamar Lewin, "Obama Signs Order to Limit Aggressive College Recruiting of Veterans," *New York Times* (April 28, 2012); Tamar Lewin, "Rifts Show at Hearing on For-Profit Colleges," *New York Times* (October 1, 2010). These outsized, subsidized, guaranteed revenue streams failed to raise much concern among economists about the problem of moral hazard. FPCUs, from the perspective of moral hazards, lacked incentives to guard against the risk of student loan defaults and dismal placement rates. Taxpayers and students absorbed those risks. Instead, for-profits faced strong incentives to prioritize profit-making through new student recruitment over positive outcomes for existing students.

14. Margaret Isa, "Where, Oh Where, Have All the Corporate Raiders Gone?," *New York Times* (June 30, 1996); Elaine X. Grant, "TWA—Death of a Legend," *St. Louis Magazine* (July 28, 2006); Blumenstyk, "Private Equity Juggernaut"; Chris Kirkham, "With Goldman's Foray into Higher Education, a Predatory Pursuit of Students and Revenues," *Huffington Post* (October 14, 2011).

15. Goldie Blumenstyk, "The Chronicle Index of For-Profit Higher Education," *Chronicle of Higher Education* (August 11, 2006); Goldie Blumenstyk, "Private Education Company Sold," *Chronicle of Higher Education* (June 9, 2006); Blumenstyk, "Private Equity Juggernaut."

16. Matt Taibbi, "The Great American Bubble Machine," *Rolling Stone* (April 5, 2010); Jeffrey Selingo, "2 Companies Plan to Buy a Chain of For-Profit Colleges for $3.4-Billion," *Chronicle of Higher Education* (March 17, 2006); Jeffrey Selingo, "Education Management Corp. Agrees to a Buyout Deal that Would Take the Company Private," *Chronicle of Higher Education* (March 7, 2006).

17. Goldie Blumenstyk, "The Chronicle Index of For-Profit Higher Education," *Chronicle of Higher Education* (February 29, 2008).

18. Chris Kirkham, "Buying Legitimacy: How a Group of California Executives Built an Online College Empire," *Huffington Post* (May 25, 2011); Blumenstyk, "Private Equity Juggernaut"; Goldie Blumenstyk, "The Chronicle Index of For-Profit Higher Education," *Chronicle of Higher Education* (November 9, 2007); Blumenstyk, "Chronicle Index" (August 11, 2006); Goldie Blumenstyk, "Capella U. Plans Public Stock Offering," *Chronicle of Higher Education* (November 10, 2006); Goldie Blumenstyk, "Laureate Education Agrees to $3.8-Billion Buyout by Private Investors" *Chronicle of Higher Education* (January 30, 2007).

19. Aisha Labi, "American For-Profit Universities Plan Push into British Market," *Chronicle of Higher Education* (October 12, 2007); Blumenstyk, "Chronicle Index" (November 9, 2007); Goldie Blumenstyk, "Laureate Education's Doug Becker Is Moving to China to Focus on Asia," *Chronicle of Higher Education* (July 24, 2007); Goldie Blumenstyk, "The Chronicle Index of For-Profit Higher Education," *Chronicle of Higher Education* (August 17, 2007); Goldie Blumenstyk, "Chronicle Index" (February 29, 2008).

20. Blumenstyk, "Private Equity Juggernaut"; Audrey Williams June, "Apollo Group Enters a New Market, Buying a Company That Provides Online High-School Education," *Chronicle of Higher Education* (January 11, 2007); Audrey Williams June, "Apollo Group Buys Online High School," *Chronicle of Higher Education* (January 26, 2007); Blumenstyk, "Chronicle Index" (November 9, 2007); Michael Stratford, "For-Profit Colleges' Marketers Generate Leads, and Controversy," *Chronicle of Higher Education* (October 22, 2012); Goldie Blumenstyk, "Marketing, the For-Profit Way," *Chronicle of Higher Education* (December 1, 2006); Stephen Burd, "'The Washington Post' and the Perils of For-Profit Colleges," *Chronicle of Higher Education* (November 7, 2010).

21. David Halperin, "For-Profit Colleges Attack New Effort to Prevent Fraud with $32 Billion of Your Tax Dollars," *Huffington Post* (April 20,

2012), www.huffingtonpost.com/davidhalperin/forprofit-colleges-attack_b _1440781.html; *For Profit Higher Education: The Failure to Safeguard the Federal Investment and Ensure Student Success, Prepared by the Committee on Health, Education, Labor, and Pensions, United States Senate,* 4 vols. (Washington, DC: Government Printing Office, 2012), I: 7, 291 (hereafter, *HELP*).

22. Goldie Blumenstyk, "First Report from Research Center Created by U. of Phoenix Attacks Critics of For-Profit Education," *Chronicle of Higher Education* (September 2, 2010); Goldie Blumenstyk, "For-Profits Develop More-Forgiving Measures to Tally Graduates," *Chronicle of Higher Education* (March 2, 2012); Donald E. Heller, "A Study to Measure Value of Community Colleges Falls Short," *Chronicle of Higher Education* (October 14, 2013).

23. Blumenstyk, "Marketing, the For-Profit Way"; Stratford, "Marketers Generate Leads."

24. Goldie Blumenstyk, "Fast-Growing U. of Phoenix Calculates a More Careful Course," *Chronicle of Higher Education* (February 6, 2011); Tamar Lewin, "Senate Committee Report on For-Profit Colleges Condemns Costs and Practices," *New York Times* (July 29, 2012); Goldie Blumenstyk, "The Chronicle Index of For-Profit Higher Education," *Chronicle of Higher Education* (February 9, 2007).

25. For a brief overview of the kinds of litigation FPCUs faced during the first decade of the twenty-first century, see Amanda Harmon Cooley, "The Need for Legal Reform of the For-Profit Educational Industry," *Tennessee Law Review* 79 (2012): 515–571.

26. Susan Cullen et al. vs. Whitman Medical Corporation, No. 98-CV-4076, 2, 9–10; "Sandals & Langer, LLP Announces Approval of Record $7.3 Million Settlement of Fraud and Racketeering Claims against Trade School," *PR Newswire* (October 6, 2000).

27. Syracuse University, "Federal White Collar Crime Prosecutions at 20-Year Low," Transactional Records Access Clearinhouse, http://trac.syr .edu/tracreports/crim/398; on lackluster Wall Street prosecutions, see Darrell Delamaide, "Even Bernanke Asks How Bankers Avoided Jail," *USA Today* (October 6, 2015).

28. Hendow and Albertson filed a complaint against the University of Phoenix on March 7, 2003. The US Department of Justice joined Hendow's case the following year in a second amended complaint: United States of America ex. rel. Mary Hendow and Julie Albertson vs. University

of Phoenix, No. Civ. S-03-0457 GEB DAD (E.D. Cal. 2004). The case centered on illegal use of incentive-based pay for recruiters, given bans that had been in place for more than a decade as a result of the work of Senator Nunn and other lawmakers. Tamar Lewin, "For-Profit College Group Sued as U.S. Lays Out Wide Fraud," *New York Times* (August 8, 2011); Kelly Field, "Compensation in the Spotlight," *Chronicle of Higher Education* (June 29, 2009); Dan Carnevale, "U.S. Education Dept. Accused of Stacking the Deck on a Controversial Rule," *Chronicle of Higher Education* (March 8, 2002); Anne Marie, Stephen Burd, and Dan Carnevale, "Education Department Seeks to Ease Rules on Student Aid," *Chronicle of Higher Education* (August 16, 2002); Stephen Burd, "Aid Expert Picked for Key Post at Education Dept.," *Chronicle of Higher Education* (October 26, 2001); "Bush Appoints Longtime Critic of Education Department Official," *Chronicle of Higher Education* (July 13, 2001); Charles Huckabee, "Sally Stroup Is Named to Key Post in Group Representing For-Profit Colleges," *Chronicle of Higher Education* (July 5, 2012).

29. Henry Weinstein, "University of Phoenix Case to Stand," *LA Times* (April 24, 2007); Doug Lederman, "$78.5M Settles U. of Phoenix Case," *Inside Higher Ed* (December 15, 2009). See full "Order of Dismissal": United States of America ex. rel. Mary Hendow and Julie Albertson vs. University of Phoenix, No. Civ. S-03-0457 GEB DAD (E.D. Cal. December 17, 2009).

30. Field, "Compensation"; Blumenstyk, "Chronicle Index," (February 29, 2008); "Fraud by University Owner Is Found," *New York Times* (January 17, 2008); "Court Approves $145 Million Apollo Settlement," *Inside Higher Ed* (April 25, 2012); Teamsters Local 617 vs. Apollo et al., No. 06-cv-02674-RCB (D. Ariz. 2006), 2; see also, Teamsters Local 617 Pension vs. Apollo Group, 633 F.Supp.2d 763 (2009) and Teamsters Local 617 Pension vs. Apollo Group, No. 2:06-cv-02674-DLR (D. Ariz. 2015); Blumenstyk, "Chronicle Index," (February 9, 2007); Christine Caufield, "Judge Pares Down Backdating Suit vs. Apollo Group," *Law360* (April 1, 2009), www.law360.com/articles/94871/judge-pares-down-backdating-suit -v-apollo-group; Ben Conarck, "U. of Phoenix Parent Drops $13.1M to Settle Backdating Suit," *Law360* (February 24, 2015), www.law360.com /articles/624724.

31. Howland-Justice and Gatsiopoulos filed the original complaint (No. 06-1452) on November 2, 2006 in the US District Court of Western Pennsylvania. Citations refer to the unsealed second amended complaint:

United States ex rel. Gatsiopoulos et al., vs. Kaplan, No. 09-CV-21720-PAS (S.D. Fla. 2011), 6–7.

32. Ibid., 8.

33. Ibid., 13. Case settled for undisclosed amount in March 2012.

34. Mary Spicuzza, "Students File Class-Action Lawsuit against California Culinary Academy," *SF Weekly* (October 10, 2007); Amador vs. California Culinary Academy, No. CGC-07-46770 (Cal. Super. Ct. San Francisco County 2007); Matt Smith, "California Culinary Academy Settles Lawsuit with Students for Millions," *SF Weekly* (May 4, 2011); Erica Perez, "For-Profit College Company Inflated Job Placement Rates," *California Watch* (August 10, 2011), http://californiawatch.org/dailyreport/profit-education -company-inflated-job-placement-rates-11987; "A. G. Schneiderman Announces Groundbreaking $10.25 Million Dollar Settlement with For-Profit Education Company that Inflated Job Placement Rates to Attract Students," NY Attorney General Press Releases (August 19, 2013), www .ag.ny.gov/press-release/ag-schneiderman-announces-groundbreaking -1025-million-dollar-settlement-profit.

35. Lewin, "For-Profit College Group Sued"; Washington and Mahoney originally filed a complaint against EMC on April 5, 2007. United States ex rel. Washington et al. vs. Education Management Corp. et al., Civil No. 07-461 (W.D. Pa. 2011), 5, 32; on the trajectory of investigations and lawsuits against for-profits, see Robyn Smith, *Ensuring Educational Integrity: 10 Steps to Improve State Oversight of For-Profit Schools* (Boston: National Consumer Law Center, 2014), especially Appendix A.

36. State of California vs. Corinthian Colleges, No. BC374999 (Super. Ct. of Cal., Los Angeles County 2007), 3; Henry Weinstein, "School Chain to Settle Lawsuit," *LA Times* (August 1, 2007); Xiao-Bo Yuan, "Disputes over Regulating For-Profit Colleges Come to a Head in California," *Chronicle of Higher Education* (August 11, 2006); Goldie Blumenstyk, "ITT Educational Services Says It Will Pay $725,000 to Settle California Complaint," *Chronicle of Higher Education* (October 18, 2005).

37. Goldie Blumenstyk, "N.Y. State Assails For-Profit College," *Chronicle of Higher Education* (December 16, 2005); Sara Hebel, "N.Y. Regents Place Moratorium on New or Expanded For-Profit Colleges," *Chronicle of Higher Education* (February 3, 2006); Goldie Blumenstyk, "New York Regents Adopt Tougher Restrictions on For-Profit Colleges," *Chronicle of Higher Education* (June 2, 2006); Kenneth I. Shulman to

Richard P. Mills and James C. Ross, August 14, 2008, https://osc.state.ny .us/audits/allaudits/093008/07t6.pdf; Steven E. Sossei to Richard P. Mills and Michael R. Wilton Jr., March 7, 2005, http://osc.state.ny.us/audits /allaudits/093005/04t1.pdf; Goldie Blumenstyk, "N.Y.'s Interboro Institute to Close on Friday," *Chronicle of Higher Education* (December 17, 2007).

38. Goldie Blumenstyk, "Attorneys General in 10 States Mount Joint Investigation into For-Profit Colleges," *Chronicle of Higher Education* (May 4, 2011); Jack Conway et al. to Bernie Sanders et al., March 11, 2013, http://ag.ky.gov/pdf_news/financial-aid-letter.pdf.

39. Conway et al. to Sanders et al., March 11, 2013.

40. Ibid.

41. See SEC filings of Form 8K for ITT (January 27, 2014), www.sec .gov/Archives/edgar/data/922475/000092247514000004/form8_k.htm; EMC (January 24, 2014), www.sec.gov/Archives/edgar/data/880059/0000 88005914000002/a124148-k.htm; CEC (January 24, 2014), www.sec.gov /Archives/edgar/data/1046568/000119312514021303/d663039d8k.htm; and Corinthian (January 6, 2014), www.sec.gov/Archives/edgar/data/1066134 /000110465914000595/a14-1250_18k.htm.

42. Krippner, "The Financialization of the American Economy"; Epstein, *Financialization;* Gerald Epstein and Jessica Carrick-Hagenbarth, "Financial Economists, Financial Interests and Dark Corners of the Meltdown: It's Time to Set Ethical Standards for the Economics Profession," Working Paper No. 239 (Amherst, MA: Political Economy Research Institute, October 2014); Sumit Agarwal, Gene Amromin, Itzhak Ben-David, Souphala Chomsisengphet, Douglas D. Evanoff, "Predatory Lending and the Subprime Crisis," Working Paper No. 19550 (Cambridge, MA: National Bureau of Economic Research, October 2013); Eryn Brown, "Can For-Profit Schools Pass an Ethics Test?," *New York Times* (December 12, 2004); Bleak, *When For-Profit Meets Non-Profit,* 5; Wilson P. Dizard, "Doubt Lingers over Bona Fide Unaccredited Schools," *Newsbytes* (May 12, 2004).

43. Goldie Blumenstyk, "For-Profit Outlook," *Chronicle of Higher Education* (November 25, 2005). Blumenstyk estimates the FPCU industry at $48.75 billion in 2005. Wilson's "For-Profit Colleges" puts the figure at $26 billion in 2009. See also *HELP.* Molly Redden, "Supreme Court Decision on Arbitration May Have Eroded For-Profit Student Right to Sue," *Chronicle of Higher Education* (June 21, 2011).

Conclusion

1. *For Profit Higher Education: The Failure to Safeguard the Federal Investment and Ensure Student Success, Prepared by the Committee on Health, Education, Labor, and Pensions, United States Senate,* 4 vols. (Washington, DC: Government Printing Office, 2012), I: 70 (hereafter, *HELP*).

2. Ibid., I: 67–75.

3. Steve Eisman, "Subprime Goes to College," testimony at hearings before the US Senate, Health, Education, Pensions, and Labor Committee (June 24, 2010); *HELP,* I: 92–101; Kathleen Tighe, "Statement of Kathleen S. Tighe, Inspector General, U.S. Department of Education," testimony at hearings before the US Senate, Health, Education, Pensions, and Labor Committee (March 10, 2011); Tamar Lewin, "Senator Calls for New Rules for For-Profit Colleges," *New York Times* (June 25, 2010); Editor, "For-Profit Schools Major in Harvesting Federal Money," *USA Today* (July 31, 2012); Tamar Lewin, "Rifts Show at Hearing on For-Profit Colleges," *New York Times* (October 1, 2010); Tamar Lewin, "Flurry of Data as Rules Near for Commercial Colleges," *New York Times* (February 4, 2011); Chris Kirkham, "U.S. Targets For-Profit Colleges That Saddle Students with High Debt," *LA Times* (October 31, 2014).

4. *HELP,* I: 1–205; Daniel Golden, "For-Profit Colleges Target the Military," *Bloomberg* (December 30, 2009); Mamie Lynch, Jennifer Engle, and Jose L. Cruz, *Subprime Opportunity: The Unfulfilled Promise of For-Profit Colleges and Universities* (Washington, DC: Education Trust, 2010), 4; Gregory D. Kutz, *For-Profit Colleges: Undercover Testing Finds College Encouraged Fraud and Engaged in Deceptive and Questionable Marketing Practices,* GAO-10-948T (Washington, DC: Government Accountability Office, 2010), 7. The US Department of Defense, citing bribery and other violations of recruitment rules, put Apollo's University of Phoenix on probation in 2015. This prevented the institution from participating in veteran loans programs. See Paul Fain, "Defense Department Puts U of Phoenix on Probation," *Inside Higher Ed* (October 9, 2015).

5. The People of the State of California vs. Heald College, LLC, et al., Super. Ct. of CA, San Francisco, No. CGC-13-534793 (2013), 2, 10; Commonwealth of Massachusetts vs. Sullivan and Cogliano Training Centers, Super. Ct. of MA, Plymouth, No. 13-0357B (2013), 1–2; "Attorney General Kamala D. Harris Issues Statement on the Announced Closure of Corinthi-

an's California Campuses" [Press Release], Office of the Attorney General, State of California (April 27, 2015), https://oag.ca.gov/news/press-releases /attorney-general-kamala-d-harris-issues-statement-announced-closure -corinthian%E2%80%99s; "Brockton For-Profit School to Repay Students $425,000 Following Claims of Misleading Ads, Inflated Job Placement Rates: Sullivan & Cogliano to Change its Advertising and Recruiting Practices" [Press Release], Office of the Attorney General, State of Massachusetts (October 31, 2013), http://www.mass.gov/ago/news-and-updates /press-releases/2013/2013-10-31-sullivan-cogliano-consent-judgment.html; Andrew M. Harris, "Career Education Settlement Gets Preliminary Approval," *Bloomberg* (November 7, 2013). More recently, Massachusetts received a $2.3 million settlement from Kaplan Career Institute and Lincoln Technical Institute for false placement claims and unfair recruiting practices. See Andy Thomason, "2 For-Profit Colleges Will Pay Former Students $2.3 Million in Settlement," *Chronicle of Higher Education* (July 30, 2015).

6. Consumer Financial Protection Bureau vs. ITT Educational Services, US Dist. Ct. of Southern IN (2014), 1, http://files.consumerfinance.gov/f /201402_cfpb_complaint_ITT.pdf; American Association of Community Colleges, *2014 Fact Sheet*, www.aacc.nche.edu/AboutCC/Documents/FactSheet _2014_bw_r2.pdf.

7. *ITT Educational Services*, US Dist. Ct. of IN, 2.

8. Ibid., 3; Consumer Financial Protection Bureau vs. Corinthian Colleges, US Dist. Ct. of NE Ill., No. 14-7194 (2014), 3, 23, 31. See the case's "Default Judgment and Order" filed on October 27, 2015.

9. Tom Harkin, "For-Profit Colleges and the Threat of a New Bubble," *LA Times* (July 13, 2010); Derek Thompson, "For-Profit Colleges: First and Last Victims of Higher Education 'Bubble'?," *Atlantic* (June 1, 2011); Jordan Weissmann, "Did the For-Profit College Bubble Just Go Pop?," *Atlantic* (October 25, 2012); Martha Coakley, "Familiar Warning Signs in For-Profit Schools," *Boston Globe* (April 10, 2013); Stephanie Gleason, "Corinthian Colleges Files for Chapter 11 Bankruptcy," *Wall Street Journal* (May 4, 2015). In July 2015, the Federal Trade Commission opened a sweeping investigation into virtually all of the University of Phoenix's business practices, giving further reason for students, investors, and regulators to question the viability of the for-profit model. For more on the general trajectory of sixty of the most publicized investigations and suits against FPCUs between 2009 and 2014, see Robyn Smith, *Ensuring Educational*

Integrity: 10 Steps to Improve State Oversight of For-Profit Schools (Boston: National Consumer Law Center, 2014), especially Appendix A.

10. J. W. McClung, *Minnesota as It Is in 1870* (St. Paul, MN: Press Printing, 1870), 10; *Abuses in Federal Student Aid Programs: Report Made by the Permanent Subcommittee on Investigations of the Committee on Governmental Affairs, US Senate* (Washington, DC: Government Printing Office, 1991), 9–10 (hereafter, *AFSAP*); Cheesman Herrick, *Meaning and Practice of Commercial Education* (London: Macmillan, 1904), 189–190; Harvard University, "Treasurer's Statement" (Cambridge, MA: Harvard University, 1858–1859); see Harvard's "Treasurer's Statement" (Cambridge, MA: Harvard University Archives) of the 1850s and 1860s for salaries archived at http://hul.harvard.edu/lib/archives/refshelf/AnnualReportsSearch .htm. David Halperin, "For-Profit Colleges Attack New Effort to Prevent Fraud with $32 Billion of Your Tax Dollars," *Huffington Post* (April 20, 2012), www.huffingtonpost.com/davidhalperin/forprofit-colleges-attack_b _1440781.html; *HELP*, I: 7, 291.

11. Goldie Blumenstyk, "Why For-Profit Colleges Are Like Health Clubs," *Chronicle of Higher Education* (May 5, 2006); Yuen Ting Liu and Clive Belfield, "Evaluating For-Profit Higher Education: Evidence from the Education Longitudinal Study," CAPSEE Working Paper (New York: Center for Analysis of Postsecondary Education and Employment, 2014), http:// ccrc.tc.columbia.edu/media/k2/attachments/capsee-evaluating-for-profit-els .pdf. See, for instance, their concluding discussion: "For this [high level of] borrowing to be worthwhile, one should expect a strong labor market advantage from attending a for-profit college. As such an advantage is nowhere evident, the net returns to attending a for-profit college are considerably lower than those to attending an alternative college type. The returns to community college dominate the returns to for-profit college" (17).

12. Board of Education, *Special Reports on Educational Subjects*, vol. 2, *Education in the United States of America, Part 2* (London: Wyman and Sons, 1902), 235; City Club of Chicago, *A Report on Vocational Training in Chicago and in Other Cities* (Chicago: Henry O. Shepard, 1912), 255–256; "Original Sound Intent of the Servicemen's Readjustment Act," Joint Report of the House of Representatives, Doc. No. 466 (February 13, 1950), 2; *HELP*, I: 7, 291.

13. *AFSAP*, 7–9; see also Osamudia R. James, "Predatory Ed: The Conflict between Public Good and For-Profit Higher Education," *Journal of College and University Law* 38 (2011): 45–105; Goldie Blumenstyk, "U. of

Phoenix Looks to Shrink Itself with New Admissions Requirements and Deep Cuts," *Chronicle of Higher Education* (June 30, 2015).

14. Todd L. Savitt, "Abraham Flexner and the Black Medical School," in *Beyond Flexner: Medical Education in the Twentieth Century,* ed. Barbara M. Barzansky and Norman Gevitz (Westport, CT: Greenwood Press, 1992), 69–70; Alfred Z. Reed, *Present-Day Law Schools in the United States and Canada* (New York: Carnegie Foundation for the Advancement of Teaching, 1928), 100.

15. "Fear and Frustration: Faculty and For-Profit Colleges," *Chronicle of Higher Education* (July 10, 2011).

16. The literature on higher education history, its faculty, and professional academic standards is vast. For one of the most recent and comprehensive studies, see Roger L. Geiger, *The History of American Higher Education: Learning and Culture from the Founding to World War II* (Princeton, NJ: Princeton University Press, 2014).

17. City Club of Chicago, *Vocational Training;* Bertha Stevens, *Private Commercial Schools, Manhattan and the Bronx* (New York: New York Public Education Association, 1918); *Report on Education and Training under the Servicemen's Readjustment Act, as Amended from the Administrator of Veterans' Affairs* (Washington, DC: GPO, 1950), 57–59; Michael Winerip, "Overhauling School Grants: Much Debate but Little Gain," *New York Times* (February 4, 1994); Kelly Field, "Compensation in the Spotlight," *Chronicle of Higher Education* (June 29, 2009).

18. *HELP,* I: 15–19; Lewin, "Rifts Show at Hearing"; Eric Lichtblau, "With Lobbying Blitz, Profit-Making Colleges Diluted New Rules," *New York Times* (December 10, 2011).

19. American Association of Community Colleges, *2014 Fact Sheet;* Donald Trump's candidacy for president in 2015 brought about renewed attention to his troubled for-profit university venture. See Caroline Howard, "Donald Trump University Lawsuit is Lesson for All For-Profit Colleges," *Forbes* (August 27, 2013).

20. Andres Bernasconi, "The Profit Motive in Higher Education," *Inside Higher Ed* (September 10, 2012); Richard Hall, "The Profit Motive Is Threatening Higher Education," *University World News* (November 18, 2012); James, "Predatory Ed."

21. Michael Lewis, *The Big Short: Inside the Doomsday Machine* (New York: W. W. Norton, 2011); Simon Johnson and James Kwak, *Thirteen Bankers: The Wall Street Takeover and the Next Financial Meltdown* (New

York: Vintage, 2011); Thomas Picketty, *Capital in the Twenty-First Century* (Cambridge, MA: Harvard University Press, 2014); Michael Sandel, *What Money Can't Buy: The Moral Limits of Markets* (New York: Farrar, Straus and Giroux, 2013).

22. Johnson and Kwak, *Thirteen Bankers,* 115–116. See also Thomas Philippon and Ariell Reshef's description of the overcompensation of financial industry executives as "rents" in "Wages and Human Capital in the U.S. Financial Industry: 1909–2006," Working Paper No. 14644 (Cambridge, MA: National Bureau of Economic Research, 2009), 1–42, www.nber.org/papers/w14644.pdf.

23. John Hechinger and John Lauerman, "Executives Collect 2 Billion at For-Profits," *Bloomberg* (November 10, 2010); Lynn O'Shaughnessy, "Is Any University President Worth $42 Million Dollars?," *CBS Money Watch* (November 10, 2010); *HELP*, I: 713–727; "Salaries of Private-College Presidents, 2009: Almanac of Higher Education, 2012," *Chronicle of Higher Education* (December 5, 2011); "Compensation Leaders among Public-Institution Presidents," *Chronicle of Higher Education* (January 18, 2010).

24. For more on this point, see James, "Predatory Ed," and Geiger, *History of American Higher Education.*

25. Shahien Nasiripour, "Tom Harkin Wants to Take Money from College Students to Pay Reviled Loan Contractors," *Huffington Post* (December 6, 2014); Danielle Douglas-Gabriel, "Congress Cuts Federal Financial Aid for Needy Students," *Washington Post* (December 10, 2014). See also David Carpenter and David Moss, eds., *Preventing Regulatory Capture: Special Interest Influence and How to Limit It* (Cambridge: Cambridge University Press, 2013), for a discussion about the problem of "regulatory capture" and trends in how it has been commonly studied. Andy Thomason, "Gainful-Employment Rule Survives For-Profit Group's Court Challenge," *Chronicle of Higher Education* (June 23, 2015); Marc Perry, "No Financial Aid, No Problem: For-Profit University Sets $199-a-Month Tuition for Online Courses," *Chronicle of Higher Education* (March 29, 2012); Goldie Blumenstyk, "Meet the New For-Profit: The Low-Profit," *Chronicle of Higher Education* (October 10, 2012).

26. Jorge Klor de Alva and Mark Schneider, *Do Proprietary Institutions of Higher Education Generate Savings for States? The Case of California, New York, Ohio, and Texas* (San Francisco: Nexus Research and Policy Center, 2014); Jonathan Marino, "Some on Wall Street Say $1.2 Trillion in Student Debt Could Trigger the Next Market Crash," *Business Insider*

(April 29, 2015), www.businessinsider.com/student-debt-crisis-could-trigger -crash-2015-4.

It's worth noting two common responses to charges made against the for-profit sector. First, FPCUs argue that they must charge high tuition when compared with community colleges ($44,000 vs. $7,000) because community colleges are heavily subsidized. We don't see additional costs factored into community college tuition, FPCU lobbyists claim, because they're picked up by taxpayers through subsidies. The second response has to do with the for-profit sector's legal standing in light of the flurry of lawsuits they face. FPCU attorneys argue that most settlements come without the admission of wrongdoing.

Both responses, however, tend to ignore vital points of interest to the public. They overlook FPCU expenditures on marketing and profits that dwarf those for instruction. The point here is that the sector's high tuition doesn't necessarily reflect their concern for student outcomes or comparability to subsidized community colleges. The responses also ignore the fundamental changes in FPCU business practices demanded and agreed upon in the terms of lawsuit settlements. These agreements have become a de facto proxy for identifying fraud perpetrated against students, taxpayers, and federal student aid programs.

27. For more on agnotology and its study of the social construction of ignorance, see Robert Proctor and Londa Schiebinger, eds., *Agnotology: The Making and Unmaking of Ignorance* (Stanford, CA: Stanford University Press, 2008); Kevin Elliot, *Is a Little Pollution Good for You? Incorporating Societal Values in Environmental Research* (New York: Oxford University Press, 2011); Naomi Oreskes and Erik M. M. Conway, *Merchants of Doubt: How a Handful of Scientists Obscured the Truth on Issues from Tobacco Smoke to Global Warming* (New York: Bloomsbury, 2011); Casey High, Ann H. Kelly, and Jonathan Mair, eds., *Anthropology of Ignorance: An Ethnographic Approach* (New York: Palgrave, 2012); Philip Mirowski, *Never Let a Crisis Go to Waste: How Neoliberalism Survived the Financial Meltdown* (New York: Verso, 2013); A. J. Angulo, ed., *Miseducation: A History of Ignorance-Making in America and Abroad* (Baltimore: Johns Hopkins University Press, 2016).

American Legion, 75
American Management Association, 35
American Marketing Association, 35. See also *Journal of Marketing*
American Medical Association (AMA), 22, 37–38
American Revolution, 1
American Social Science Association, 22
American Society of Mechanical Engineers, 22
American Veterans of World War II, 75. See also World War II
American Vocational Association, 70
Andrade, Jeffrey, 124. See also Career College Association (CCA)
Ann Arbor, Michigan, 78, 82
Apollo Group, xi, 114–115, 119–120, 122–125, 138. See also Aptimus; Axia College; Carlyle Group; de Alva, Jorge Klor; Insight Schools; Nexus Research and Policy Center; Sperling, John G.; University of Phoenix
apprenticeship, 2–4, 15–16, 21, 31–32, 34, 36, 44–45
Aptimus, 120. See also Apollo Group; marketing; recruitment
arbitration, 131
Arizona State University, 145
Ashford University, 118, 134. See also Bridgepoint Education
Asia, 109, 118
Association of American Law Schools (AALS), 30–34, 141
Association of Independent Colleges and Schools, 111. See also Career College Association (CCA); National Association of Trade and Technical Schools (NATTS)
Association of Land-Grant Colleges and Universities, 70
Association of National Advertisers, 35

Association of Private Sector Colleges and Universities (APSCU), 142
asymmetric information relationships, 94, 96–97
attendance requirements, 34, 48, 68, 74, 76, 106, 129
attorney general: state, 63, 128, 129, 131, 135; of the United States, 70
Auburn University, 145
Axia College, 119. See also Apollo Group; Carlyle Group; Sperling, John G.

backdating, 125
Baltimore, Maryland, 16, 38
bankruptcy, 16, 105–106, 137, 147
barbershop training academies, 27
Barbour, Haley, 110
bar exam, 33–34. See also American Bar Association (ABA)
Barnard, Charles, 26–27
Bartlett's Commercial College, 18
Basic Educational Opportunity Grant, 86–87. See also Pell Grant
Bates, Charlie (*Oliver's Twist*), 14
Beckel, Bob, 110
Behn, Julie Albertson, 124. See also Apollo Group; whistleblowers
Bell's Commercial College, 5, 19–20
benefit corporations (L3Cs), 147
Bennett, Bill, 91–94, 98–99, 104, 110, 113. See also National Endowment of the Humanities; Pelavin Report of 1988; Reagan, President Ronald; United States Department of Education
Bevan, Arthur Dean, 39–40. See also American Medical Association (AMA); Council on Medical Education
Blair, Stephen, 110–113
Bloom, Thomas B., 113
Boston, Massachusetts, 2, 5, 25, 48, 116

New Orleans, Louisiana, 5, 24
New York, state of, 5, 9–10, 18,
20–21, 48, 52, 54, 60–62, 89,
95–96, 114, 118, 123, 126–129,
142, 147
New York City, 5, 89
New York Education Department, 62
New York tuition assistance, 89
New York University, 35, 145
Nexus Research and Policy Center,
120–121. *See also* Apollo Group;
de Alva, Jorge Klor; University of
Phoenix
9/11 GI Bill, 115. *See also* Servicemen's Readjustment Act of
1944
90-10 rule, 104, 116, 136
N. O. Nelson Manufacturing
Company, 27
nonprofit colleges and universities,
xi–xiii, 4, 6, 8, 10, 13, 17–18, 24,
36, 75–78, 85, 87–88, 102–103,
118, 120–121, 144. *See also
specific colleges and universities*
North American Training Academy,
102
North Dakota, state of, 60–63
Northern Indiana Normal School, 19
Northwestern University, 146
Notre Dame University, 8
Nunn, Senator Sam, 91, 98–100,
103–111, 113
Nunn Investigation of 1990, 91,
98–100, 103–104
Nunn Investigation of 1995, 91,
104–108

Obama, President Barack, 123
Oberlin Commercial College, 5
Ohio, state of, 5, 13, 19, 94, 147
Ohio State University, 145
Oliver Twist, 14
on-site inspections, 38–40, 65, 94,
106–107, 115
Oregon, state of, 60–61, 63

Orwell Normal Institute, 13
Osbourne, Lloyd, 14
outsourcing, 124
Ovid, 1
Owens, Robert, 27

Packard's Commercial College, 5
Paine's Commercial College, 5
Parent Loans for Undergraduate
Students, 96
Parish's Commercial College, 5
Parrott, Sharon, 111
patient capital, 117
Pearl Harbor, 57
Pelavin Report of 1988, 93–94,
96–98, 110
Pell Grant, 86–88, 90, 93, 104–107,
115, 146. *See also* Basic Educa-
tional Opportunity Grant
Pennsylvania, state of, 18–19, 26,
60–61, 75, 96
Philadelphia, Pennsylvania, 5, 48, 75
Philadelphia Academy, 4
philanthropy, xiii
Pond, George E., 13
Poston, Rebekah, 101
Post University, 118
poverty, ix–x, xiv–xv, 39, 43, 53, 76,
93, 95, 102, 114, 143, 147
predatory lending, x, xii, 96–97,
136–137
Princeton University, 121, 145
*Private Commercial Schools: Manhat-
tan and the Bronx* (1918), 52
Procter and Gamble, 27
professionalization, 2–4, 6, 8, 10, 12,
21–23, 26, 28–38, 40, 42, 47, 78,
139–141
professors. *See* faculty
profits: academic standards and, 126,
134, 140–142; asymmetrical
information relationships and,
131, 143; budget for, 120–122;
children and, 97–98; cost cutting
and, 50–51, 53, 106, 140; culture

and, 100–101; deregulation and, 109; easy, 115; finance sector and, 130; franchise, 9; labor and, 27; large-scale, 85–86, 90, 146; pain and, 133; privileging of, 148; skeptical views on, 7–8, 26–27, 66, 79, 93–94, 100–101; stock manipulation and, 117; student performance and, 129, 135 progressivism, 29–30, 32, 34, 37, 40, 43–44, 48

Proposals for the Education of Youth of Pennsylvania (1749), 4

Providence Equity Partners, 117–118. *See also* Educational Management Corporation (EMC); investment firms

Public Law 81-610, 68

Quayle, Senator Dan, 90
QuinStreet, 120. *See also* marketing; recruitment

Reagan, President Ronald, xv, 92, 110
recitation, 5
recruitment, 48, 51, 54, 56, 76, 94–96, 98, 101–102, 119–121, 124–125, 128–130, 133–134, 142, 145
regionalism, 21, 23, 26, 28
regulation, xiii, 2, 23, 34, 55–61, 63, 65, 69, 72, 77, 79–80, 83, 94, 96–97, 104, 109, 111–113, 123, 127–128, 131, 133, 136, 142, 144–147
religion, 24, 38–39, 42, 80–82, 104
Rensselaer Polytechnic Institute, 6, 145
research, x, xiii, xvi, 55, 93–94, 96, 114, 120–121, 139–140, 142, 144
retention, 48, 55, 66, 101, 130, 140
right-to-know legislation, 112, 142
Robert Fiance Beauty Schools, 90

Rockefeller, John D., 19
Roosevelt, President Franklin D., 57, 78

safe harbor rules, 124
Sagemont Virtual, 119
Salisbury, David, 130–131
Sandquist, Representative Elroy C., 60–61
San Francisco, California, 116, 126
San Jose State University, 114
Sawyer's Commercial College, 5
Schofield's Commercial College, 5
Schwarzenegger, Arnold, 128
Scientific American, 8
Scribner's Magazine, 26
Scripps, James E., 19
Scripps College, 19
Scripps Institute of Oceanography, 19
search engine optimization, 21
secondary education, xv, 16, 29, 42–47, 49, 52, 54–55, 68, 85, 97, 111, 118–119, 128
Servicemen's Readjustment Act of 1944, xiii, 58–59, 60, 63–78, 83, 85, 139. *See also* 9/11 GI Bill; World War II
Sex in Education (1873), 25
Shakespeare, William, 7
sham degrees, 12–13
shareholders, 117, 120, 125, 127, 131, 140, 146, 148
Shylock, 7
Silberman, Robert, 145–146
Smith, Adam, xv, 8
Smith, Senator Hoke, 45
Smith-Hughes Act of 1917, 45, 47
Socrates, 7
solicitation, 48–52, 54–55, 61
Soros, George, 119
Soule's Commercial College, 5, 24
South Brooklyn Legal Services, 99
Soviet Union, 144
Spencer, Herbert, xv
Spencerian Business College, 21